# THE WESTERN ANGLER

*also by Roderick Haig-Brown*

A RIVER NEVER SLEEPS

FISHERMAN'S SPRING

FISHERMAN'S SUMMER

# THE
# WESTERN
# ANGLER

*An Account of Pacific Salmon &*

*Western Trout in British Columbia*

## by Roderick Haig-Brown

*Illustrated by T. Brayshaw*

*A Totem Book, Toronto*

First published 1939
Second edition published 1947
Third edition published 1968
Re-issued in 1981
by TOTEM BOOKS
A division of Collins Publishers
100 Lesmill Road, Don Mills, Ontario

Cover illustration by Louis Darling

**Canadian Cataloguing in Publication Data**

Haig-Brown, Roderick L., 1908-1976.
    The western angler

Originally published: Toronto: Collins, 1968.


ISBN 0-00-216826-X

1. Pacific salmon fishing — British Columbia.
2. Trout fishing — British Columbia.   I. Title.


SH572.B8H34 1981        799.1'755        C81-094161-9


Printed and bound in Canada by
T. H. Best Printing Company Limited

# DEDICATION

*To General Money of Qualicum Beach,
finest of western anglers, and to his own Stamp River,
loveliest and most generous of western streams*

# CONTENTS

# PART IV. *The Pacific Salmon*

# PART V. *General Again*

# PREFACE

## *to the Third Edition*

IT IS NOW almost thirty years since *The Western Angler* was first published and many things have changed in the world of angling and fisheries management. One could write a whole new book with the same title without repeating a word of this one. One thing that does not change, though, is that anglers like old books and continue to find good things in them even in a new age.

I did make some minor changes in the second edition of *The Western Angler*, which was published in 1947. This time it seems better to let the book stand as it is. Much of the basic information is still sound and still has not been gathered together in convenient form elsewhere. My readers will know that I have supplemented the book in the "Fisherman" series —Spring, Summer and Fall—in *A Primer of Fly-Fishing* and in a small pamphlet written for the Canadian government, *Canada's Pacific Salmon.*

But I should like to note briefly here some of the more significant changes of the past thirty years to put things in proper perspective. Some changes are in myself; I am now more dedicated to fishing in rivers, to fishing only with a fly and to observing the fish rather than fishing for them. A lot has happened in thirty years and much of it has not been good for fish or the waters that nourish them.

The principles of fisheries conservation and management have not greatly changed in thirty years; the base of good management was ecology then, and it remains so to-day. We know more about habitat and have cheaper and more effective means of manipulating it or protecting it, even though we are woefully reluctant to apply them.

Because the Pacific salmons make a great commercial industry, we have immensely improved our knowledge of their migrations and we have developed quite spectacular means of managing the runs. Balancing of catch against spawning escapement is now pretty well taken for granted and is achieved with a high degree of accuracy. I would no longer subscribe to the theory that an excess of spawners is harmless, as suggested on p. 251. The proper relationship of spawning numbers of each species to available gravel areas is now well understood, and regulated escapement produces better returns than excessive escapement.

In the United States, hatchery techniques have been developed to remarkable efficiency, mainly to compensate for high dams and other destructive watershed uses. In Canada, where we are not yet affected by such problems on the main anadromous watersheds, emphasis has been on artificial spawning channels and flow control. I must admit to the gravest reservations about hatcheries, however great their apparent successes, because of their critical, if not fatal, tendency to select out and foster grossly inferior stocks. Artificial spawning channels and even flow control may have similar, though less drastic effects, but I believe there is an excellent chance of reducing these to a minimum and so of maintaining hardy natural stocks.

These thirty years have seen pathetically small advances in knowledge of the fundamental biology of steelhead and migratory cutthroat trout. We know a little more, it is true—for instance, that the summer steelhead and winter steelhead are physiologically different fish and that the scale readings of migratory cutthroats offered in this book are probably unsound. But we do not begin to know enough to ensure the protection, let alone the proper management, of either species.

These sad deficiencies are due to the continuing failure of both governments and public to understand the economic and social values of recreational fishing and, particularly, the high and irreplaceable values of quality fishing. Anglers and hunters, as well as governments, still seem to believe that publicly-owned stocks and habitat can continue to produce sport without significant expenditure of money and human effort. They cannot.

Fishing tackle has also changed substantially since this book was written. With nylon monofilament and the bale pick-up, spin-casting (referred to in this book as "thread-line fishing") has come into its own. This is probably good in that it has introduced many anglers to the sport who might not otherwise have found it. But in capable hands the gear is far too easy and too deadly and it is an unhappy fact that many cling to it when they should have graduated to more demanding and less destructive methods long ago.

Fly-fishing tackle also has improved out of all knowledge. Modern glass rods are very good, very powerful and very light. I would no longer dream of recommending an eleven-foot Wye rod weighing over twelve ounces for steelhead fishing, simply because one can buy a nine-foot, five-ounce glass rod that will throw a number ten line and therefore handle any fly up to 2/0 with at least equal ease and effect.

Modern fly lines are beautifully finished and offer the fisherman an almost infinite choice—floating, intermediate, sinking, fast sinking, sinking tip or sinking head. They can be maintained with a minimum of care. And I believe the modern forward taper offers many advantages over the old double taper under most fishing conditions. This is not to say that the old gear was not pleasant to use and effective. It was, and is, both. But the modern fly fisherman can buy many things that he formerly had to do for himself. The advantages, in my opinion, are in no way detrimental to the sport, which remains demanding and fascinating. To consider one example, sinking lines and lighter fly rods that will carry heavy flies have made winter steelhead fly-fishing a practical proposition for many who might have hesitated to try it under the old conditions.

I trust that the reader who comes to *The Western Angler* in the late sixties instead of the late thirties will hold some of these thoughts in mind and use them to temper the advice and information that is offered. Thirty years of Pacific Coast angling history has produced new record fish, new fly patterns, at least some new fishing techniques. It has also opened up many areas of lake and stream and salt water that were once remote. And it has brought to most of them a degree of angling pressure far beyond any I had imagined. This last is the most significant change of all and it is the fact we have to live with. I do not find it discouraging. Only a large and interested body of anglers can hope to preserve the stocks and habitat on which the sport depends from the careless encroachments of industry and population. If anglers themselves can learn to accept the challenges of the sport instead of its easy ways; to honor its traditional courtesies and generosities instead of crowding and competing; and above all to respect and protect the fish themselves and the waters on which they depend, I believe we can always expect good fishing in the west.

I wish future generations the same joy in the sport that I have found. And this is no small thing, for in all its history angling has brought delight and pleasure to many and harm to no one.

*27 September 1968.*                    *Roderick Haig-Brown.*

# PART ONE

*General*

# I

## Setting & Circumstances

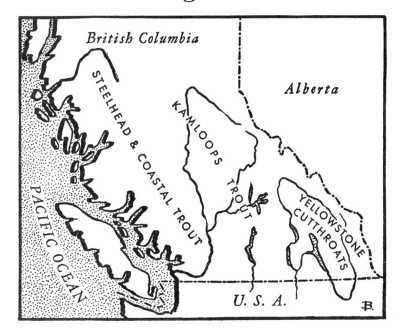

B RITISH COLUMBIA is a big Province, it is sparsely settled, it contains a lot of fresh water and it is bordered on the west by a lot of salt water. Perhaps figures make it clearer. The area of the Province is 350,000 square miles. Its population is something under a million. One tenth the area of the United States with one-one-hundred and thirtieth of its population—three people to each square mile as against forty in the United States and four hundred in Great Britain. The United States has a mile of road to every square mile; Great Britain has one and a half miles of road to every square mile. British Columbia has one mile of road to each twenty square miles of country.*

From the fisherman's point of view, three other factors multiply the size of the Province—its geological youth, heavy rainfall and long coast line. The young mountains break the country into hollows and grooves and depressions of every shape and size. Heavy rainfall keeps the depressions filled, forming lakes and potholes and inland seas, and drives stream and river systems down along the grooves. The coast line, hugely indented, broken by islands, adds thousands of miles of good fishing water to those of the lakes and streams.

Perhaps the best way to get an idea of what a fisherman may find in British Columbia is to sit back and look up at a fair-sized wall map of the whole province. First, in the southwest corner there is Vancouver Island, and round it an area of salt water that plays a big part in the life histories of the steelhead and the five varieties of Pacific salmon. To the east coast of the Island flow such streams as the Cowichan, the two Qualicums, the Courtenay, the Oyster and the Campbell, all accessible by road and most of them draining chains of lakes. North of the roads, still on the east coast are the Salmon, the Nimpkish, the Cluxewe, the Keogh and others. Down the west coast are a dozen deep sounds, fed by such rivers as the Gold and the Stamp. All through the centre of the Island are tributary streams and lakes—hundreds, perhaps thousands, of lakes.

East of the summit of the Coast Range is another district of many lakes, centring on Kamloops. Between Vancouver and Kamloops it is a district reasonably well served by roads; many of the important lakes can be reached by car, and where there are no roads there are pack trails. The fish of the country is the Kamloops trout, perhaps the finest of British Columbian

*Good maps of the province are obtainable from the Ministry of the Environment, Survey and Mapping Branch, Parliament Buildings, Victoria, B.C.

game fish, and in his honour it is a fisherman's country; every man in it seems to be an angler of one sort or another, and there is fishing talk in all the hotels, in every barber shop and general store, at the butcher's and the baker's and the grocer's and at every street corner. Famous and familiar names are on the signposts along the road—Paul Lake and Knouff Lake, Little River, Adams River and all the others.

North of Kamloops the roads are fewer, but it is still fisherman's country, and the lakes have names just as famous; fewer men may have wet lines in HI-Hiume and Myrtle and Mahood and Babine and Stuart than in Paul and Pennask and La Jeune, but those few have told the tale, and others make their plans with an enthusiasm that grows rather than fades as they count the miles of trail or water that lie between the lakes and the nearest road.

North of the road from Hazelton to Prince George there is still nearly half the Province. Through it there now runs a five hundred mile section of the Alaska Highway from Dawson Creek through Fort St. John, Fort Nelson and Liard River to Watson Lake on the Yukon boundary. This can be reached by automobile from Edmonton, but from the United States or from most parts of Canada the Alaska Highway is so long a drive that most vacations would be largely used up in the journey out and home. Even from the Alaska Highway only a small section of Northern British Columbia and that probably not the best of it, is accessible. It is still a country for air travel and the man who has a seaplane of his own or can afford to charter one can find great sport there. On the Arctic watershed there are char and pike and grayling, on the Pacific slope cutthroat and steelhead. All through the country there are lakes, large and small, many of which will probably make fishing for future generations only when the roads go in and proper plantings of fry can be made.

If this great northern part of the Province is only for the very wealthy or the very venturesome of this generation, the rest is large enough and full enough of good water to make sport for half a continent of anglers. And the fish native to that water are good fish; at least three of them—the coast cut-throat, the steelhead and the Kamloops—are really fine game fish. The Yellowstone cutthroat of the southeastern part of the Province is also a good fish, and the Pacific salmon, though its freshwater habits leave something to be desired, keeps saltwater anglers busy enough. If there is a man who feels that *Oncorhynchus* and *Salmo* are not enough, he can turn his attentions to the two native char and to the mercifully few non-native species that the authorities have from time to time thought fit to import.

British Columbia, then, is a vast area of country, sparsely settled, not too well served by roads, dotted and seamed with water of every kind, most of which either can or does support worthy game fish. The second point that strongly influences any consideration of its fishing possibilities is the fact of public ownership. There is no privately owned fishing water in the whole Province. Obviously this is a fine thing and a desirable thing. True, public ownership has proved elsewhere in the past, and it may yet prove in British Columbia, a catastrophe so far as conservation is concerned. Private ownership in Great Britain has preserved and often improved good fishing from generation to generation—but only the few get the good fishing. Public ownership in most states of the Union and most provinces of the Dominion has allowed stocks of both fish and game to fall far below safe or valuable limits—but at least everyone has had a chance at the fish and game. British Columbia, as the last corner of the west, has the evil of a whole continent before her. She has only to examine the record to learn what abuse of public ownership can do; and on the positive side she has the collective and ever increasing experience and knowledge of the rest of the continent to draw upon when she wishes to take steps to improve or preserve what she has.

Nothing about public ownership is inherently incompatible with conservation. Rather the opposite. Under public ownership plans can be worked out on a large scale and experiments can be carried out over large areas. A government can employ good scientists and initiate research work; it can think in terms of decades rather than in terms of seasons, in terms of whole watersheds rather than in terms of little stretches of water here and there. It can legislate according to the advice of its scientists and it has the means to enforce its legislation. It can (or should be able to) build steadily and solidly on its work from year to year.

Unfortunately governments have only recently begun to realise their responsibility to their electors for what may well be termed the recreational resources of the country—fish, game and wild life generally, lakes and streams, mountains and swamps and forest lands, beaches and rivers and bays, even the winds that blow and the sun that shines and the rain that falls; for these things too may come within the scope of government at some future stage of the atomic era. Even today governments, especially in a pioneering country such as Canada still is in many ways, treat recreational resources as a very unimportant side issue when commerce becomes involved. The plain truth is that sensible regulation and control of commercial interests can nearly always preserve a country's recreational assets at insignificant cost compared with the potential cost of restoring them at some later date. And there is little to be said for making a people prosperous through commercial effort if there is nothing left for them to enjoy in prosperity.

Commercial exploitation, particularly of fish and timber, has been ruthless in British Columbia, and were it not for a commercial aspect of the game fishery this resource would probably be in far worse state than it is today. The commercial aspect is what is known as "the tourist trade" and this is the third major factor that must be considered in any discussion of the British Columbian game fishery.

British Columbians generally are quite strongly interested in the tourist trade. The Province is competing against powerful rivals and in general she cannot offer as much as they do. Washington, Oregon and California have better roads, comparable scenery, better hotels and accommodations, better entertainment facilities, greater variety and more dependable climate. And they are more accessible. As against this, British Columbia is wild and in parts unspoilt; accommodations are improving and roads are improving slowly. This is not enough to draw tourists in important numbers. What does draw them is rod-fishing—better rod-fishing than anywhere else in North America and more of it. Left to itself the water of the country cannot provide enough really good fishing, nor will it provide good fishing for an indefinite number of years. Even a commercially inclined government can be made to appreciate this. Small business men can appreciate it and make their weight felt. And the ordinary local angler can see in it his main hope of ensuring good fishing for himself and his visiting friends.

These three factors, the size of the country, the fact of public ownership and the economic importance of the subject through the tourist trade, have influenced this book. Because the country is so large and because conditions change so frequently, this is in no sense a guide book to the fishing waters of the Province. Rather it is an attempt to give an accurate general picture by treating typical waters in some detail. Because the fishing is publicly owned, such scientific and administrative work as has been done is of real importance to other areas of North America. If the tourist trade gives the ring of dollars and cents to a page here and there, at least it is in a good cause—my own interest in it is purely academic.

My own fishing habits have undoubtedly had their influence and I may as well be frank about them from the start. I am at least as interested in fish as I am in fishing. I am a fly fisherman by preference, simply because I have found far more pleasure in flyfishing than in any other method. When flyfishing is hopelessly unproductive—which it seldom is in British Columbia —I am perfectly willing to try other methods. I have never learned to enjoy trolling or still fishing, probably because I am still too young and too impatient. On all these points I am, no doubt, prejudiced, and I have made little effort to control my prejudices; tackle and methods and pleasure in fishing are essentially matters of opinion and prejudice; true statement here is a matter of a man's close examination of himself and can be checked by no one outside himself.

But in matters of observation and natural history and conservation methods there can be exact truth, often hidden and confused but always discoverable in the end. In such matters I have tried honestly, to the limit of my powers, to be without prejudice and to restrain myself from too easy conclusions. Because I feel that these things are important to every fisherman both for the enjoyment of his sport and its future security, I hope that trollers and baitfishers and all other anglers will overlook my prejudices and preferences and stay with me through the book.

# 11

# *The Trout of British Columbia*

A<sup>S</sup> recently as 1930 some authorities recognised no less than thirty-three species of trout from the waters of British Columbia and western North America. Since then, thanks partly to some brilliant research work and partly to what seems a more sensible attitude, those leading authorities most closely connected with

British Columbia have driven through a mass of superficial dis-
tinctions and have reached the conclusion that British Columbia
has only two native species of trout, the cutthroat and the rainbow. Working in much the same way, European authorities
have reduced the number of recognised species of trout in
Europe from some scores to exactly one, the brown trout. Thus
the present position—accepted, I think, by the majority of scientists—is that there are in the world only three species of trout,
each of which has a few, but only a few, recognised variations.

Since this position has been adopted so recently, it seems
important to explain in some detail how it has been reached,
as well as exactly what it is. Of all fish, trout are probably the
most subject to variation in colour and appearance, and it is
this fact that generally misleads anglers, as it has in the past
misled scientists. It is important to realise from the start that
trout, no less than sheep or cattle, are individuals. The shepherd or the cowman is able to recognise each animal in his
charge by some difference in it from the rest of the flock or
herd; in the same way an angler can, if he takes the trouble,
find individual peculiarities in every one of the ten or a dozen
fish of his catch—different markings or arrangements of spots,
different body shape, different colouring. The differences may
be slight if the fish all come from the same part of a single body
of water, but they will be there. And they will probably be
quite clearly marked in two fish from different lakes or from
different parts of the same lake.

Such individual peculiarities are generally due to different
environment or different feeding habits, and it is easy to see
that they may become exaggerated as these two conditions
become set. Trout from a brown-water lake, for instance, will
be very unlike those from a clear lake; a trout in the habit of
cruising over a pale, sandy shallow may be quite unlike its own
brother who has lived all his life in the depths of the same lake.
These differences are obviously superficial and subject to
change in one generation or even within the lifetime of the

individual. Conversely, they will become more marked as generation after generation of fish is reared under certain conditions of feed and environment. In many thousands of years they may produce a new species; it is the scientist's job to decide in certain cases whether or not they have already done so.

Since it is the accepted theory that not only trout, but all other fish, are descended from some single, original species, a scientist will first look for evidence of different habits of breeding or feeding. These are really the fundamental things which make necessary the differentiation between species. But the ultimate test of such differences of habit is in the effect they have had on the structure of the fish; and the scientist of today desiring to describe a new species is under obligation to show structural differences between it and species already described —differences which are, as far as can be ascertained, hereditary and permanent.

It must be admitted that scientists are not yet agreed on what constitutes sufficient difference to necessitate the naming of a new species. Some scientists are what is known as "lumpers," some are "splitters"—which is natural enough, in view of the prevailing belief that all species are the result of evolution and that evolution is still going on. It is even arguable, I suppose, that a certain variety, differing widely from the rest of its species, will tomorrow or next week or next year or in a hundred years' time have reached the point at which its difference demands the naming of a new species. There must be a dividing line somewhere, but exactly where to set it can only be a matter of opinion. So there is justification for both "lumpers" and "splitters," and a course between the two, somewhere nearer the "lumpers" than the "splitters," is probably the most defensible logically. Certainly the average angler —and I think the fish-culturist also—will do best to pin his faith on the fairly broad and definite differences that most modern scientists insist upon before admitting a new species.

In differentiating between species of trout and between varieties of those species, the scientist seeks structural peculiarities that have become hereditary, and this necessitates close examination of many individual specimens of each possible species. Such examination usually includes the counting of scale rows, fin rays, gill-rakers and pyloric caeca (blind pouches attached to the intestine), as well as certain measurements of head and fins in comparison with the length of the body. Sometimes, as between trout and char, these differences will be very marked, and there may actually be major structural differences to confirm them.

Differentiation between the species of trout in British Columbia has been a matter of some difficulty and controversy. Cutthroat trout have always been well and clearly separated from steelhead or Kamloops or rainbow, but differences among the three latter groups are slight or non-existent. Only the Kamloops trout was distinguished from the others by differences that seemed to justify its classification as a separate species. This led to the opinion, widely and reasonably held only a few years ago, that British Columbia had three species of trout: cutthroat, steelhead and Kamloops. The relationship between steelhead and Kamloops was recognised, but a difference in the number of scales along the lateral line from gill-cover to tail (usually 135 or less in the steelhead, 140 or more in the Kamloops) was believed by most authorities to be constant and unchangeable, and so was considered sufficient cause for a separation of species.

In 1934, in a paper read before the American Fisheries Society, Dr. C. McC. Mottley of the Pacific Biological Station, Nanaimo, British Columbia, showed that the number of scale-rows in Kamloops trout can be reduced by raising the temperature of the water in late embryonic development. From this he concluded that "differences in the number of scale-rows are determined largely by environment," not constant and unchangeable as had been supposed. This conclusion was con-

firmed in practice by the discovery that Kamloops trout introduced into coast waters lost all distinguishing characteristics
and were no longer separable from steelhead and coast rainbow.
Justification for specific differentiation fades altogether with
this, and it is now commonly accepted that rainbow, steelhead
and Kamloops belong to the same species.

It may be asked, Which species? Even on this point there
was, and possibly still is, some difference of opinion. The general custom in adopting scientific nomenclature is to apply to
the whole species the name given to the first properly described
member of a species. Rainbow trout were classified as *Salmo
iridea* by Dr. W. P. Gibbons in 1854. This was revised to
*Salmo irideus* by Jordan in 1878. The Kamloops trout was not
named until 1892, when Jordan called it *Salmo kamloops*. But
the first of all the rainbow group to be described was a steelhead sent to Richardson by Dr. Gairdner from Fort Vancouver
on the Columbia River in 1836. Richardson named the fish
*Salmo gairdneri*, and, since the specific interrelationship of
steelhead, Kamloops and rainbow is accepted, there can be no
reasonable doubt that this is the only correct name of the
species.* Anglers may regret the passing of *irideus*, but since
the differences between steelhead and rainbow are not even
subspecific, no useful purpose can be served by perpetuating it.
And the gain in clarity from the new classification is very
great.

The cutthroat, the only other species of trout native to
British Columbia, was also first described in 1836 by Richardson from specimens collected in the region of the Columbia
River, and the correct name is *Salmo clarkii*. These are the
only two species of trout native to British Columbia as far as
is known at present; it is altogether improbable, though per-

---

* The suggestion that the fish sent to Richardson by Gairdner was a
sockeye (*Oncorhynchus nerka*) and not a steelhead at all will not bear
serious consideration. The oncorhynchids had been properly described more
than a century before and the mistake is not one that could have been made
even by a layman.

haps not impossible, that a new species will be discovered, so
anglers will be well advised to accept this position. It is simple,
as logical as any such position can be, and it has the support of
good naturalists.

There are recognised in British Columbia also, three varieties
of each of these species. The separation is based on differences
caused by variations in climate and other conditions, which

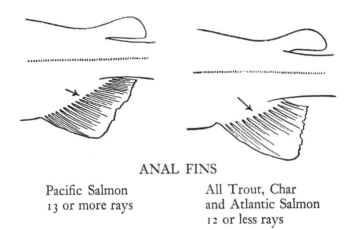

ANAL FINS

Pacific Salmon                    All Trout, Char
13 or more rays                  and Atlantic Salmon
                                 12 or less rays

are in turn due to differences in physical geography, chiefly
altitude, so that the pattern is still neat and easily remembered.
To consider the rainbow group first, *Salmo gairdneri* is the
steelhead or coastal form, *Salmo gairdneri kamloops* is the
Kamloops trout of the interior, and *Salmo gairdneri white-
housei* is the alpine form, usually called "mountain Kamloops."

Mottley notes that the Kamloops is different from the steelhead, and that the mountain Kamloops is progressively different from the Kamloops in the following ways:

"1. An increase in the number of scale-rows.

2. A decrease in the average number of gill-rakers, bran-
chiostegal rays, dorsal and anal fin rays.

3. An increase in the relative length and depth of head.

4. An increase in the relative length of the maxillary process.

5. A decrease in the relative width of the head and body.

6. An increase in the relative height of the dorsal and anal fins.

7. An increase in the relative length of pectoral, ventral, and caudal fins.

8. In general, a greater tendency towards the retention of juvenile characteristics—namely, parr marks, brighter colours, larger heads and fins, and a more terete body form."

GILL-RAKER COUNT

Sockeye                          Dog Salmon
30-39                            20-26

Mottley adds: "An experiment in which mountain Kamloops were planted in a barren lake at a lower elevation has shown that many of these characters may change in the first generation. The notable features were the reduced scale count, reduced proportions of the head, deeper and wider body and decreased fin proportions."

Actually, most British Columbian anglers will be concerned chiefly with the first two varieties, the steelhead and the Kamloops, and will seldom or never be called upon to differentiate between them. But it is fortunate that, having somewhat different habits and providing somewhat different types of sport, the two fish have developed sufficient physical differences to justify the use of different subspecific names as well as different common names.

In the case of the non-migratory coast rainbow and the steelhead, the position is not so fortunate. Some coast rainbows are definitely landlocked in lakes or streams that are shut off from the sea by impassable falls; anglers are justified in referring to these as rainbow trout rather than steelhead, but close examination reveals no marked difference in physical charac-

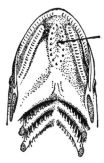

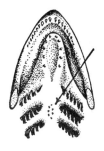

Upper jaw of trout. Note boat-shaped vomerine bone extending about half-way to gills.

Lower jaw of Cutthroat showing hyoid teeth.

teristics between these fish and steelhead. And it is fairly certain that the migratory habit persists whenever possible, even under landlocked conditions, with the lake in the place of the sea, and the streams that flow into it representing coastal rivers. In the coastal streams themselves there are rainbow trout which, though having free access to the sea, apparently spend their whole lives in fresh water; and others, again, which migrate to sea as immature fish, often very small, and return only as mature fish when the spawning urge drives them. Between two fish of such widely differing habits there is no scientific distinction, nor is it yet known whether the migratory habit is hereditary or not. It seems fairly certain that the position is further confused by fish having the migratory habit in varying degrees; some go to sea as fingerlings and return only as mature adults, others, perhaps, feed within a fairly short radius of the parent stream and may return when still immature, others, again, may be estuarial feeders in much the same way as the cutthroat are, and may return to fresh water at any time.

This is upsetting to the angler who would like to know, for instance, whether to consider his five-pound rainbow, caught on

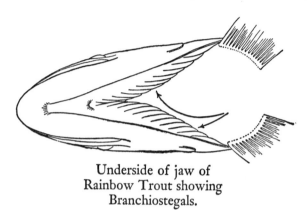

Underside of jaw of
Rainbow Trout showing
Branchiostegals.

the fly in May, a record trout for the river or just a small steel-head. If there is a fair-sized lake at the head of the river, his fish may well be a fresh-water trout. If there is no such lake it is almost certainly a sea-run fish, since the feed in coast streams is not likely to produce or support such a fish. But in neither case is the answer conclusive or satisfactory. Further research work will undoubtedly produce much information about the habits of both migratory and non-migratory rainbows, and it may yield some means of identification. But in the meantime anglers cannot profit greatly by discussing individual fish, and may avoid some hot and unpleasant arguments by writing off their "record rainbows" as "small steelheads." This is one of the very few instances where different habits have not produced struc-tural differences in fish, and it seems reasonable to suppose from this that the habits are not hereditary.

The cutthroat trout of British Columbia are divided into three varieties, almost exactly as are the rainbows. The coast cutthroat originally described by Richardson is *Salmo clarkii*. The Yellowstone cutthroat of the interior—or, rather, the southeastern part of the Province—described by Girard in 1865, is *Salmo clarkii lewisi*. And the mountain cutthroat, described by Dymond in 1931, is *Salmo clarkii alpestris*. These three varieties, like the three varieties of rainbow, are well separated geographically, and anglers are not likely to be worried much by problems of identification. Again, as in the case of the varieties of rainbow, the three varieties may be considered to be altering gradually in response to environmental influence; they are, in fact, slowly forming the characteristics of what may one day be different species.*

I have dealt with these points at some length because there has been much confusion about them. Anglers are—and I believe they should be—much interested in the fish they catch and in proper identification. Probably the worst means of identification is what is known as experience. True, the experienced angler can nearly always tell what his fish is from looking at it; but he should also be able to prove his identification when it is questioned. In the case of British Columbian trout this is not usually difficult; as I have said, the angler will not often be called upon to differentiate between varieties, as these are for the most part widely separated. And when they have been transplanted it may easily be found that characteristics have changed so that even scientists cannot differentiate between the transplanted fish and the native variety. But the angler may be called upon to differentiate between Kamloops trout and char, between coast rain-

* Kamloops and cutthroat trout have been successfully crossed to produce what is known as the Cranbrook trout. A cross of this type can only be maintained and established by selective breeding and I understand the virtues of the Cranbrook trout are not such as to justify the expense of this. The apparent susceptibility of hybrid Pacific salmon to furunculosis suggests that any experiments with hybrids should be very cautiously conducted.

bow or coast cutthroat and either char or Pacific salmon, and, finally, between coast rainbow and coast cutthroat.

The difference between trout and char is nearly always marked and quite evident, as the char have smaller scales, rounder bodies and either pink or red spots in the case of the Dolly Varden or the Eastern brook, large, pale spots in the case of the Great Lake trout. If for any reason these differences are not apparent, the final test is the bone in the centre of the roof of the mouth, known as the vomer. In the case of the trout this runs back from the palatine bone almost halfway to the gill arches, and has teeth all along it. In the case of the char there are a few teeth on the front end of the bone only, and the after part of the bone is sunken and invisible.

A quick and almost invariably sound method of differentiating between any trout—including brown trout and Atlantic salmon—and any Pacific salmon is to count the rays in the anal fin. Only fully developed rays are counted—that is to say, rays at least two-thirds as long as the longest. Trout will be found to have fewer than thirteen rays. Pacific salmon almost invariably have more than thirteen.

Between cutthroat and rainbow, the cutthroat's red under-mandible is usually distinctive, but it is sometimes extremely pale, particularly in the case of sea-run fish. A quick test is to run a finger back along the fish's tongue; in both fish there is a group of small teeth on the tip of the tongue, but the cutthroat has almost invariably a second group farther back, on the base of the tongue. These are known as the hyoid teeth, and are never present in rainbow trout. Another quick test is the length of the jaw, which in the cutthroat usually extends well behind a line drawn vertically through the rear margin of the eye. A rainbow's jaw barely reaches this line.

It may also be necessary to distinguish between native trout and the brown trout or Atlantic salmon. Each of the latter usually has only eight or nine fully developed rays in the anal fin, whereas the native trout practically always has ten or more.

To distinguish the brown trout from the Atlantic salmon, there is a quick test much used in Great Britain. The salmon has thirteen or fewer rows of scales between the adipose fin and the lateral line, while the trout has fourteen or more.

This is very far from being a complete list of counts or peculiarities by which the species may be recognised, but it is an effort at simplification. All the tests suggested can be made without instruments and by the water-side, and they are conclusive enough to settle the normal doubts in an angler's mind. A full list of scale counts and fin-ray counts is better left in the library than carried in the mind or stowed in the fishing bag. But quick differences such as the cutthroat's hyoid teeth or the Atlantic salmon's few anal fin rays are remembered without effort when they have been found once or twice, and recognising them may add considerably to the satisfaction of a day's sport.


## REFERENCES

Dymond, J. R. Trout and Other Game Fishes of British Columbia. Ottawa. Biol. Bd. Can., Bull. 32, 1932.

Dymond, J. R. Description of Two New Forms of British Columbia Trout. Contr., Can. Biol. Fish. N.S. 6(16), 1931.

Mottley, C. McC. The Origin and Relations of the Rainbow Trout. Trans. Amer. Fish. Soc. (Vol. 64), 1934.

Mottley, C. McC. The Effect of Temperature During Development on the Number of Scales in Kamloops Trout. Contr., Can. Biol. Fish. 8(20), 1934.

Mottley, C. McC. The Number of Vertebrae in Trout (Salmo); Journ. Biol. Bd. Can., Vol. III, No. 2, 1937.

Mottley, C. McC. The Classification of the Rainbow Trout of British Columbia. Progress Reports, Pacific Biol. Stn. No. 27, 1936.

# | | |

# *The Salmon of British Columbia*

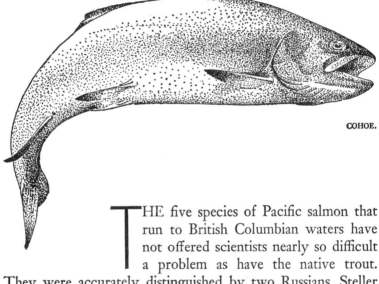

COHOE.

THE five species of Pacific salmon that run to British Columbian waters have not offered scientists nearly so difficult a problem as have the native trout. They were accurately distinguished by two Russians, Steller and Krascheninikov, in the early 1730's—which sheds a faintly interesting light on the alleged decadence and backwardness of those bad old tsarist days. The common names given to these five species were properly adapted to scientific purposes by Walbaum in 1792, and are still used.

The common use of the word "salmon" in describing these fish has unquestionably caused much unnecessary confusion, but the name has been used, is used and undoubtedly will be used until the end of time, or until the last of the genus is prevented from laying her eggs in the last stream by nets or traps

or dams. Pacific salmon are not particularly close relatives of
the Atlantic salmon, nor even of Pacific coast trout, and so are
not classed in the genus *Salmo*. I do not wish to suggest by this
that Atlantic and Pacific salmon have not had a common ancestor somewhere along the line of evolution, because they
undoubtedly have had one. But at the present time the habits
and characteristics of Pacific salmon differ so widely from those
of Atlantic salmon that no useful purpose is served by calling
attention to the relationship. If the former must be called salmon
—and obviously they must be—it is as well to keep in the back of
one's mind the name of the genus, *Oncorhynchus*, as a qualification.

In discussing British Columbian game fish it is not usual to
include more than two of the five species of Pacific salmon.
Anglers have been very slow to learn the sporting qualities and
possibilities of even these two, and still have not learned nearly
all there is to be known. But at least three of the five species are
now commonly caught by rod-fishermen, and there is every
reason to suppose that the other two may sooner or later provide
some type of sport; even if they do not, it is quite impossible to
disregard them in any thorough consideration of the game fish
of British Columbia, because they strongly influence the habits
and movements of the native trout.

These five species of Pacific salmon, roughly in the order of
their present importance to anglers, are: *Oncorhynchus kisutch*
(the cohoe), *O. tschawytscha* (the spring salmon), *O. gorbuscha* (the humpback), *O. nerka* (the sockeye) and *O. keta* (the
dog salmon). It is necessary to consider each species separately,
as their habits vary greatly. In the following account I have
endeavoured to include as many of the common names as possible, giving first those most commonly used in British Columbia.

The Cohoe, or Silver Salmon, is also known in its immature
saltwater stages as the blueback, and the precocious males
which ascend with the spawning run are generally called grilse.
United States commercial spring-salmon trollers, fishing north-

ern waters, refer to cohoes rather slightingly as "snakes." The reason for this contempt is that the fish do not keep well enough to be carried back to Seattle on ice and so must be returned to the water, but I have not been able to learn exactly why the trollers chose the word "snake" to express their feelings. Cohoes are valuable game fish, as they take the fly particularly well either in fresh or salt water and are extremely fast and active when hooked. Through their willingness to ascend streams of every size and type in their spawning migration, they are the most generally distributed of all Pacific salmon. The majority of the young spend at least one year in fresh water, and a few spend two years; it is possible that some migrate to the sea in their first summer, but this has not yet been definitely proved or disproved. During their first year in salt water the small fish feed chiefly on *Euphausids* and other small crustacea. Towards the end of this second year of their life, or early in their third, considerable numbers of the young cohoes leave coastal waters for the open sea, and do not return until they are maturing, towards the end of their third summer; others, perhaps a greater proportion, spend their whole saltwater life in the Strait of Georgia. This third year is the period of rapid growth. A blueback of 1¼ lbs. in February weighs about 3 lbs. by the beginning of May, 4½ lbs. by June 15 and anything between 5 and 12 lbs. by the middle of September. The great majority of cohoes mature, spawn and die towards the end of their third year, though a few fish mature at two years and fewer still at four years.

The angler's chief concern is the maturing third-year fish, as they begin to work towards their spawning streams in July, August and September. In these months they are still feeding fish, and are generally to be found in the tidal eddies formed by large bays and long points, where the shoals of herring and needlefish (*Ammodytes personatus*) collect. The majority of fish caught in August and September weigh from 5 to 8 lbs., but there is a very noticeable increase in the average weight all through these two months, and in the latter part of September 9 and 10 lb. fish are common; individual fish, late in the season, weigh as much as 15 to 18 lbs., and it seems probable that some of these are four-year-olds.

The SPRING SALMON is or becomes the famous tyee; the name tyee is properly applied only to fish over 30 lbs., maturing and almost ready to leave salt water. Scientifically, the name is of no importance and merely causes confusion, as a maturing spring salmon may weigh anything from 2 lbs. or less up to 100 lbs.; but the use of the name is so common that it is necessary to emphasise that there is no valid difference between a tyee and any other spring salmon. Other names of the spring salmon are "king," "chinook" and "quinnat," all three of which are used more frequently in the United States than in British Columbia; a name sometimes used by the Indians is "sachem."

Sufficient work has not yet been done to make it possible to generalise very comfortably about the life history of the spring salmon. It seems probable that in British Columbia about eighty per cent go to sea early in their first year and may be called "ocean-type," while the remaining twenty per cent stay in the rivers for a full year and are "stream-type." They mature after spending anything from two to seven years in salt water, though the majority—in British Columbian waters, at least—probably mature at the end of the fourth or fifth year in salt water; thus an ocean-type fish will probably spawn late in its fourth or fifth year, while a stream-type fish may not spawn until its fifth or sixth year.

The spring salmon has a tendency to ascend only the more considerable streams and rivers, and therefore is not so generally distributed as the cohoe. I can find no figures which indicate that the size of individuals in the run varies markedly with the rivers, but there is almost conclusive evidence that fish from northern streams tend to spend a longer period in fresh water and to mature later than those from southern streams; thus, the great majority of fish from the Yukon River in Alaska spend at

# YOUNG SALMON AND STEELHEAD

**SPRING SALMON.** Heavy parr marks, extending about half their length below lateral line. Short first ray of anal fin. Fins not usually colored.

**COHOE SALMON.** Long whitish first ray of anal fin. Lower and probably also caudal fins tinged orange and tipped with white.

**SOCKEYE SALMON.** Parr marks short and oval, extending little, if at all, below lateral line. Gill-rakers about 18 11.

**DOG SALMON** or **CHUM.** Bright mottled green back (parr marks as above), greenish sides. Gill-rakers about 14 10.

**HUMPBACK SALMON** or **PINK.** Absence of parr marks.

**STEELHEAD.** Parr marks similar to Spring but usually more heavily spotted. Distinguished from all salmon by short anal fin.

All fry shown are approximately natural size except the humpback salmon. The humpbacks migrate to the sea almost at once and would seldom or never be seen in a river at more than half the length shown in the drawing.

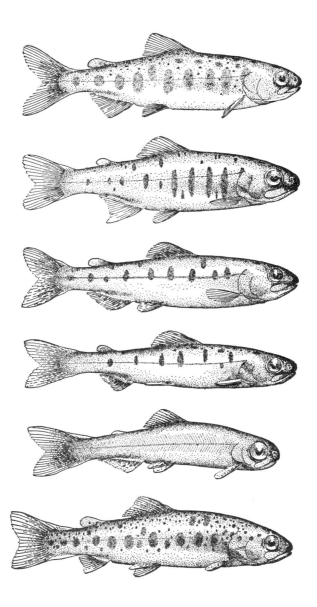

least one year in fresh water and mature at the end of the seventh year, and a fair proportion mature at eight years after spending two years in fresh water.

The angler's chief concern with these fish is their size. From scale readings of nearly a hundred large fish I believe that the great majority of spring salmon weighing over 30 lbs. that are caught south of Queen Charlotte Sound are ocean-type, five-year fish; and that the larger individuals will be found to have made exceptional growth in the early saltwater years. Maturing fish of twenty pounds or less are usually, though by no means always, at the end of their fourth year. I have not seen the scales of any fish larger than 64 lbs., but such fish may be late in maturing and so have had an extra year of saltwater growth.

The HUMPBACK or PINK SALMON is the smallest of Pacific coast salmon, averaging from three to six pounds at maturity, and has the simplest life history. The fry drop down the rivers to the sea almost as soon as they are free-swimming, spend their first summer, their first and only complete winter and part of their second summer feeding in the salt water; towards the end of this second summer they mature, and less than two years after hatching they have spawned and died. Humpbacks appear to spend most of their sea life in the open ocean, and the angler is not likely to meet with them until they have started their spawning migration. In the course of this migration they pause to feed in the bays where the cohoes are feeding, and often the humpback take the fly quite well. They cannot be said to make important game fishing by themselves, but often enough when the cohoes are not taking well a poor day is made a good one by the willingness of a few humpbacks to take hold. They do not fight as spectacularly as the cohoes, but run strongly, like spring salmon, to a considerable depth, rarely jumping. The humpback is surprisingly powerful for his 4 or 5 pound weight, and if the angler allows him to do so will take charge of a slow fight and hold out for a long while.

The influence of the humpback on the movements of migratory cutthroats is probably more important to anglers than is his value as a game fish. In streams where there is no early sockeye run, the first schools of mature humpbacks to ascend usually draw considerable numbers of trout up after them. The emergence and seaward migration of the fry in spring are even more important, and in many streams make extremely good trout fishing in the years when the hatch is large. It is perhaps worth noting that humpback fry may be easily distinguished from all other trout and salmon fry by the complete absence of parr marks.

The SOCKEYE SALMON is the blueback of the Columbia River (not to be confused with the immature cohoe of the Strait of Georgia) and the red salmon of Alaska. It is the most important commercial species of the five, and for this reason has inspired some extremely brilliant and detailed research work. Its life history is almost as variable as that of the spring salmon, and generalisations are equally dangerous. The sockeye seems especially dependent on freshwater life, and perhaps for this reason the mature fish seldom run to a stream that has no lake; it is often stated that they never run to such a stream, but this is not the case; and though the generalisation is not unreasonable, it occasions some confusion.

A majority of the adults spawn in streams tributary to the lakes along their watershed, and the fry drop down to the wider area offered by the lake, where they feed on crustacean plankton, chiefly *Daphnia* and *Diaptomus*. This freshwater life lasts normally one year, frequently two years and occasionally three; some of the fry go to sea in their first year. Work at Cultus Lake has shown that about 7% of the total migration leave fresh water in the first year, 90-92% in the second year, and from 1 to 3% in the third year. These figures are for one lake only, but they are the result of very detailed work and probably give a sufficiently accurate idea of the proportions in most other waters.

The majority of the migrants return to their rivers after three or four years in the sea, at four or five years of age, and generally weighing between 5 and 8 lbs. A few, chiefly males, mature at three years and are comparable to cohoe grilse; some individuals mature at six, seven and eight years. From this it may be seen that the tendency to regard the sockeye as a fish having a four-year life-cycle is not altogether sound. The proportion of five-year-olds in the Cultus Lake run was not shown to be particularly high, though it apparently varies from year to year, but in some important streams five-year-olds make up a strong percentage of the runs. About 40% of the sockeyes running to Rivers Inlet and Skeena are five- or six-year-olds and in the Nass River over 80% of the fish are five years of age or older.

It is rather widely believed that sockeyes are never, under any circumstances, known to take a fly or lure or bait. Actually, this is not the case at all. Their habit of feeding entirely upon crustacea, from the free-swimming stage until maturity, reduces the likelihood of their striking at spoon-baits, but even so sockeyes are occasionally caught by commercial trollers. This has been noticed for many years in Alaskan waters, and recently in British Columbian waters commercial trollers have been catching them more frequently; individual boats have brought in as many as five fish in one day. Whether this is due to the greater intensity of the fishing effort or to the working of new localities or to some change in the feeding habits of the fish it is hard to say, but if this last possibility proves correct it may be of considerable importance to anglers. But in spite of this, and in spite of the fact that mature fish have at times been taken on the fly in fresh water, sockeye cannot yet be considered angler's fish. Their habit of feeding in salt water on what is known as the "pink-feed" or the "pink-shrimp," generally *Euphausia pacifica* or *Thysanoessa spinifera*, suggests that it should be possible to catch them on flies tied to imitate this feed. I have several times taken cohoes on pink or red or orange shrimp imitations when they refused everything else, and have found from stomach examination that they were feeding exclusively on crustacea.

The seaward migration of sockeye fry, yearlings and two-year-olds, particularly of yearlings, is extremely important in influencing the movement of Kamloops trout in waters such as Little River. The spawning migration of the adults and the emergence of alevins also influence the movements of trout, though they provide less satisfactory fishing.

The Dog or CHUM SALMON is almost as generally distributed as the cohoe, and probably runs in greater numbers than any of the other species. It is considered less valuable commercially than the others, and the runs have not been over-fished to the same extent. Ten years ago dog salmon still almost literally "covered the bottom" of some streams during November and December, but heavy fishing has had a noticeable effect since then.

Dog salmon fry apparently go to sea as soon as they are free-swimming, and feed in the ocean until they are three, four or five years old, though the great majority mature at the end of their fourth year at a weight of 8 or 10 lbs. Though they do not feed extensively on herring and pilchard and needlefish as the cohoe and spring salmon do, I believe their feeding habits differ from those of the sockeye and humpback and that they feed quite largely on jelly-fish, squid and marine forms other than crustacea. This statement is based only on examination of the stomachs of a few individuals and on the paleness of the dog salmon's flesh; but on such evidence as is obtainable it seems that the sockeye is the only Pacific salmon that keeps really closely to crustacean feed throughout its life.

Dog salmon take the spoon fairly frequently in salt water, and occasionally take the fly. It seems probable that more would be taken by anglers if they did not run to the rivers so late in the year. I have found them by far the most violent and active of all Pacific salmon, and for this reason, if for no other, feel bound to consider them angler's fish. Actually, they are—

in some rivers, at least—game fish in every sense of the word. We used to catch them in the tidal water of the Nimpkish, chiefly with the idea of salting them down for winter use, by casting an ounce lead with a small treble hook about four feet below it, and working the hook near the bottom until a fish was foul-hooked. We noticed that a very high proportion were hooked near the jaw, and by watching the lead on a bright day were able to see that the fish were striking at it. This suggested the use of dull metal devons and we found that the fish took them quite well, though they were still inclined to strike at the lead rather than the devon. Eventually we learned to use a one-ounce crescent-shaped lead with the hook attached directly to it, and frequently had extremely good sport when the fish were just in from the sea.

Many dog salmon spawn in the tidal water of their rivers, and the emerging alevins draw migratory cutthroats in the spring. In rivers with large dog-salmon runs this fishing is likely to be more important than that made by the emergence of the humpback alevins.

The KOKANEE, known also as "Kennerly's salmon," has a great number of local names which are better forgotten, as most of them are based on false information and are confusing. The kokanee is simply a sockeye that never leaves fresh water, and is recognised as a subspecies under the name *O. nerka kennerlyi*. It is found in many lakes in the interior and on Vancouver Island, particularly the large lakes, and its life history is probably much like that of the migratory sockeye, with the lake playing the part of the sea. After hatching out in the streams tributary to the lake, the fry drop down to the lake and feed there until they mature at four or five years of age and ascend the streams again to spawn.* It is believed that they all die after spawning. They are small fish and seldom grow to more than a pound in weight; the average weight in many lakes is only a

---

* When conditions are particularly favourable some kokanees may, as anadromous sockeyes do at times, spawn in the lakes.

## PACIFIC SALMON–SALTWATER CHARACTERISTICS

COHOE. Feeds closest to surface, upper half of tail sometimes spotted.

HUMPBACK. Also caught on fly, oval markings on tail.

SPRING. "TYEE" when over thirty pounds. Largest of the group, plentifully spotted tail.

SOCKEYE and DOG SALMON. Almost indistinguishable from each other in salt water. Of limited interest to anglers.

few ounces.* For this reason, if for no other, the kokanee cannot be considered an important game fish, but it is a vitally important forage fish and without it the very large rainbows of the big lakes would probably not occur. Its potential importance is even greater than this because, after proper research, it may be found desirable to introduce it into smaller Kamloops trout lakes with a view to increasing their productivity.

The kokanee occurs in some lakes from which there is free access to the sea. Why it chooses to remain in fresh water in these circumstances is not exactly known; but sockeye are likely to follow a temperature belt of between 45 and 50 degrees F. in their seaward migration, and it seems possible that this belt occasionally lies deeper than the outlet of the lake at the time when the fry are inclined to migrate. In such circumstances they would not find the way out, and so might remain in fresh water either until the following spring or permanently. Whether or not the colonies in the interior lakes were originally formed in this way has not yet been shown.

In considering Pacific salmon it is necessary also to mention the possible occurrence of hybrids. Fishermen have frequently reported the capture of fish that seemed to be hybrids, and in 1927 experiments were carried out at Cultus Lake to determine whether or not cross-breeding is a possibility. These experiments proved conclusively that it is possible to produce fair to good hatches of healthy fry from crosses between sockeye, humpback and dog salmon; except in the case of the cross between a male humpback and a female sockeye it seemed to matter little which species supplied the male or the female to the pair. A male spring salmon was also crossed with these varieties and gave good results, though reciprocal crosses, except the male humpback–female spring, produced practically no results. The cohoe appeared to be the only species that could

* I have heard recently that kokanees weighing up to 3 lbs. have been taken in Woods Lake near Vernon. Unfortunately I have not been able to obtain proper confirmation of this in the shape of measurements or specimens.

not be successfully mated with other species as either male or female.

Since the three species that cross most readily—sockeye, humpback and dog—are also the three most likely to be on the spawning beds at the same time, there is a possibility that hybrids occur naturally. The pairing of separate species on the spawning beds has never been recorded, but normal pairs of different species frequently spawn at the same time within a few feet of each other. Hobbs's exact observation of the spawning habits of salmon and trout, and his demonstration of the high efficiency of natural fertilisation, suggest that cross-fertilisation under such conditions is unlikely to occur. The eggs are held closely and firmly in the spawning pocket and the milt of the spawning male is held down on them by the same flow of current, so that the chance of milt from another male reaching the eggs first would be extremely small. The very few eggs that escape from the spawning pocket, though they might possibly be fertilised by the milt from another male, would be unburied and have a practically negligible chance of survival. But in spite of these facts the occurrence of cross-fertilisation between pairs of different species spawning at the same time cannot be considered absolutely impossible.

Foerster, in discussing his experiments, emphasises the fact that more value must be placed on the positive results than on the negative, since other factors than the species difference of the parents may have caused poor hatches; but it seems to be shown fairly conclusively that the cohoe does not cross readily. Although it was proved that—in some cases, at least—hybrids are fertile, Foerster also concludes that "the possibility of a distinct run of hybrid fish developing is highly incredible," since hybrids returning to the spawning grounds would be almost certain to mate with normal individuals of the opposite sex and their progeny would thus gradually revert to the normal strain. On the whole, I believe anglers should be extremely sceptical about apparent hybrids, and should seek to prove them normal rather than abnormal. Such peculiarities as spots and other marks, size, shape, colour, fighting qualities, even colour of flesh, are not satisfactory proof of abnormality; this can only be supplied by proper examination of the constant structural characteristics.

The whole question of the identification of the various species of Pacific salmon is finally dependent on these characteristics. Normally, the species can be separated without much difficulty, particularly when approaching maturity. The spring salmon, for instance, has a heavily spotted tail with a slender caudal peduncle or wrist, whereas the cohoe has no spots on the tail or only a few along the upper edge, and the caudal peduncle is thick. The humpback is usually more heavily spotted on the back than either of these fish, and has distinctive oval spots on the tail. It also has a deeper, narrower body and smaller scales. The dog salmon and the sockeye are extremely hard to separate by superficial characteristics when immature, but may be readily recognised when approaching maturity.

Such superficial characteristics are better illustrated than described, and they can be used satisfactorily only by a man who has had at least some personal experience with the species concerned. And no matter how experienced a fisherman may be, he will do well, when any doubt arises, to refer to the constant structural characteristics. I have given at the end of this chapter a fairly complete table of these for both trout and salmon, but for positive identification in most circumstances it is only necessary to use one or two of the outstanding characteristics of each species, and these are fairly easily remembered.

Pacific salmon are distinguished from all trout by lack of spots on the dorsal fin and by the number of rays in the anal fin—14 or more as against 13 or less. The sockeye, including the land-locked variety, may be distinguished from all other Pacific salmon by the high number of its gill-rakers—normally about 36 as against 30 or less for the other species. The humpback is distinguished by its high scale count—170 or more in the first row above the lateral line, whereas all other varieties have 153 or less. The cohoe is distinguished from all species—except possibly the humpback—by having 80 or less pyloric caeca—small blind pouches attached to the intestine at the point where it joins the stomach. The dog salmon and spring salmon, thus separated from the other species, are more difficult to separate exactly from each other, though they are seldom likely to be confused. The spring salmon is extremely likely to have more anal fin rays than any other species, including the dog—16 or more. The dog salmon is likely to have fewer branchiostegals than the spring—13 or 14 instead of 16 or more; and the black spots on the tail of the spring salmon, combined with one or other of the above characteristics, may generally be considered positive identification.

The British Columbian fisherman is probably faced with more difficult problems of identification than any other fisherman in the world, and perhaps chiefly for this reason, I believe he takes a more acute interest in the fish he catches than does the average fisherman. This fact and the innumerable fishermen's discussions I have listened to and taken part in are my excuses for these two long chapters of life histories and scale counts and other anatomical details.

## REFERENCES

Clemens, W. A. The Pacific Salmon in British Columbia Waters. Rept. Prov. Fish. Dept., for 1934, Victoria, B.C. 1935.

Clemens, W. A. Pacific Salmon Migration: The Tagging of Spring Salmon on the East Coast of Vancouver Island in 1927 and 1928, Together With Notes on the Incidental Tagging of Other Fish. Biol. Bd. Can. Bull. 27, 1932.

Clemens, W. A. Pacific Salmon Migration: The Tagging of the Cohoe Salmon on the East Coast of Vancouver Island in 1927 and 1928. Biol. Bd. Can. Bull. 15, 1930.

Clemens, W. A. and Williamson, H. C. Pacific Salmon Migration: Report on Tagging Operations at Quatsino and Kyoquot in

1927, with Additional Returns from the Operations of 1925 and 1926. Biol. Bd. Can. Bull. 26, 1936.

Foerster, R. E. An Investigation of the Life History and Propagation of the Sockeye Salmon at Cultus Lake, B. C. No. 4, Contr. Can. Biol. Fish. N. S. 8(27), 1934.

Foerster, R. E. The Same: No. 5 Biol. Bd. Can., 1936.

Foerster, R. E. Inter-specific Cross-breeding of Pacific Salmon. Trans. Roy. Soc. Can. Series 3, Sec. 5, Vol. 29, 1935.

Foerster, R. E. and Pritchard, A. L. The Identification of the Young of the Five Species of Pacific Salmon, With Notes on the Fresh-Water Phase of Their Life History. Rept. Prov. Fish. Dept., for 1934, Victoria, B. C., 1935.

Hobbs, D. F. Natural Reproduction of Quinnat Salmon, Brown Trout and Rainbow Trout in Certain New Zealand Waters. New Zealand Marine Dept. Fish. Bull. No. 6, 1937.

Mottley, C. McC. Pacific Salmon Migration: Report on the Study of the Scales of the Spring Salmon Tagged in 1926 and 1927 off the West Coast of Vancouver Island. Contr. Can. Biol. Fish. N. S. Vol. 4, No. 30, 1929.

Pritchard, A. L. Pacific Salmon Migration: The Tagging of the Spring Salmon in British Columbia in 1929 and 1930. Biol. Bd. Can. Bull. 41, 1934.

Pritchard, A. L. Pacific Salmon Migration: The Tagging of the Cohoe Salmon in British Columbia in 1929 and 1930. Biol. Bd. Can. Bull. 40, 1934.

# IV

## Other British Columbian Game Fish

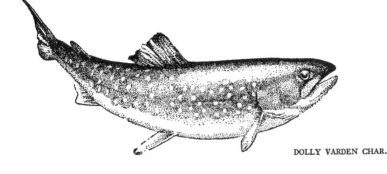

DOLLY VARDEN CHAR.

THE most important native "other fish" of the Province are the two native chars (*Salvelinus malma* and *Cristivomer namaycush*), the grayling (*Thymallus signifer*), and the Rocky Mountain whitefish (*Prosopium williamsoni*). Five aliens have been introduced, each of them a game fish of the highest quality: The Atlantic salmon (*Salmo salar*), the brown trout (*Salmo trutta*), the Eastern brook trout (*Salvelinus fontinalis*), the small-mouth bass (*Micropterus dolomieu*) and the large-mouth bass (*Aplites salmoides*). Because it is necessary to complete the picture of game fish available in British Columbia, I propose to discuss each of these rather fully in this chapter; none of them seems to be of sufficient importance to need a chapter of its own later in the book.

There is comparatively little risk of confusion between trout and char. Char have finer scales than trout, and their spots are pink, red, orange or pale yellow, never black or dark brown. As a general rule they are more vividly coloured than trout and have a more rounded body form. A final and positive means of identification is the presence or absence of teeth on the shaft of the vomerine bone, as described in a previous chapter.

Char are essentially cold-water fish and do best in a temperature of well below 60 degrees F., but in spite of this the Dolly Varden (*Salvelinus malma*) is the most generally and widely distributed game fish in the Province. Dymond states that this fish in British Columbia is very little different from the seagoing char of northern Europe, Asia and North America, and should probably be considered a sub-species, *Salvelinus alpinus malma*. In British Columbia the Dolly Varden is found landlocked in many watersheds, but where it has access to the sea it may be migratory or non-migratory. The angler is likely to meet with it at any size from ½ lb. up to 20 lbs. or more. Small specimens often take the fly fairly well, but the larger fish are nearly all caught by trolling or spinning. They are voracious fish, and take with rather contemptible lack of caution; in most waters they are slower than trout when hooked but they can put up a remarkable fight at times; their appearance when landed is, in spite of their bright colours, somehow unattractive.

The smaller individuals compete directly with trout for food. Larger individuals are more predatory than trout and undoubtedly account for considerable numbers of salmon fry, trout fry and forage fish such as kokanee. They also account for some numbers of chub (*Mylocheilus*), but even in this they are competing with trout. There seems little to be said for them except perhaps that in coast streams they may help to keep down the numbers of the bullhead (*Cottus asper*); but they may possibly be helping, in some way not yet determined, to preserve a natural balance in the lakes and streams they frequent, and organised efforts to reduce their numbers should only be made after really thorough investigation.

The Great Lakes trout (*Cristivomer namaycush*) may be

distinguished from the Dolly Varden by its many large, pale spots and by its strongly forked tail. It is found in most of the large lakes north of Kamloops and grows to a tremendous size, probably to at least 60 and perhaps to 80 pounds. In spite of this, it really has not much claim to be considered a game fish, as large specimens are taken only by deep trolling, and are sluggish when hooked. Most of what I have said of the feeding habits of the Dolly Varden probably applies also to this species, especially to the smaller individuals. I understand that the smaller fish do at times—usually for a short period in the spring—take the fly fairly well. I have never caught them in this way myself, but Bergman, in his excellent book JUST FISHING, states that they give really good sport. The larger specimens may possibly be considered of some value as, in many of the large lakes, they utilise wide areas of water too deep to attract trout.

The third char to be found in British Columbia today is also the first of the alien, or rather non-native, game fish. It is the Eastern speckled or Eastern brook trout (*Salvelinus fontinalis*), incomparably the best and most beautiful of North American char, and in its native waters a splendid game fish. It may be readily distinguished from the Dolly Varden by its mottled back and dorsal fin.

The introduction of the speckled trout to British Columbian waters has not been an unqualified success. Sufficient attention has not been paid to the char's preference for very cold, clear streams, and in most of the waters in which it has been planted the speckled trout is definitely a slower, less active fish when hooked than is the Kamloops. As is often the case with introductions of non-native species of both fish and animals, the speckled trout at first appeared able to attain greater weight and to thrive better than trout native to the water in which it was planted. But, again as is usual, the abnormal results of the first few years have not lasted, and, in many cases, a stream or lake which produced annually a fair weight of native fish before the introduction is now producing a lesser weight of both species. It seems probable that the speckled trout, when first introduced, finds a built-up stock of some particular type of feed which is available to itself but not available to the native trout. As long as this stock holds out the results are remarkable. When it is exhausted or reduced to normal proportions the speckled trout begins to compete with the native fish, to the detriment of both; in other words, the introduction eventually produces what amounts to an overstock of fish in the lake or stream of the planting.

Such results seem clear enough demonstration of the inadvisability of introducing speckled trout to waters which are too warm for the native species or in which a good native species is already doing well. But when the road goes on north of Hazelton and the time comes to plant the colder northern streams and lakes, it may well be that the speckled trout will come into its own in British Columbia and show even finer sport than it has shown so long in the eastern streams of the continent.

A last word on char: The Dolly Varden is called also "bull trout." *Namaycush* is the Great Grey Trout, the Mackinaw trout, the Great Lakes trout. *Fontinalis* is the speckled trout or the Eastern brook trout. But why? I have no wish to be controversial, certainly no wish to detract from the noble qualities of *Fontinalis*, but the fish are, after all, char. There are plenty of trout in the province, and they need the name. It would save quite a lot of confusion and trouble if anglers would use the word "char" more frequently and let us have, say, a plain "Dolly Varden," a perfectly reasonable "Great Lakes char" or "Mackinaw char," and a wholly admirable "Eastern speckled char."

I have not yet caught grayling (*Thymallus signifer*) in British Columbian waters, but I have had splendid sport with them in the Coppermine River, within ten or twelve miles of the Arctic Ocean. In Canada they are native to the Arctic watershed only, but they rise as freely and well to a dry fly as

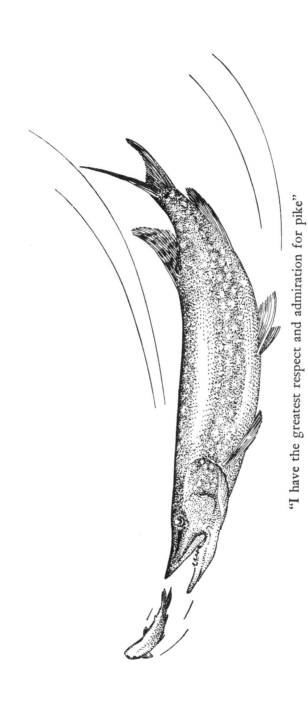

"I have the greatest respect and admiration for pike"

do the grayling of England and Scotland and they put up as good a fight when hooked. They are also fully as graceful and lovely as the grayling of the United Kingdom, with the same splendidly developed and colored dorsal fin, the same tiny mouth and slender silver body. For my money they are worth a northern trip at any time and as the country opens up they will certainly prove their attraction.

The common pike (*Esox lucius*) is another northern fish that I have not yet caught in British Columbian waters. Apparently they are fairly plentiful in the Arctic watershed of the Province and should be well worth investigation. Asst. Commr. Sandys-Wunsch of the R. C. M. Police has told me of seeing really large specimens in the Yukon River, and it seems altogether possible that some of the northern British Columbian lakes hold record fish. Half the appeal of the pike has always been in the mystery that builds around him and the hope that a monster of the species will be lying under the next patch of lily pads or hovering in the dark backwater of the next deep pool.

The Rocky Mountain whitefish (*Prosopium williamsoni*) is the last of the natives with much claim to be considered as a game fish. Dymond writes of this fish, after emphasizing that it must not be mistaken for a grayling: "It somewhat resembles the common whitefish, the valuable food fish of the Great Lakes and other large Eastern lakes, but is not so closely related as the name suggests. It too is often regarded as belonging to the trout and char family, but sometimes is placed with the ciscoes or lake herrings in a separate family, the *Coregonidae*. The Rocky mountain whitefish will often rise to an artificial fly, and in swift, cold mountain streams shows some of the spirit characteristic of a game fish."

The small-mouth bass (*Micropterus dolomieu*), like the speckled char, is a great game fish in its native waters, but, unlike the speckled char, it is not, even in its own waters, a game fish comparable to the true trouts, because it is not a fish that comes really well to either the dry fly or the ordinary wet fly. It is also a frequenter of warm and sluggish waters, which are not normally as attractive to the angler (or to fish) as clear, cool waters. If there were in British Columbia extensive areas of warm, sluggish water unsuited to other game fish, the small-mouth bass might be a desirable introduction. But the small-mouth is so voracious a fish that his introduction must always be a dangerous experiment; an unforeseen spread of the original planting may wipe out excellent and thriving colonies of native fish. Since there is relatively little water in British Columbia in which one or another of the native species will not thrive, this danger makes the planting of small-mouth bass anywhere in the province practically indefensible. Actually, they have been planted with some success, notably in Spider Lake on Van-couver Island, and provide some sport; I understand that a fish of over 11 lbs. was taken from Spider Lake a few years ago. They are also spreading from adjacent waters into Kootenay Lake, where they may serve a useful purpose. There is in this lake, at certain seasons, a strong shoreward movement of coarse fish which is apparently little attended by trout. Small-mouth bass might use this potential source of food and interfere very little with the trout in the lake. But these are exceptional con-ditions, and the danger of spread to valuable waters is such that plantings should be made only after the most careful examina-tion of the risk entailed and of all other possibilities of using the water in question.

The large-mouth bass (*Aplites salmoides*) is present in Koo-tenay Lake, in Osoyoos and Vaseaux lakes on the Okanagan watershed and in Mary Lake on Saltspring Island. Most of what I have written of the small-mouth bass applies to the large mouth also. He is generally considered somewhat inferior to the small mouth in game qualities but in one important respect, his greater readiness to respond to artificial lures, he is superior. Since there is in Kootenay Lake, and perhaps also in some of the other large lakes of the province, an abundance of forage fish not at present utilised the desirability of planting some large predator, such as one or other of the bass or the pike or the muskellunge, is well worth considering. To reach a proper decision on this point it will be necessary to measure the probable efficiency as a predator of the fish to be introduced, his game qualities, the danger of his spreading to waters where he would be undesirable and the possibility that he may exhaust the supply of forage fish available and become either a predator or a competitor of more desirable species. No large scale introduction should be undertaken until these points have been weighed in the light of all available knowledge; and if the knowledge available seems insufficient to justify a decision whatever research work is necessary should be undertaken.

There remain two last non-natives which, for sentimental and most practical reasons, I should like to see successfully planted in the province. The first of these, *Salmo salar*, the Atlantic salmon, is the equal of any fish that swims for gameness, for beauty, for the traditions that surround the sport of catching him and for the multitude of truly delicate methods to which he succumbs. His is also the only species which gives an angler a worthwhile hope of raising to the fly a forty, fifty or sixty-pounder in the fast, good water of a river. He is, as everyone knows, a migratory fish, and normally goes to sea at the beginning of his third year; since the resources of the sea are certainly great enough to provide for a few more salmon, he would be competing with native fish only in the first two years of his life; and even in those he would probably provide more in forage for the native trout than he took from them. So it seems unlikely that his introduction would be dangerous to native species unless he gave up his seagoing habit, and the food supply of coast streams is not such as to make this at all probable.

But unfortunately there is little to suggest that Atlantic salmon can be successfully established in Pacific Coast waters. Annual plantings were made in the Cowichan, and occasional plantings in other Vancouver Island streams, for a sufficient number of years to give the experiment a good chance of success, but there have not been more than two or three properly authenticated returns. A certain number of anglers have reported captures from time to time, but identification has usually been based on general appearance, colour of flesh, fighting qualities, table qualities or other such valueless observations. Since there is still some hope of returns from the most recent plantings and since differentiation between Atlantic salmon and steelhead may be an extremely difficult matter even for a trained biologist, anglers would be well advised to submit specimens about which there is any question to the Fisheries Research Board at Nanaimo. If this is impossible it should be remembered that identification is usually made by anal fin ray and vertebrae counts. The Atlantic salmon normally has 9 or less anal fin rays, whereas the steelhead normally has 10 or more; the steelhead usually has 62 or more vetebrae, whereas the Atlantic salmon normally has 59 or less. Even in these counts there is some danger of overlap, and in the case of the Atlantic salmon, a possibility of environmental modification. A more thorough knowledge of the factors influencing salmon migration may one day reveal some flaw in the method of planting used or the type of stream chosen for the experiment and so justify further attempts to introduce Atlantic salmon. But in the present state of knowledge there is nothing to suggest that future plantings would be more successful than those already made.

The introduction of the brown trout, *Salmo trutta*, has been more successful—perhaps too successful. The brown trout is unquestionably a fine fish and a better surface feeder than any other trout. Though not the equal of the Kamloops in swiftness and vigorous activity, he is essentially the finest trout from a fly fisherman's point of view, not only because he rises so freely to even the smallest types of surface feed, but because his habit of hovering or cruising just under the surface of the water instead of rising from a depth makes him much more difficult to stalk or deceive.

I should like to enlarge on this point and bring some further evidence in support of it, because if a certain species of trout is more difficult to catch than other species, clearly that is the best trout to plant in waters that are subject to extremely heavy fishing—provided always that the species can be produced and planted as cheaply as other species. The eastern United States are already faced with this problem; in a paper read before the American Fisheries Society in 1935 Henry C. Markus of the United States Bureau of Fisheries gave some interesting facts about a stocking of brown trout in a heavily fished water. At the start of the paper he quotes the late Mr. R. B. Marston, editor of *The Fishing Gazette*, on the brown trout in American waters: "Given fairly pure running water," Mr. Marston wrote in 1895, "and our trout do well anywhere if they have a good supply of food. Although varying in colour and marking, wherever he is found, *S. fario*, in good condition, is as handsome, as game and as good a fish in every way as anglers could wish to catch. That is why so many thousands of our best anglers wish to catch him, and why he is so difficult to catch. And it is this very difficulty that places him so high in our esteem. Our trout are so well educated that the angler who can with the fly kill a few brace of them in a day must be a good hand."

Mr. Markus goes on to state that in an endeavour to check these claims 2,700 10-inch brown trout were released in 2½ miles of stream in New York State on 25th April, 1935. 470 daily fishing permits were issued between May 1st and July 1st to 311 different anglers. Artificial fly and lures only were allowed. There was a daily limit of 8 fish, or 5 pounds. The resulting catch by 311 anglers, fishing a total of 470 days, was 185 trout; of these, 100 were taken by 5 anglers. On the opening day 40 fishermen took 4 fish.

These figures are not quite complete. One would like to

know, for instance, how many days the 5 anglers spent in catching their 100 fish. But the conclusions are obvious: The brown trout can take good care of himself, yet by the use of fine tackle and a decent skill he may be caught. Since angling is a test of skill rather than a means of filling the pot, it would seem that the brown trout is an extremely valuable fish for stocking purposes in heavily fished waters.

But he should not be planted in waters where he will be competing with fish that are already providing satisfactory sport. The risk is too great. Unfortunately, the boards of trade and the individuals who persuaded the authorities to plant brown trout in British Columbia chose Vancouver Island waters for the experiment. These waters are already used by cut-throat, steelhead and the five Pacific salmon. That the feed in them is insufficient to support a heavy fish population is clearly shown by the migratory habit of the cutthroat trout. So it was, or should have been, sufficiently obvious that if the brown trout were able to establish itself it could only be at the expense of some native species. The only question was, which species?

The brown trout apparently has established himself in the Cowichan and Little Qualicum Rivers, from the plantings of 1932, 1933 and 1934. He seems to have adopted sea-running habits, not the true migratory habits of the steelhead and salmon, but the estuarial and inshore feeding habits of the cutthroat. For two reasons this should be a good thing: He will not be competing so strongly within the narrow confines of the river itself, and he will probably show the game qualities of the European sea-trout and so win the hearts of many anglers who might otherwise find him sluggish in comparison with the best of the natives. But there is already some evidence that the brown trout preys particularly upon young cohoes in British Columbia. This is altogether likely, since cohoe salmon spend a full year in fresh water before migration, but the charge is not yet fully proved, so there can be little point in discussing it further; within the next few years it will be fully

proved or disproved, and in the meanwhile any further introductions to waters already carrying stocks of desirable fish
should be avoided.

I do not wish to suggest that there is no place for the brown
trout in British Columbian waters. He can serve a useful purpose in heavily fished waters near large towns, so long as those
waters are land-locked. And there should certainly be a place
for him in some of the "barren" lakes of the interior, again
land-locked lakes, well separated from those which already
hold good stocks of Kamloops trout. In such lakes, particularly
if they were chosen for the quantity of surface feed available,
or first stocked with mayflies, sedges, stoneflies, alders or other
fauna that provide good surface feed, he would provide a type
of fishing different from anything at present available in the
Province, and in many ways a superior type. If the plantings
were calculated to produce a 1½- or 2-pound average, it would
be possible to make in this way a few dry-fly lakes of the highest quality, because the brown trout is, whatever his deficiencies as a fighter or sins as a predator, at once the boldest and
wariest riser of all trout. And, given a fair chance, he provides
a finer test of the angler's skill than any other fish that swims.

I hope I have not been too hard on the non-natives. All four
have such excellent qualities that any keen angler must hate to
be without them. But the native fish also are good, probably as
good as any fish anywhere when every quality is exactly
weighed. Certainly, it is important never to risk displacing them
for any non-native unless it can first be proved that the non-
native will provide better fishing and more of it.

### REFERENCES

Bergman, Ray. *Just Fishing*. Penn Pub. Co., 1932.

Dymond, J. R. The Trout and Other Game Fishes of British
    Columbia. Ottawa. Biol. Bd. Can., Bull. 32, 1932.

Foerster, R. E. Sockeye Salmon Propagation in British Columbia. Biol. Bd. Can., Bull. 53, 1936.

Markus, Henry C. Americanized Brown Trout Retain European Characteristics. Trans. Amer. Fish. Soc., Vol. 65, 1935.

Mottley, C. McC. The Introduction of Brown Trout (*Salmo trutta* L.) into British Columbia. Proc. Fifth Pac. Sc. Congress, Vol. V, p. 3801. 1933.

# PART TWO

*The Interior of the Province*

# The Fish & the Water

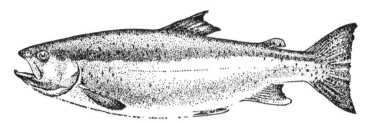

THE fish of the interior is the Kamloops trout. As we have decided, the Kamloops is, strictly speaking, simply a subspecies of the steelhead. He is a rainbow trout which has certain slight structural differences from the originally described member of the species, but none that may not be readily modified by change of environment. From the point of view of the scientist and the naturalist, this is a thoroughly logical and desirable simplification, and the loop-hole left by the subspecific rating is all that the angler needs. An angler's view of his fish, though it should be at least related to that of the scientist, is not necessarily identical with it. Differences of habit, of habitat, of those qualities which go to make up what he considers a game fish—even superficial differences in appearance—naturally mean more to the angler than the slight structural differences that separate two closely related fish. In a comparatively few years the Kamloops trout has won for himself a place in the average angler's list of good fish quite apart from that already held by the rainbow and the steelhead.

It is not easy to describe the typical Kamloops, because his colours and markings vary greatly with environment and the stage of maturity at which he is caught. From the fisherman's point of view he is probably at his best as a maiden third- or fourth-summer fish, in a clear-water lake where feed is plentiful. Under these conditions a sixteen-inch fish will often weigh as much as two pounds, which means, in a trout, a very beautifully shaped fish, short and thick and deep. His back will be a strong steel-grey, changing rather sharply to silver-grey a little above the lateral line and shading gradually from there to pure silver on the belly; set in the steel-grey of his back, and often scarcely noticeable, there will be a good number of small, black spots. Ideally, in the perfect Kamloops, there should be, I believe, no faintest trace of the pink iridescence along the lateral line and on the gill-covers which is the rainbow trout's mark. This colouring, particularly in its early stages, is extremely beautiful, but it is always an indication of approaching maturity; the trout that shows it will almost certainly spawn within twelve months and to me, at least, it is a reminder of the vivid red lateral band, the sunken flanks and dirty belly of the spawner; it is a refinement of beauty yet a warning of decay, so that the trout which shows it must always seem ever so slightly less close to perfection than his steel-grey and silver brother who has no look of maturity.

The beauty of the perfect Kamloops trout is clean and firm and strong, a beauty of both line and colouring probably equal to that of any of the other salmonidae. He also has what are to the angler three other essential qualifications: He is to be found in pleasant and beautiful places, he rises at least sufficiently well to the artificial fly, and under the right conditions he grows to a great size. These excellences would be enough to make him a highly valued fish, but no Kamloops trout fisherman would suggest that these are his outstanding qualities; his greatest quality, the one that has really given him his place apart, is his gameness.

This quality of gameness in trout—and in other game fish, for that matter—is not by any means a simple one or easy to measure. Perhaps the angler's usual approach to it, when he speaks of "fight" and "courage," and sometimes even of "pugnacity" or "ferocity," is unsound; it reflects the hunter's natural tendency to praise himself by the indirect but effective method of praising his conquered quarry. The ultimate projection of this idea can become a little ridiculous; at times, after reading accounts of the savage qualities of the fish of this lake or that stream, one begins to feel that the intentions of the average one-pound trout are at least homicidal; that an angler, wandering alone near the edge of the lake or stream towards dusk of a murky evening, might be set upon by a brace of such creatures and most foully destroyed. A hooked fish does, in fact, "fight" the restraint of rod and line, I suppose. But substitution of "flight" for "fight," "fear" for "courage," "determination to live" for "pugnacity," seems generally to give a clearer picture of what is taking place. The effect is the same—one of violent movement calculated to defeat the fisherman's aim—but the words substituted lend themselves less to over-emphasis and match better the factors which influence gameness.

These factors—condition, maturity and habitat—are so important that they may at times quite outweigh the natural difference in game qualities between two species of fish. A fish will not show proper gameness unless he is in really good condition; a fish that has never spawned will normally be more active and stronger than one that has spawned and recovered; a fish approaching maturity will be less active than an immature fish. Water temperature, also, is often a fairly important factor. The angler's tackle must be approximately proportionate to the size and strength of the fish. And if the fish is to run and jump and turn quickly, he must be hooked in such a way that he can use muscles and fins and gills freely.

When these conditions are fulfilled, a trout of any species should prove active and vigorous and perhaps spectacular in his attempts to escape. How effective these attempts will be is another matter. The most difficult trout in the world to land, even when they are properly hooked, are the big brown trout of the English chalk streams. These fish are not as active and perhaps not as strong in proportion to their weight as are Kamloops trout, but to hook them one must use 3x or 4x gut and flies tied on No. 16-18 hooks; and there is nearly always a weed-bed, a stake, a strand of barbed wire or some other obstruction within reach of a first short rush. The Kamloops, on the other hand, will tolerate 2x gut, and generally prefers large flies; nine times out of ten he must show his qualities in the open water of a lake, without even a current to help him. In these conditions he does surprisingly well, and I have very little doubt that if comparable figures were available it would be found that the average, skilful fly fisherman loses a higher percentage of Kamloops, simply through the activities of the fish, than of any other trout.

The maiden Kamloops of two or three pounds, in good condition, is a very strong and active fish. He can take out yards of line against heavy pressure on the reel. He can change direction surprisingly fast, and he is always likely to turn and swim directly towards the fisherman. He jumps spectacularly, repeatedly and in spite of gentle handling, often swimming down to a considerable depth to turn, rush towards the surface and fling himself high out of the water. And, unlike many other vigorous and spectacular fish, he does not tire easily or quickly. It is this splendid speed and strength and violence that have done more than anything else to make the Kamloops a popular game-fish, and I have used a great number of words to describe it and emphasize it because I believe it is a real thing and not simply the burden of an angler's tale. I believe, also, that the excitement of those spectacular few moments after the fish feels the hook is to the average angler the highest point in his day's fishing, and that the Kamloops, under like conditions, will yield more excitement for each moment that he is on the end of a line than will any other trout.

There are in the interior of British Columbia both native and planted stocks of Kamloops. The history of the early days has been so casually recorded that it is not always easy to tell which waters have been planted and which have always held trout. But it is probable that most plantings have been made in the land-locked, so-called "barren" lakes. These "barren" lakes before planting held no fish of any kind, but in other respects most of them are far from barren; they carry an extremely heavy growth of bottom weed, usually chara or lime-weed, and a teeming stock of crustacea, mollusca, insecta and other highly important trout foods; such food supplies, built up through thousands of years, together with the absence of all competing and predatory species, made conditions for stocking almost ideal. And though the early stocking was extremely haphazard—a matter of three or four pairs of breeding fish, a coal-oil can of fry or a few handfuls of eyed ova, turned down by Indians or small groups of anglers—the immediate results were, almost inevitably, extremely good.

How long these results lasted usually depended on a single factor, the extent of the spawning grounds available to the lake in question. The Kamloops, unlike the cutthroat, will spawn properly only under almost ideal conditions of running water and clean gravel beds. When these were available the lake soon built up an overstock of fish which reduced the food supply to normal or subnormal proportions, and the average size of the fish to a half pound or less. When a limited extent of good spawning ground was available the stock built itself up to reasonable proportions and held there, so that lakes of this type produced fair numbers of sizeable or smaller numbers of really large fish. The stock in lakes which had no good spawning grounds accessible to the trout usually died out within a few years.

But the successes in these haphazard activities were, naturally enough, more clearly remembered and more frequently dis-cussed than the failures. By the time Kamloops trout fry and eggs were readily available from government hatcheries, anglers and others had deduced from the successful plantings at least two conclusions that were absolutely false. Studying the records of lakes of the intermediate type, those with good spawning grounds of limited extent, they decided either that these were "big-fish lakes" or that the stock of trout in them was a "big-fish strain." They called for heavy plantings of fry and eggs in the "big-fish lakes" or for heavy plantings of the "big-fish strain" in lakes that were producing only small fish. As a result, many good lakes were ruined by overstocking and some plantings were completely wasted on lakes which already held an overstock.

This brings us within reach of the present time. In the past few years a great deal of valuable scientific work has been done by Mottley, Rawson, Dymond and others. Many lakes have been stocked, a few have been settled on a sound basis of annual production, and a few more, in spite of the knowledge available both to anglers and to the authorities, have been ruined by popular request. For the future there are still many "barren" lakes that are unstocked, some that are coming into production, and others that have been producing either below or within their capacity for many years. Even the lakes that are now overstocked do not present a hopeless problem, nor are they in their present state a complete loss.

But the future of most of the more accessible lakes depends on the next few years. It is still far too generally believed by anglers, resort-keepers and local organisations of all kinds that heavy stocking is the solution of every problem, and that it is a simple matter to produce permanently beneficial results by stocking "barren" lakes. More enlightened opinions are gaining ground everywhere, but the demand for quick results is against them. Unless this handicap can be overcome, many valuable waters are likely to be ruined, at least temporarily and perhaps permanently, by overstocking.

Meanwhile, research work has ceased. There is no money. Even comparatively enlightened anglers would rather see their dollars spent upon fry than upon research work, for the fry are something they can touch and understand. Research work too often seems pointless, a government excuse for "stalling." In this lie the real tragedy and the real danger, for there is so much still to be learned before stocking can be at once safe and efficient, and the learning can only be slow and costly.

The life history of the Kamloops trout, like that of British Columbia's two other most important trout, the steelhead and the cutthroat, is little understood. It seems fairly clear that they retain to some extent the migratory habit of the steelhead, and normally run from lakes to streams or rivers to spawn. The spawning period extends from April until June, though the heaviest part of the run is likely to occur in most lakes between May 5th and May 25th. Mottley has shown that migration is directed and stimulated by currents in the lake set up by wind action on the surface water, that streams draw migrants approximately in proportion to their volume of water and that the migrants prefer, and probably follow through the lake, a temperature band from 45 to 50 degrees F. The eggs are spawned in gravel and covered, and hatch after about 40 days at a water temperature of 52 degrees F. By August the fry from eggs spawned in May should be 1½ to 3 inches long.

From scale reading it is evident that there are both "stream-type" and "lake-type" Kamloops trout, just as there are "stream-type" and "ocean-type" spring salmon. Probably the large majority of Kamloops trout drop back to the lake as fry, during their first year. But a considerable proportion spend a full year in the streams and some—perhaps corresponding to the non-migratory rainbows of the coast streams—spend their whole lives in the streams. The "lake-type" fish—that is, those which descend to the lake as fry—are probably preferable to the "stream-type" in that they make faster growth and are likely to be larger at maturity, but this is the sort of question that can be answered only by exact and comprehensive research. For instance, it is possible that the "stream-type" have a better chance of survival than the "lake-type," since they are not so much exposed to the attacks of larger fish when in the fry stage; and it is possible that the "stream-type" tend to mature a year later than the "lake-type," as is the case with spring salmon. Early stream-feeding may produce hardier fish or fish that rise more freely. And possibly the "stream-type" fish, by utilising the food supply of the spawning streams and so reducing the drain on the food supply of the lake, may increase significantly the total productivity of the lake.

Once the fish are past the fingerling stage, the growth of Kamloops trout, as is the case with all trout, varies tremendously, but probably in exact proportion to the amount of food available. In Paul Lake, which may be considered fairly typical, a fish hatched in July will probably be 6 inches long by the following July, and by September of the same year should weigh about ½ pound. By the following July, as a two-year-old it should weigh from 1 to 1¼ pounds and a normal three-year-old should weigh over 2 pounds. The few four- five- and six-year-old fish in the lake normally weigh between 2½ and 5 pounds.

Paul may be considered an "in-between" lake, neither large nor small and carrying a reasonably heavy stock of fish. Many lakes have shown much better figures, and the really large lakes consistently produce fish, many of them probably three-year-olds, weighing 10 pounds or more. The smaller lakes which show better figures than Paul are usually carrying smaller stocks of fish, while the large lakes have native stocks of kokanee, the land-locked sockeye, which make excellent forage for Kamloops of 2 pounds or more and produce rapid and sustained growth. It is significant that most of the big trout in the large lakes—and they at times reach weights of over 20 pounds—are caught by trolling.

The Kamloops normally matures and spawns for the first time at four years; a few, usually males, mature at three years, and some individuals mature at five years. Size seems to make little difference in the age of maturity; trout weighing ½ pound or less, in an overstocked lake or a small stream, will mature at four years of age just as surely as will 5- or 10-pound trout in a really good lake. Mortality after spawning appears to be very high. This is perhaps to be expected in view of the close relationship of the Kamloops trout to steelhead and Atlantic salmon, but it is probably dependent more on the rate of growth than upon any inherent disability to withstand the loss of weight and condition caused by spawning. Fish that have made rapid growth under good feeding conditions are more likely to die after their first spawning than fish that have made slow growth; I believe that a majority, perhaps a large majority, of the fish that spawn for the first time at a weight of 3 pounds or more fail to recover; in other words, the average Kamloops in a good lake is not likely to live much longer than four years. There are exceptions to this; some fish live to spawn two or three times, and fish that have made slow growth may live perhaps as long as twelve years, though this is an extreme figure.

The Kamloops trout is likely to be found almost anywhere in British Columbia to the east of the summit of the Coast Range, except perhaps in the extreme north of the Province. But the great fishing waters are for the most part along the Fraser and Okanagan watersheds, particularly along the Fraser watershed north from Hell's Gate Canyon to Stuart and Takla Lakes. A considerable part of this country can be reached by road, either the fairly good main road that runs from Vancouver to Hazelton or by one or another of the usually extremely bad automobile tracks tributary to the main road. Some of the famous lakes are a few miles away from the roads, and to fish them properly it is necessary to camp for a night or two. Some lakes are so large or so far in that they are well worth the questionable comfort of an extended camping trip.

Unfortunately, most of the fishing is lake fishing. There is some river fishing in streams such as the Adams above Shuswap

Lake, the Stellaco River, the streams flowing into Takla and
Stuart Lakes and most of the streams that flow between two
good Kamloops lakes. But river fishing is hard to find in most
parts of the Kamloops trout country and is not nearly as popular or well known as the lake fishing—at least partly, I think,
because the best streams are not opened up. There are few
good trails along them, the pools are hard to find, and to travel
from one pool to another is seldom easy and too often entails
something approaching really hard work.

Of the trout taken in the lakes a very good proportion are
taken on the fly, for the Kamloops is a really good wet fly fish,
and a fair dry fly fish when there is anything big on the surface
to tempt him. The best fly-fishing months are April, May,
June, September and October. Many of the best lakes offer
absolutely no fly fishing at all in July and August, though it is
possible to find fly fishing in these months in the lakes at higher
elevations. It is simply a matter of temperature; lakes such as
Paul (elevation 2,600 feet) have a surface temperature of 70
degrees F. or more all through July and August, which is ten
or fifteen degrees too high to suit trout. It has been well said
that when the water in a lake is warm enough for swimming
it is too warm for fly fishing.

Probably more Kamloops trout are caught by trolling than
on the fly. In the very large lakes trolling is the only method
that can be depended upon to take sizeable fish at all consistently, but in small and medium-sized lakes this is not true, and
a good fly fisherman, so long as the surface temperature is not
above 55 to 60 degrees F., will take more and better fish than
the troller. Actually, the popularity of trolling is decreasing
every year as more and more fishermen realise that fly fishing
is not difficult and yields more satisfaction for every fish
caught. Trolling will always have its place in the interior lakes,
for the big trout of the large lakes, and for those months at
the smaller lakes when the surface is too warm for fly fishing.
Certainly, there is room in most lakes for both troller and fly

fisherman, since the troller takes many fish that are habitually deep feeders, and considerably more than his share of the mended spawners, which are undesirable fish. There are some lakes which could, and perhaps should, be reserved for the fly fisherman, but in the majority of lakes which have considerable depth such a ruling would create a selective fishery which might eventually produce undesirable results. And in those lakes which are carrying something approaching a capacity stock of fish the fly fisherman needs the troller's help, particularly during the warm months, to produce an annual catch large enough to keep down the stock and maintain the average size. The man who enjoys trolling can feel sure of his sport with Kamloops trout at any time in the season, and need seldom fear that he is spoiling the other man's sport. The fly fisherman can find his sport somewhere in the interior all through the season, and need only be careful to avoid planning to fish some of the lakes at lower elevations during July and August.

# 11

## *Paul Lake*

HAVE said that Paul Lake is the most dependable of the artificially stocked Kamloops trout lakes. In this, therefore, it is not typical; but there are a number of purely artificial reasons for this dependability which are extremely important in any consideration of Kamloops lakes, and close examination of these reasons shows more clearly than could anything else what may be expected of such lakes. In purely natural and physical characteristics Paul Lake is fairly typical of the so-called "barren" lakes; there are many lakes like it in size, depth, elevation and surroundings; many lakes which show approximately the same water conditions in respect to oxygen, temperature range, carbonates and the other values that affect fish; many lakes which would show approximately the same varieties of plankton and bottom fauna; and, consequently, many lakes that are capable of approximately the same annual yield of trout in pounds to the acre.

For these reasons, and because the conditions and fauna of Paul Lake have been more closely examined than those of any other interior lake, Paul is the obvious yardstick by which to measure such lakes; and a statement of its history and characteristics will give a fairly accurate general picture of the others. The fact that its present stock of fish is dependent upon the almost complete prevention of natural spawning and upon a carefully calculated annual planting of fry does not affect the value of such comparisons, because control of this sort is the only means of ensuring consistently good fishing in almost any barren lake for more than a few years after the first stocking.

The early history of Paul Lake, like that of many of the barren lakes, is a little vague. The Indians claim to have been the first to stock it with Kamloops trout, but such a claim is often made in order to establish a right to spear the fish when they run up the creeks to spawn. It seems probable that Paul Lake held no fish of any kind until 1909, when it was stocked by white men. In the first ten years after this stocking it produced some splendid fishing. Between 1920 and 1930 the fishing was still good, but perhaps less consistently satisfactory than in the previous decade, although the percentage of big fish was good and quite a few three-, four- and five-pounders were taken every season. In 1931 Mottley came to the lake and began to develop it to its present yield.*

Paul Lake has a length of 3.8 miles, an average width of about three-tenths of a mile and a total surface area of approximately one thousand acres. The fact that it is a long, narrow lake is of some importance, as a lake of this shape will have a

---

* A better reference for details of the work done at Paul Lake than any of those given at the end of this chapter is Mottley's paper *Production of Rainbow Trout at Paul Lake,* which appeared in Trans. Amer. Fish Soc., Vol. 70, 1940.

far greater length of shoreline in proportion to its surface area than will one that is more nearly circular; Paul Lake has a shoreline more than five and a half times as long as the minimum (a perfect circle) needed to enclose its area of water, so that a high percentage of the water is close to shore and very productive of fish and insect life.

Paul is rather a deep lake, having a maximum depth of just over 180 feet off Gibraltar Rock and an average depth of over 100 feet; its water is clean and clear, and these factors of depth and clearness have a material effect on the colour and probably on the markings of the fish. But in spite of this considerable average depth the lake has a gradually sloping shore, particularly at the ends, and a good area of comparatively shallow water. About 70 per cent of its total area may be considered really deep water, over 60 feet; of the remaining 30 per cent about 18 per cent is between 35 and 60 feet deep, rather more than 7 per cent is between 3 and 35 feet deep, and the remaining 4 per cent is less than 3 feet.

Rawson, in his extremely valuable "Productivity Studies in Lakes of the Kamloops Region," names these zones respectively "Profundal," "Lower Sublittoral," "Chara Zone," and "Shore Zone," and gives the population of fauna, in pounds dry weight per acre, as 19.5 for the Profundal, 36.3 for the Lower Sublittoral, 105 for the Chara Zone and 87.3 for the Shore Zone. I have given these figures in some detail because they serve to break up a good lake into its component parts and because they so strongly emphasise the importance of the Chara Zone. This is so called because the bottom of the lake at this depth—on the slope between very shallow water near shore and the limit of the penetration of light, which is about 35 or 40 feet—is covered with a heavy growth of chara weed or stone-wort. This growth growth is a green mass of vigorous plant life, sometimes lime-coated, and often as much as 5 feet thick, in which insects and aquatic fauna of all kinds can live and breed with a very large measure of protection from enemies. Thanks to this protection, the population of the chara beds has a good chance to maintain itself at a maximum, and the excess population, chiefly the amphipods, *Gammarus* and *Hyalella*, is constantly being forced out to the edge of the shelter or into the open water above, where it becomes available to trout.

The extensive range of deep water in the lake is also highly important to both trout and insect life. Trout will do really well only at temperatures below 60 degrees F., and in all lakes which have a high surface temperature during the summer months the larger fish are forced down to deeper water in search of the 55 to 60 degrees F. optimum. In Paul Lake this optimum can be found at the surface and below it to a depth of 12 to 35 feet through the early months of the season, until towards the end of June; in July it is usually between 20 and 45 feet, in August between 30 and 60, and in September between 50 feet and the surface. Thus, the fish are never forced altogether away from the most productive parts of the lake. In many lakes the range of trout into deep water is limited by the low oxygen content and the high acidity of the bottom water. The water of Paul Lake is well charged with oxygen even at the greatest depths and in the warmest months; it is also hard or alkaline, having a pH value of 8 at the surface and 7.5 at 160 feet throughout the summer.* Summering fish therefore have a range of at least 60 or 70 per cent of the lake's area.

The importance of these conditions is even greater since *Gammarus limnaeus* (the "fresh-water shrimp") which, with *Daphnia pulex* (the water-flea), is the main food of Paul Lake trout, also needs low temperatures, ample oxygen saturation and probably some degree of alkalinity, to do really well.

It is as well to avoid detailed discussion of Paul Lake fauna until its importance to the fisherman as well as to the fish can

---

* These values express the relative amount of positive hydrogen ions present in the water. Water with a pH value of 7 is neutral. Values below that figure are from acid water. Trout cannot live where the pH value is 5.4 or lower.

be considered. After the crustaceans, *Gammarus* and *Daphnia*, the most important trout foods are Insecta (chiefly dragon-fly nymphs, caddis grubs, true midges and water bugs), fresh-water snails, leeches, and terrestrial insects blown on to the water. These between them make up over 90 per cent of the food normally found in Paul Lake fish.

In 1931 the fish population of the lake was comparatively small, and the daily catch per boat throughout the season averaged less than four fish. The fish were fairly large, but, even so, the lake was probably yielding less than six pounds of fish per acre each year. These were the conditions that Mottley found when he first went to Paul Lake to work on the life history of the Kamloops trout. He decided that the lake was capable of an annual yield of between eight and ten pounds of trout per acre, and it seemed fairly evident that on account of its size and popularity—fishermen come to Paul from all over the world and many Kamloops residents have summer cottages on the lake—it would be wise to take this yield in fish averaging about one pound.

Since the area of the lake is almost exactly one thousand acres, this programme called for the production each year of about 10,000 fish, varying in size between the legal limit of 8 inches and a probable maximum of 4 pounds, but averaging as nearly as possible one pound. If the average proved to be higher than one pound the lake could stand a proportionately heavier stock of fry; if lower, the annual plantings would have to be reduced.

Allowing for a survival of approximately 5 per cent from planted fry, the lake was stocked in 1931 with 200,000 free-swimming fry. In 1932 the total catch from the lake was 3,000 fish. In 1933, the first planting made itself felt, and the total catch was 6,000 fish; from then on the lake began to assume its present character.

Mottley worked at Paul Lake every year until 1936, gradually learning more about the fish and the possibilities of the lake. His first conclusions as to the potential productivity of the lake and the probable survival from plantings of fry proved essentially sound, though he modified them slightly and developed them in greater detail as time went on. Paul Lake has fairly good spawning beds in Paul Creek, and an insignificant number of fish spawn in Agnes Creek, which has only about one-fiftieth of the volume of Paul Creek. A hatchery on Paul Creek handles all the fish that run there to spawn, so that natural spawning was a minor factor in the problem; it was a simple matter to plant the lake each year with 200,000 fry raised at the hatchery and leave the small Agnes Creek run to take care of itself.

Mottley decided that the lake should carry a total abundance of between twenty and twenty-five thousand yearling, two-year-old and three-year-old fish, and that ideally it should yield each year to anglers 2,500 yearlings averaging 0.5 lbs., 3,000 two-year-olds averaging 1.0 lbs., 1,500 three-year-olds averaging 2.0 lbs., and 1,000 four-, five- or six-year-olds averaging from 2.5 to 5 lbs. These figures give a total of 8,000 fish weighing 10,500 lbs., or a productivity of ten and a half pounds to the acre. Actually, this ideal has been pretty well realised; in 1936 the lake yielded 10,000 fish averaging almost exactly one pound each, thus giving a productivity of ten pounds to the acre. It was found that the potential productivity of the lake is actually somewhat greater than this figure, since the abundance of *Hyalella*, a crustacean about half the size of *Gammarus* present in the lake, is not available to the trout. *Hyalella* has a burrowing habit, whereas *Gammarus* is more inclined to swim away from the protection of weeds and bottom detritus. In the hope of utilising this abundance, Mottley suggested the planting of crawfish, which would probably feed largely on *Hyalella* and be themselves readily available to trout. In 1936 a planting of *Astacus trowbridgi* was made, but I have not yet heard whether there is any indication that they have established themselves; it is too soon, in any case, to judge the effect of the experiment. The introduction of forage fish is a further possible means of increasing the productivity, but it is altogether too dangerous an experiment to be attempted until extensive research work, to determine the effect on the general balance of the lake, has been undertaken and completed.

Meanwhile, there is good reason to suppose that the productivity of the lake may continue to improve. Though the annual planting of fry was kept at 200,000 until 1937, there is strong evidence that the survival from the plantings has varied from year to year. The survival is largely dependent upon the stock of yearlings in the lake, since these make the greatest attack upon the young fry. Thus, in 1931, the first year of the programme, the lake was understocked, and a small number of yearlings probably permitted a survival of about 10,000 fry instead of the 5,000 allowed for in estimating the stocking figure. In 1932 these 10,000 survivors were yearlings, and probably reduced the survival of that year's planting to something like 6,000. From then on the survival probably varied by alternate years more or less as follows:

In 1933,   6,000 yearlings allowed 10,000 fry to survive.
In 1934, 10,000 yearlings allowed   5,000 fry to survive.
In 1935,   5,000 yearlings allowed   9,000 fry to survive.

The survival figures of 1935 were the beginning of an expected break in the more or less exact alternation. The high survival of the 1933 planting had produced an overstock and a temporary shortage in the food supply of the lake during 1935. As a result, the 1935 yearlings were so hard put to it to find adequate feed that 5,000 of them only allowed 9,000 fry to survive, though 6,000 of their forebears had allowed 10,000 fry to survive in 1933. By 1936 the food supply had again built itself up to something approaching the normal, and it seems probable that the survival figures will have been approximately as follows since then:

In 1936, 9,000 yearlings allowed 6-7,000 fry to survive.
In 1937, 6-7,000 yearlings allowed 8-9,000 fry to survive.
In 1938, 8,500 yearlings allowed 8,500 fry to survive.*

The two figures have gradually drawn closer together, and in 1938 should have been approximately equal. From this point on, as long as there is no change in the size of the annual planting—which, at Mottley's suggestion, was reduced to 175,000 in 1937 to allow for the natural spawning in Agnes Creek and any that might take place in Paul Creek—there is no reason to suppose that the survival figures will vary materially from year to year. At the same time, there is reason to hope that the food supply of the lake, depleted by the overstock of 1935, will build itself up sufficiently to increase fairly considerably the average weight of the fish taken.

The effect of the improvement is very clearly shown by the yearly figures of the spawning run and total catch from the lake between 1932 and 1936:

| 1932 | Spawning run to Paul Creek | 500 |
|---|---|---|
| | Catch by lodge boats | 2,000 |
| | Estimated total catch from Paul Lake | 3,000 |
| | Average catch per boat per day | 4 |
| 1933 | Spawning run to Paul Creek | 850 |
| | Catch by lodge boats | 4,300 |
| | Estimated total catch from lake | 6,000 |
| | Average catch per boat per day | 6 |
| 1934 | Spawning run to Paul Creek | 1,500 |
| | Catch by lodge boats | 5,700 |
| | Estimated total catch from lake | 8,000 |
| | Average catch per boat per day | 8 |
| 1935 | Spawning run to Paul Creek | 2,300 |
| | Catch by lodge boats | 8,700 |
| | Estimated total catch from lake | 12,000 |
| | Average catch per boat per day | 10 |

* Estimates of survival in the years 1931-1935 were made by Knut Dahl's method. Their accuracy is therefore dependent upon the assumption that the fall catch by anglers of two-year-olds at Paul Lake is a true sample.

| 1936 | Spawning run to Paul Creek | 2,500 |
| | Catch by lodge boats | 7,000 |
| | Estimated total catch from lake | 10,000 |
| | Average catch per boat per day | 9 |
| 1937 | Spawning run to Paul Creek | 3,000 |
| | Catch by lodge boats | 7,100 |
| | Estimated total catch from lake | 10,000 |
| | Average catch per boat per day | 9 |

Since 1937 there has been little close scientific observation of the lake, but the levelling off process is quite apparent in the figures given above. The drop in total catch in 1936 and 1937 indicates that a corresponding drop should have occurred in the spawning runs of 1939 and 1940, with a steady production from then on of about 9,000 fish for the year's catch and some 2,000 spawners. Apparently this was the case, because Heber Smith, one of the best all-around guides in British Columbia, wrote me from Paul Lake in June 1941: "The fish are in exceptionally good condition this year, averaging nearly a pound and a half. I've had two maiden fish of three and three-quarters and several over three." Of the spawning run earlier in the same year he wrote: "The creek is as full as a humpback stream. Beautiful fish. Some must weigh six or seven pounds."

Paul Lake's annual spawning run of about 2,000 fish gives a yield of 1,200,000 eggs—a by-product of over a million eggs for planting elsewhere. An annual planting of 175,000 in the lake itself should have held a really satisfactory balance and produced fishing of the type described by Heber Smith, year in and year out. I understand, though, that some time during the war years the annual planting was increased to 200,000 fry and that there has since been a drop in the quality of the fishing. In spite of this, Paul can be considered a safe and dependable lake. There will be no great variation from year to year in either size or numbers of fish, and the lake is now producing a type of fish good enough to satisfy both local and visiting fishermen in the largest numbers that it safely can. It is a natural resource that is being farmed on a maximum sustained yield basis.

In the first edition of *The Western Angler* I discussed another lake, whose proper value I felt had been ruined by poor management, in some detail. Reports I have had from this lake even as late as this year (1946) confirm my original opinion, but I feel that a brief description of what happened to the lake and why will make my point at least as clearly as the more detailed account I wrote before.

Lake X—let it be anonymous this time—is not far from Paul Lake. Its fish were of similar quality but considerably greater size. But the most important thing about the lake was its sedge hatches, which brought the largest fish up to free surface feeding. Lake X was, in the late twenties and early thirties, one of the finest, if not the finest, dry fly lake in the world. As such it was worth thousands of dollars a year to the country in free advertising. And it gave fishing of wholly exceptional quality to a few really skilful local flyfishers and to any visitors who were good enough to take it. It is a small lake, some distance from any large centre of population, and accessible only by rather bad roads. Chance made it what it was—the chance of a limited first stocking, very limited spawning areas, extensive shallows and ample feed, including the sedge hatches. There could have been no more fortunate chance; the value of the lake, as it was producing in the late twenties and early thirties, to the Province's game fishery was far out of proportion to its size or normal importance. It was something unique, on its way to becoming a famous name among anglers all over the world.

The sort of fishing that produced this fame was truly remarkable. Fish of six, eight and ten pounds were commonly taken on the dry fly. In 1930 a fish of 17¼ lbs. came up to a dry sedge. Most days yielded only a fish or two even to the best fisherman, but I have the record of two outstanding single day catches before me as I write—in 1931 fifteen fish weighing

60 lbs., best fish 5 lbs.; and in 1933 seven fish weighing 43 lbs., excluding a spawned fish of 8 lbs. returned unharmed to the water. On both days only the dry fly was used. The fisherman concerned—it was the same man each time—caught his fish by waiting quietly well down in the bottom of a skiff anchored over the sunken islands. He cast only when a good fish arrived within reach of a short line, played his fish hard but quietly and netted them with the least possible disturbance.

The change in Lake X dates from 1933 when, through someone's "mistake," "about 75,000 fry" were released. Lake X could have taken a stock of 75,000 fry, or possibly even more, if the whole natural spawning run had been stripped for artificial hatching. Unfortunately this was not done—some 30 pairs of spawners were stripped and the rest spawned naturally in a good year of ample water in the creeks. Several high water years followed, with good spawning in each. The average size of fish caught in the lake dropped from over 5 lbs. in 1933 to a little over 1 lb. in 1936 and the lake entirely lost its character.

Three groups of fish from Lake X, checked by the writer in 1936 averaged from 16% to 20% below the normal scale of weight for length relationship in Kamloops trout. More significantly, check of their stomachs showed far less both in quality and variety of feed than did the stomachs of trout from near-by lakes. The hatches of travelling and other sedges that had brought big fish to the surface in good years gradually disappeared and I have not met a single guide or fisherman who has seen a real hatch of travelling sedge at Lake X in the last ten years. Nor have I been able to pick up any evidence that the lake is likely to return to its former excellence.

The lesson of Lake X is that a single slip in management can cause irreparable damage. Clearly there is a place for lakes such as X under public ownership. True, they will not yield limit catches, even to good fishermen; but there are plenty of other lakes that will, and there are plenty of fishermen who would far rather catch one or two really good fish under ideal circumstances than several times the daily limit of small fish. Such men have a right to sport of their choice in a fishery as generous as British Columbia's could be.

Even more important, from the dollars and cents viewpoint in the management of the fishery, is the publicity value of the lake. Lakes that consistently yield five- and ten-pound trout to the dry fly are mighty rare. They get talked about and written about and so they advertise the rest of the fishery in a natural, unpaid way that is worth far more than ordinary commercial advertising ever can be. This value also was destroyed when the stock of fish in Lake X built up sufficiently to wipe out the breeding stock of the good sedge hatches.

There may be another lake like X in British Columbia—if so I have not heard of it. It is possible to imagine that Lake X could be built back to its former quality by an expensive and lengthy period of careful management, but there is nothing in the present handling of the Province's game fishery to suggest that anything of the sort is likely to be attempted. The loss seems permanent, in many ways comparable to the extinction of some valuable species of bird or animal.

## REFERENCES

Mottley, C. McC. The Spawning Migration of Rainbow Trout. Trans. Amer. Fish. Soc., Vol. 63, 1933.

Mottley, C. McC. Fluctuations in the Intensity of Spawning Runs of Rainbow Trout at Paul Lake. Journ. Fish. Res. Bd. Can. 4(2), 1938.

Rawson, Donald S. Productivity Studies in Lakes of the Kamloops Region, B. C. Biol. Bd. Can. Bull. 42, 1934.

# | | |

## *Future Possibilities*

GRAYLING.

I HAVE said already that it would not be wise to attempt to make this in any way a guide book to the waters of British Columbia. This is doubly true of the Kamloops trout waters of the interior. Certain generalisations may be made safely enough, but the whole picture is a changing one and any angler planning a trip should make every effort to get recent and reliable information.

This is not to suggest that good Kamloops trout fishing is hard to find. There is every reason to suppose that lakes like Paul, Fish (Lac le Jeune), Pinantan, Beaver (near Kelowna) and many others accessible by road will continue to yield dependably good fishing. The big lakes like Okanagan will continue to grow twenty-pounders and even larger trout for the troller. And there will always be new lakes, recently stocked, just coming into their best production for the fly fisherman.

It is these last that are the greatest risk. Almost any interior lake is capable of producing great fishing three or four years after its initial stocking, no matter how carelessly that initial stocking has been undertaken. What happens from then on is dependent on an infinity of variables, because the initial or subsequent stocking of new lakes is seldom or never calculated closely against such factors as the lake's potential productivity, its natural spawning yield or the probable survival of fry.

Probably the best advice for a visiting fisherman is that he should not expect too much of the new lake where his friend found such wonderful sport a year or two ago. It may still be fishing well or it may have started into rapid deterioration. He should remember also to find out from his friends whether the fish were coming well to the fly or only to the troll and in exactly what month of the year it was that all this happened—the matter of a few weeks can make all the difference between good fly fishing and none at all in some lakes.

The virgin lake coming into its first fishing, filled with monster fish of gleaming silver that roll and plunge all over the surface in eager search for both natural and artificial flies must always be an angler's dream. A very worthy dream, too, and a thrilling experience when realised. Yet it is very, very easy to become surfeited with such fishing; and fine fish, even record fish, lose something of their value when caught under such circumstances—the circumstances rather than the angler are responsible. So there is much to be said for lakes that are passing out of their first fine flush and finding their natural level—lakes today (I am writing in 1946) such as Peter Hope and Tawheel and Devick's Beaver which may at times prove disappointing but which hold a lot of fish and some really big ones that can be taken on the fly. Lakes such as these have been in production long enough to have developed a standard against which the visiting fisherman can measure his prowess, and that is a point of some importance to most of us.

There are in the interior both lakes and streams that owe nothing to artificial stocking and these are as dependable and as variable as fishing streams and lakes are everywhere. The great fly fishing at Little River and the mouth of the Adams,

in the two Shuswap lakes, is dependent on the seaward movement of sockeye and spring salmon yearlings; at both places
there is flyfishing only slightly less good when the alevins are
coming out of the gravel and when the mature fish are going
up to spawn. At some times in every season there will be good
fishing, even spectacular fishing, but I know of no one who
would venture to predict from season to season just when those
times will be. It is enough to say they are worth a wait of
almost any length.

There are plenty of fish in lakes such as Mahood and Canim
up the Cariboo Highway, and in the big northern lakes, Stuart,
Babine and Trembleur. There is a worthwhile trip through the
great circle of easily travelled water made by Ootsa and Eutsuk
and Whitesail and the other lakes south of François. Bryan
Williams' *Fish and Game in British Columbia* (1935) lists these
places and many others, with a mass of information compiled
from the records of the British Columbia Game Department.

In the original edition of *The Western Angler* I discussed at
some length various possible methods of developing and improving the Kamloops trout fishing of the interior. Such a
thorough discussion can have only an academic interest for
most anglers and, I am afraid, for many of those now entrusted
with game-fish management. But some aspects of the discussion
are important to any keen angler, not only because they contribute to his understanding of his sport and his influence in
conserving it and improving it, but because knowledge of the
factors involved is likely to be his surest guide in choosing a
place to fish.

It is quite obvious that in considering Kamloops waters one
must differentiate sharply between those carrying a native
stock and those dependent upon artificial planting, even though
these latter may have developed a native stock of their own
after the initial planting.

Of the two the native-stock waters present by far the more
complicated problem, and since the natural balances controlling

life in such waters are at present only improperly understood, it is impossible to judge what developments may eventually become possible. The necessary research work will be gradually undertaken and completed, and the resulting knowledge will undoubtedly suggest ways of improving very considerably the fishing in both streams and lakes. But such improvements can only be economically possible if, in the meanwhile, breeding stocks of fish are maintained at a safe level.

All policy in the immediate future should be directed towards ensuring this maintenance of adequate breeding stocks. It is too often said by anglers, and by others who should know better, that fished-out streams or lakes can readily be restocked. In the United States this wretchedly persistent idea has again and again been proved utterly fallacious. The stocking or restocking with trout of a water that already carries an established population of fish is in itself a complicated and difficult piece of work. When, as must be the case, there is also in the district a sufficient human population to cause depletion, the water cannot possibly be built up again unless it is closed to angling for several years. Local resistance is fairly certain to prevent such a policy, and the only remaining course is to stock, and keep on stocking, the water with sizeable fish. Such practice is extremely expensive and quite unsatisfactory. In very heavily populated areas such as New York State there is probably no alternative, and the system does at least provide fishing of a sort. But in countries which are not yet heavily populated and whose waters carry adequate stocks of native fish, it is obviously more desirable to ensure the preservation of these stocks by proper restrictive legislation. Then, as the population grows and justifies the expenditure, they may be built up by increasingly intensive cultural work.

Conditions vary greatly in different waters, and the restrictive legislation necessary to ensure an adequate escape must vary with the conditions. This is an axiom of fish culture widely disregarded in the new world, for various reasons, but chiefly because it is difficult to enforce local regulations. Sooner or later, if there is to be any real conservation, legislators will have to change their hearts on this point. The present bag limit of twelve trout per day, for instance, is in force practically throughout the Province; yet in most native-stock waters it is too high—no fisherman should take twelve trout in a day at Little River, or from the Adams. And in some it is too low; the Flyfish Lakes are too little fished, and good spawning grounds have produced an overstock.

Apart from such local restrictive legislation as may be found necessary, it is quite essential to prohibit the sale of trout and forbid the use or sale of salmon roe as a bait anywhere in the Province. Sale of trout is economically quite unsound, because they must always yield more in dollars and cents when caught by the sportsman, and the stock is not adequate to support both commercial and sporting fisheries. And the preservation of a breeding stock of fish in waters where salmon roe is used as a bait is quite impossible, for reasons that I shall give later in this book. It is frequently suggested that the numbers of trout in the native-stock waters can be increased by the complete destruction of coarse fish, such as suckers, squawfish, chub, carp, etc. There is at present—perhaps fortunately—no known way of achieving this complete destruction, or anything approaching it, without running a grave risk of destroying most other aquatic life at the same time. Experiments with copper sulphate have apparently caused some anglers to suppose that this chemical can be used to destroy coarse fish without injury to trout and salmon. But the experiments carried out at Jesse Lake, Nova Scotia, which are the only ones of which I have seen detailed accounts, make it quite obvious that any attempt to use copper sulphate in a lake that carries an important stock of commercial or game fish would be extremely foolish.

Furthermore, present knowledge suggests that some, if not the majority of coarse fish, provide extremely valuable forage for trout. E. R. Hewitt writes: "I regard the sucker as one of the most valuable foods for trout that we have, and I never allow them to be killed in my waters." Hewitt has shown himself a sound, practical fish culturist as well as one of the best anglers on the continent, and such a definite statement demands a good deal of consideration, especially since a major problem of future development will almost certainly be one of increasing the available food supply of many waters.

Until the experiments at present being carried out at Cultus Lake have yielded some conclusive evidence, and until a good deal more is known of the importance of coarse fish as forage, it would seem advisable to attempt only very limited control, by the use of nets rather than by chemicals. A broad rule of safety in predator control is that it should match as exactly as possible the drain upon desirable species by angling, and any more extensive control can be justified only by very exact knowledge of the habits of the predator in question. The authorities concerned will be wise to disregard completely, for the time being, the frequent and sweeping requests of local organisations for the destruction of coarse fish.

The point almost invariably forgotten or disregarded by those interested in the use of a natural resource is that depletion is always caused by exploitation; there may be other causes that contribute in some measure, but these have always existed, and the resource has not only persisted but built itself up in spite of them; when they cause serious damage they are enabled to do so only by the fact that exploitation has prepared the way for them. So it is that the logger will never face the fact that he is wasting or overcutting, the hunter blames predators or disease rather than his own gun or rifle, and the fisherman, whether he fishes for profit or sport, is always seeking other causes of depletion than the only really important one—overfishing.

In the case of fish resources there is perhaps one other danger that is potentially almost as serious as overfishing—pollution. Actually, this danger also will always arise from exploitation, even though it be of a resource other than the one that suffers, and so it is to be classed with overfishing as a danger to be met by restrictive legislation. Comparatively few waters in British Columbia have suffered from pollution yet, and comparatively few are in immediate danger. But it is necessary to guard against pollution before there is any chance that it will occur, and legislators would do well to realise that there is no conceivable excuse or justification for pollution of even the smallest stream or body of water, in this day and age of comparative enlightenment. No commercial development causing pollution is likely to benefit the country to the extent of the loss it produces. It should be a fairly simple matter to make the penalties so heavy and inevitable that pollution will never occur.

Restrictive legislation is comparatively cheap and extremely effective conservation. But if the natural resource is to support the attack of a large and rapidly growing population or to attract and satisfy a highly developed tourist industry, it must be supplemented by constructive measures. These are likely to be expensive, but will not be prohibitively so if the restrictive legislation has been effective; the growing population and the revenue from the tourist traffic will meet the expense. The time will come for wholesale constructive methods in the native-stock waters of the interior—and this fact must never be lost sight of. Much of the basic research and detailed planning must be undertaken before the time for development actually arrives and while the restrictive measures are holding the status quo.

The "barren" waters of the interior are another matter altogether. They are well able to provide for the needs of both resident and non-resident anglers at present and in the immediate future. The time is absolutely ripe for a constructive and intensive cultural programme, and restrictive legislation is comparatively unimportant. There must be some restrictive legislation, such as reasonable bag limits and the prohibition of deadly baits, to ensure proper distribution of fishing opportunity, and perhaps there should be, for advertising purposes, the reservation of certain waters for certain fishing methods. But most of the work should be directed towards obtaining a maximum sustained yield of the size and quality of fish and the type of fishing desired.

The cultural problems presented by the "barren" lakes are very much simpler than those of the native-stock waters because there is in these lakes no fish life to complicate the balances. Feed stocks have been built up over thousands of years, and both survival and growth rate of the initial planting may be expected to be extremely high. This fortunate state of affairs has led to the extremely unfortunate misconception, widely held by anglers and too often also by those in authority, that to make a barren lake produce good fishing it is simply necessary to plant a few fry or fingerlings. Actually, from a fish culturist's point of view, the real work starts when the first stocking is made.

The "barren" lakes, in their fishless condition, are a natural resource of very great value—value strictly comparable to that, for instance, of virgin forests or salmon runs. The great majority of them have water conditions particularly favourable to the multiplication and growth of trout and of the aquatic fauna on which the trout depends. In the thousands of years that they have been empty of fish they have built up great reserves of trout food, and the problem of making them produce good fishing, year in year out, is not so much one of conserving the trout population from the depredations of the human population as of conserving the built-up food supply of the lakes from the depredations of the trout. The essential point is to preserve at all times an adequate breeding stock of fauna. Ways may be found of increasing or supplementing this natural stock of feed, just as ways may be found of increasing or supplementing the numbers of trout in the native-stock waters, but if the yield is to be a sustained one—and man has no conceivable right to demand anything else of a natural resource—the breeding stock must never be reduced beyond the danger point.

As I have suggested in the Paul Lake chapters, a great deal of excellent research work in the possibilities and problems of the "barren" lakes has already been done. It is still very far from complete, and at the time of writing no further research is being conducted. Many questions remain to be answered before the lakes can be made to produce a high average yield and before even a reasonably extensive stocking program can safely be attempted; but it is not too difficult to see the lines the research must follow and, from this, approximately the type of program that will probably be shown to be desirable.

All future work must necessarily be based on Mottley's work at Paul Lake and Rawson's *Productivity Studies in Lakes of the Kamloops Region*. Mottley himself in 1932 drew up a research program from which he hoped eventually "to derive a fish-cultural formula for stocking purposes." He suggested following the life history of several generations of trout with:

1. Definite annual plantings of fry in the various lakes controlled by the fish-cultural program (Paul, Knouff, Pinantan, Pennask and Fish).

2. Determinations of the yield of Paul Lake, by an enumeration of the fish in the fishing quota and the spawning run.

3. An annual determination of growth rates in the five lakes, for signs of fluctuation in size for age.

4. Studies on the food types, for correlative fluctuations.

5. A complete "check-up" of the productive capacity of the lakes at definite intervals.

Had these suggestions been followed out, the Province would by now be well on the way to a decent knowledge of Kamloops trout and the barren lakes. The work was discontinued early in 1936, presumably for "lack of funds," and little or nothing has been done since. It will have to be done sooner or later, for without it the stocking of barren lakes can only be a haphazard proceeding, and the majority of them are likely to be spoiled very quickly. Once the life history of the trout and the influence of conditions in the five lakes is fully understood it will not be difficult to go ahead safely and sanely with a very comprehensive program. The first step will be to work out some reasonably simple formula by which the productivity in pounds to the acre of any given lake may be determined after a minimum of field work. Then surveys of all barren lakes to be stocked can be carried out, and a program worked out for each, based on this formula, the area of the lake, the extent and probable production of the spawning beds and the desired type of yield.

This last point is one to which far too little attention has been given. Each lake must be examined to determine the size of fish and the type of fishing it is best fitted to yield; and at the same time the general picture of all the producing lakes must be examined to determine the type of fishing or the size of fish needed at the moment to make that picture more complete. It is neither possible nor desirable that all the barren lakes should be made to one given pattern; within certain limits the size of fish produced by each one can be very exactly controlled, and the principal type of fishing shown by each—dry or wet fly, trolling or spinning or even bait-fishing—while it must be, to a considerable extent, dependent upon the natural characteristics of the lake, may also be materially influenced by intelligent work.

This may seem a rather extravagant claim, but actually it is not so. Control of size presupposes either prevention or exact knowledge of the yield of natural spawning. The potential productivity of the lake must also be known, as well as certain of its physical characteristics which might influence the survival of fry. Given this information, it is a simple matter to apply the standards of Paul Lake to determine what can be done. An annual planting of 175 fry to the acre in Paul Lake, with no natural spawning, gives an annual yield of about nine sizeable fish to the acre. Since the lake has a productivity of something in the neighbourhood of ten pounds to the acre, the average weight of these nine fish taken by anglers will be slightly over one pound. Any reasonably competent fisherman can catch plenty of fish on the fly in Paul Lake during the fly-fishing months, and trolling is always productive. So it is arguable that a yield of nine fish to the acre is quite enough to keep the average fisherman as busy as he needs to be.

Let us say, then, that Lake A is to be stocked. The survey has shown it to have a potential productivity of twelve pounds to the acre. It is a five-hundred-acre lake, with very poor spawning facilities, plenty of shoal water and particularly good sedge hatches. Examination of the general picture of all the producing lakes shows a lack of good fly-fishing lakes producing fish averaging two pounds, with the possibility of an occasional four- or five-pounder. Clearly, Lake A is ideal for the purpose, having the necessary physical characteristics, the right fauna and a high potential productivity. It is obvious that to get a two-pound average one must aim at a production of six fish to the acre. Using the Paul Lake figures, this means an annual planting of about 120 fry to the acre or about 60,000 to the lake.

Lake B is a large and fairly deep lake with a potential productivity of five pounds to the acre. The general picture shows a lack of good trolling lakes producing good catches of fish averaging 1½ pounds. Lake B is well separated from other lakes, and this, since the lake is to be primarily for trollers, at once suggests the introduction of a forage fish to increase productivity. It is estimated that by introducing kokanees the productivity will be increased by at least fifty per cent, perhaps doubled. So the lake is stocked with eighty or ninety fry to the acre.

Lake C is a medium sized lake, with spawning grounds capable of a heavy yield, fair quantities of shoal water, and a productivity of ten pounds to the acre. It is within easy reach of a large centre of population where there is a demand for plenty of fish of any size above the legal limit, to be caught by any and every method. The fish culturist might feel a momentary regret at sacrificing a lake of such high productivity to such a demand, but the extensive spawning ground would make it necessary to install a hatchery or to resort to some really drastic and perhaps costly expedient to reduce spawning, if the lake were to be controlled. He would probably plant about 300 fry to the acre, and hope for an average of a little less than three-quarters of a pound. He would have to pin his faith on the heavy drain on the stock by anglers to maintain that average in the face of the heavy natural seedings of subsequent years.

That is a very bare outline of the possibilities. I have already tried to show some of the more complicated factors that force the fish culturist to revise his original figures from time to time. These factors and their influence can only be discovered by a close watch of the lake, and in this the anglers and resort keepers can render great assistance by keeping a complete and accurate record of all fish caught. At present this is not at all well done, but it can only be because the average angler does not realise the value of such records or his own intimate concern with them.

Though these things will be the base of controlled production from the barren lakes in the future, new discoveries will probably have important influence. In most parts of the world a lake capable of producing ten pounds of fish to the acre every year is unquestionably an excellent water, and it seems likely that a very fair proportion of the barren lakes are capable of such a yield. If we consider ten fish to the acre a sufficient abundance to satisfy most fishermen and withstand the drain of heavy fishing, it is evident that the majority of controlled lakes will be made to produce, as Paul does now, fish averaging about one pound. To obtain an increase in weight it is necessary to sacrifice numbers—five fish to the acre for a two-pound average, five fish to two acres for a four-pound average, and so on. Good fishermen are likely to be satisfied with smaller numbers of larger fish, but, even so, lakes producing such relatively low numbers of fish might not be able to withstand the drain of very heavy fishing. So there is not much doubt that a good deal of research should be directed towards obtaining a higher yield. While ten pounds to the acre is good, much higher productivity is possible. The following short list, showing the yield of certain well-known waters, gives some indication of how flexible the figures are:

Estimated productivity, average Vancouver Island lakes, 1½-2¾ lbs. per acre.
Actual productivity, Loch Leven, Scotland, 9 lbs. per acre.*
Actual productivity, River Test, Houghton Club water, 29.8 lbs. per acre.
Actual productivity, Fish Lake, Utah, 38.3 lbs. per acre.

Some explanation of these figures is necessary. The Vancouver Island lakes are usually low in carbonates, have poor weed growth and rapid drainage; they are very much like the low-productivity lakes of Norway. Loch Leven has an area of 3,500 acres averaging 11.6 feet in depth, 1,200 of which average only four feet. It withstands very heavy fishing and yields annually about 40,000 trout averaging rather over three-quarters of a pound. It is a neutral lake, between acidity and alkalinity, and has extensive and very perfect spawning grounds, evidently capable of producing well over a million fry each year. An important characteristic of the lake is the limited size range of its fish; fish of more than a pound and a half are very rare, though the average of three-quarters of a pound would normally suggest a fair proportion of fish up to at least two pounds.

The Houghton Club water of the Test has been very highly developed by the efforts of such men as the late William Lunn,

* In the 1938 season the Loch Leven catch was 57,884 fish weighing 46,725 lbs. This represents a yield of about 14 lbs. per acre, but the year was a record one.

river keeper, and its present productivity is a comparatively new thing. The club records show an average productivity of only a little over 5 lbs. for the years 1823-1897, with a steady and rapid increase from 1897 to 1907. Much of this improvement was produced by stocking with fish raised in carriers near the main stream to a weight of 1½ lbs.; but proper weed cutting, with protection and encouragement of breeding stocks of insect life, has also done a great deal.

Fish Lake in Utah has poor spawning grounds, and the fish population is largely maintained by heavy stocking. Like Loch Leven, it is a neutral lake, but about seventy per cent of its 2,500 acres is over ninety feet deep. Aquatic plants, favoured by good soil, protected shoal areas and the type of the bottom, are very abundant, and are probably the most important factor in the tremendous productivity of the lake. Besides the native cutthroat and a native bullhead, the lake supports rainbow trout and Eastern speckled char, Great Lakes char, spring and cohoe salmon, a chub, and shiners, all of which have been introduced. The rainbow trout and the two chars provide most of the fishing and may, through their varying habits of feeding and wider utilisation of all available resources, account in some measure for the high productivity. Some of the other fish introduced undoubtedly provide forage, but at the same time must compete with the fish that make up the yield. However one examines the facts, it is quite evident that the lake is exceptionally productive, and the figure 38.3, about four times that of a really good Kamloops lake, suggests at once that ways and means may be found of increasing the productivity of these lakes very considerably, even if not to the high point of Fish Lake.

In considering methods of improving natural productivity of the lakes it is extremely important not to lose sight of the type of fishing desired from each water. Simply to offer fish to the angler is not enough; he must also get a reasonable chance to catch them by the methods he likes to use. For instance, there can be little doubt that the majority of fishermen, especially the majority of tourist fishermen, are looking for waters where they can catch large trout on the fly with reasonable certainty and frequency. A good fly lake is many times more valuable to the country than an equally good trolling lake, and it would be extremely unwise to risk spoiling such a lake. That is why the obvious suggestion that the introduction of forage fish such as kokanee, shiners or minnows might increase the productivity of many lakes must be examined very carefully. While such introductions would compete with the trout for the natural food of the lake, it seems likely that they would utilise some food not available to the trout, and so produce more pounds of trout to the acre; it is almost certain that they would help to produce larger fish. On the other hand, they might easily change the feeding habits of the trout materially, and spoil an otherwise good fly lake. In lakes required primarily for trolling they should prove highly beneficial. I believe there is room for a good deal of research on this point, since any introduction is bound to upset balances which, at the moment, are working extremely well. It seems worth suggesting that experiments should be made with very small forage fish having a preference for shoal water. Some minnows, for instance, might improve rather than spoil fly fishing, but I do not think the kokanee should be turned loose in any good fly lake. If experiments are to be made with Pacific salmon as forage fish, the humpback would seem the logical choice, since he matures at two years; this would produce a quicker turnover and the shorter period of growth might not permit him to attain the size of the kokanee. Small fish which are partially herbivorous, such as the blunt-nosed minnow (*Hyborhynchus notatus*), may also be found valuable.

Introductions of natural food other than forage fish have seldom proved very successful in lakes which already carry a stock of trout. But such introductions could be made well in advance of a first planting of trout, and the natural increase would build up a sufficient breeding stock to resist the drain put upon it by the trout; there seems little doubt that fishing, particularly fly fishing, might be tremendously improved by them. One obvious suggestion is the use of the travelling sedge, which occurs far too rarely in the barren lakes; another possibility would be the introduction of both large and small mayflies from English and Irish waters. The large mayflies (*Ephemera*), if they established themselves, would produce some very remarkable fishing; and some of the smaller *Ephemeridae*, if they hatched in sufficient numbers, might bring good trout to the dry fly all through the season. But in spite of the possibilities of highly efficient utilisation of the productivity of a water by the introduction of forage fish and fauna, that productivity must always, in the last analysis, be limited by water and soil conditions. It seems probable that considerable increase in productivity is more likely to be brought about by close attention to the chemical content of the water, the improvement of bottom soil fertility, and the encouragement of good weeds, than by any other means.

A good deal of attention has recently been paid to the selective breeding of trout for quick growth and early maturity. The experiments of Hayford and Embody in the United States have shown what can be achieved by these methods within a very few generations, and in a country that is dependent for its fishing on hatchery-raised fish from breeding stock kept in ponds the practice is undoubtedly extremely important. But British Columbia must, if it is to continue to provide a sufficient quantity of good fishing, depend upon natural spawning and upon fish raised from wild breeders and planted out at the fry stage; stocking to supply immediate fishing needs is economically unsound and quite undesirable. In these conditions, selective breeding experiments lose significance, since all of them have, as far as I know, been carried out with fish hatched and raised and fed under purely artificial conditions, and the startling improvements may be due in great measure to the adaptability of the selected fish to artificial conditions.

This is not to say that a good breeding stock is not desirable. It is, if only because large fish produce the large, healthy eggs which make care during the hatching and alevin stages a comparatively simple matter. For this reason the degeneration of the magnificent breeders of Knouff Lake is a matter for regret.

Two or three small points touching the productivity of interior lakes are worth consideration. I believe that in most artificially stocked and properly controlled Kamloops lakes anglers would do well to kill all spawned-out fish caught and, if they are insufficiently recovered to be worth keeping, cut the swim bladders and let them sink to the bottom of the lake. A Kamloops kelt recovers weight very much more slowly than a maiden fish puts on weight, and from the point of view of gameness can never be as good. The returning of the body of the fish to the lake provides valuable feed for caddis, dragon-fly larvae and other carnivorous insects on which the trout feed, and fishermen would do well to return also the entrails of any clean fish they kill.

A point of some importance in both the productivity and the control of interior lakes is a sufficient utilisation of diverse methods of capture. The troller and the fly fisherman are inclined at times to regard each other with some hostility. Actually, in most properly stocked Kamloops lakes each is vitally important to the other. True, there are some lakes particularly adapted to fly fishing, where the fly fisherman does not need the troller's assistance. And there are some lakes where the fly fisherman can do little or nothing to help the troller. But in the lakes that have a reasonable amount of water suitable for each method, proper use of both methods tends to keep the fishery from becoming too selective, and at the same time it helps to keep the stock within reasonable limits, if only because water temperatures prevent both methods from being fully effective all through the season.

The claim that some lakes should be reserved for fly fishing only has force only when such lakes are demonstrably well suited for fly fishing and when the fly fisherman is able to catch a sufficient number of fish to prevent overstocking. Such restricted waters would make extremely valuable advertising and assist materially in attracting tourists. At the same time, there are lakes particularly suited for trolling, and in developing and improving these the interests and sport of the troller should be considered in every possible way.

So much talk of planning and control, of fixed yields of fish of prearranged average weight, may sound rather depressingly cut-and-dried to most fishermen. Actually, of course, there is neither real fear nor real hope of producing a cut-and-dried result. Fish will remain, as they always have been, individuals, and there will still be infinite variations of colour and size and weight and behaviour. After all, any lake or stream holds fish of a certain average weight, whether the average is controlled or not. Proper control and development should tend to make the fishing more rather than less varied, since different lakes in the same district can be made to produce different types of fish and fishing. And whether the prearranged average weight is half a pound or ten pounds, the unexpected big one will always be there; he may be closer to the average than he would have been had there been no control, but he will still be the big one; and any fisherman knows that when he catches a three- or four-pounder in a lake of half-pounders he has caught an undesirable.

Planning in British Columbia will all be directed towards making possible the continuation of natural conditions by obtaining a maximum weight of fish from every area of water in the Province. If it fails to achieve this object—and there is no reason why it should—we shall have to plan really artificial measures, and the tank trucks will be lumbering forth from Vancouver and Kamloops and Kelowna to plant their loads of hatchery-raised quarter-pounders from hatchery-raised parents. After each truck will follow the long line of cars—perhaps yours and mine amongst them if we haven't burned our rods in disgust before then—filled with anglers wanting a first chance at the innocents because there is nothing else to fish for.

## REFERENCES

Catt, James. Copper Sulphate in the Elimination of Coarse Fish. Trans. Amer. Fish. Soc., Vol. 64, 1934.

Hazzard, A. S. A Preliminary Study of an Exceptionally Productive Trout Water, Fish Lake, Utah. Trans. Amer. Fish. Soc., Vol. 65, 1935.

Hewitt, E. R. Better Trout Streams. Scribners, 1931.

Higgins, Elmer. Progress in Biological Inquiries 1928. U. S. Bureau Fish. Doc. 1068, page 729, 1930. Same. 1930, pp. 609, 610, 1931.

Hills, J. W. A Summer on the Test. Allan. London, 1934.

Menzies, W. J. M. Sea Trout and Trout. Arnold. London, 1936.

Mottley, C. McC. The Propagation of Trout in the Kamloops District, B. C. Trans. Amer. Fish. Soc., Vol. 62, 1932.

Smith, M. W. The Use of Copper Sulphate for Eradicating the Predatory Fish Population of a Lake. Trans. Amer. Fish. Soc., Vol. 65, 1934.

Westman, James R. Studies on the Reproduction and Growth of the Blunt-nosed Minnow (*Hyborhynchus notatus*). Copeia. June 30, No. 2, 1938.

# I V

## *Tackle*

TOOLS for any type of fine work are necessarily the subject of much discussion and intimate consideration among those who do the work. Fly fishermen's tools have been developed to a high state of perfection, and every fly fisherman has his own preferences, mixed in with a few valued prejudices. I enjoy my own prejudices and believe in my own preferences too well to wish to disturb those of any other angler against his will. In writing these chapters on tackle for British Columbian waters I feel that I can give free rein to my own ideas; the tackle and methods I use have given me pleasure and satisfaction without too much straining and effort, and it seems reasonable to suppose that an account of them will be of assistance to the stranger or the novice, even though the experienced resident angler may insist, quite rightly, upon his own preferences.

There seems little to be gained by writing too vaguely and generally of tackle. To speak of a nine-foot, five-ounce rod, for instance, is to speak of an infinite number of different rods, unless the names of both rod and maker are also given. So I have not hesitated to mention makers' names, and in writing of tackle for specific types of fishing I have confined myself as closely as possible to the consideration of tackle listed by a single maker, Hardy Brothers of Alnwick, England. I have chosen Hardy's partly because they are very good makers, partly because I have had more experience with Hardy tackle than any other, but chiefly because Hardy's *Angler's Guide* gives the most comprehensive list I know of rods for every type of fishing. By referring to this guide, any fisherman will be able to find the full specifications of all rods and tackle discussed, and match them in the catalogue of his own favourite maker.

It is quite possible to fish, and fish properly, virtually any water in the interior of British Columbia with one rod. If I had to do this I should choose a 9½-foot rod weighing about six ounces, with rather a stiff action and plenty of power in the top and middle joints, and I should use with it a line not lighter than Hardy's IBI (point .024 in., centre .048 in.). Probably a majority of anglers who fish in the interior do confine themselves to an outfit of approximately this type, but I believe that to realise the utmost efficiency, comfort and satisfaction from every type of fly fishing one is likely to come across it is well to carry at least four rods. My own choice is as follows:

> 8-ft. 9-in. "Davy" rod, weighing 5¼ ounces.
> 10-ft. "Crown Houghton" rod, weighing 8¼ ounces.
> 11-ft. "Wye" rod, weighing 12¼ ounces.
> 11½-ft. "Loch Leven" rod, weighing 10½ ounces.

There are many other rods of approximately the same specifications, in Hardy's list and in the lists of other makers. These four rods of mine are probably heavier on the average than they need be and were I buying them again I believe I should aim at lighter and stiffer rods than the Davy and the Crown Houghton—rods of the Jubilee, Koh-i-noor or Rogue River type in Hardy's list are better adapted to western needs, and are more powerful in spite of their light weight. Actually, though, I have found the Davy perfectly satisfactory for dry or wet fly in smaller streams and for the dry fly in a calm lake;

and I have used it frequently enough, against my better judgment, on windy days with both wet and dry fly and have been able to make it do the work. The Crown Houghton is a very good dry fly rod under any conditions, and a rod of this type is far better than a lighter one for the wet fly in large, fast streams. It is a comfortable rod on a windy lake and it is even powerful enough for the fishing at Little River, though a longer and more powerful rod of the "Wye" or "Wood" type gives one better control of really large flies.

The "Loch Leven" type of rod is, I believe, by far the best for a man who wishes to fish the wet fly in a lake with a maximum of efficiency and ease. A properly built rod of this type is sensitive enough to handle 4x gut, powerful enough to throw a long line even into the wind, and light enough to be fished singlehanded by most men. The extra length gives a tremendous advantage in the two most difficult phases of lake fishing —working the fly and striking the fish—as well as some slight advantage in playing the fish. The 12½-ft. rod of the type is even better, but most men find it too heavy to be used singlehanded through a whole day, and one can only fish with maximum efficiency when the left hand is free to handle the line. In making roach rods Hardy has introduced a principle of hollow-built split-cane, which makes for decreased weight. Powell of Marysville, California, has made some fly rods on a similar principle, and they are extremely pleasant to use. It seems probable that the principle could be applied to produce a longer and lighter lake fly rod than any on the market at the present time.

There are plenty of good fly reels of all makes. Of those I have tried I prefer Hardy's "St. John" for most purposes, and the "Uniqua" for small and light rods. Both these reels are extremely simple and have narrow drums for quick recovery of line.

As every fly fisherman knows, lines are important. I do not think there is any substitute for a double-tapered, oiled-silk, vacuum-dressed line, and, given a line of this type properly balanced to the rod, one can make some show of casting and fishing with any type or grade of fly rod. With a poor line or one not reasonably well balanced to the rod, the best rod in the world can only be an uncomfortable and inefficient tool. Of the rods I have listed above the "Davy" carries an ICI line, the "Loch Leven" and "Crown Houghton" are best with IBI, and the "Wye" needs a No. 5, all Hardy's sizes.

Nine-foot tapered gut casts are probably the most satisfactory for all-round use, and they are better unstained, except in coloured water. 4x is seldom necessary. 2x is perhaps the best general size, but I should not care to be without 3x. A few of the larger flies should be fished with ox, and some of the Little River flies need considerably heavier gut than this. On still, bright days, in lakes such as Paul, a 14-foot cast may help to raise a few shy fish, and a sound general rule is to use gut as fine as the size of the flies will allow.

I have written so far of tackle in terms of casting and working the fly and striking the fish under varying conditions, with very little attention to the playing of the fish. This may seem an omission in discussing tackle for a fish reputed to be the strongest and most vigorous of all the trout family. But I believe that the hardest strains a fly fisherman's tackle is called upon to withstand are in the lifting and casting of the fly, particularly when these strains are accentuated by hard winds or fast water.

Most Kamloops trout fishing is done in the open water of lakes, where the fish is likely to have little help from weeds and obstructions and none from flowing water, yet hooks and gut, even rods and lines, are often broken. Some of these troubles are caused by weak tackle—gut suddenly cracked in a dry wind or grown rotten, improperly tempered hooks, and other such hidden things that catch the most careful angler at times. Others are caused by improperly balanced tackle; fine gut cannot carry a heavy hook, and a man must have sensitive hands if he wishes to use 4x gut with a powerful fly rod. But the great majority of troubles are caused by the failure of the average fisherman to realise how strong his tackle is.

Every year there are, in the interior, a great many fish hooked and lost by men fishing 2x gut with a five- or six-ounce rod. This is a powerful and well-balanced combination; good 2x gut should stand all the strain that can be put on it by a five-ounce rod handled properly, and that strain is enough to control and to check gradually the strongest rush of even a very large trout. Yet many fishermen, often experienced fishermen, when they hook a good fish on such tackle, allow him to run and jump as he pleases, without attempting to bring him under control. In other words, these men, out of exaggerated respect for the prowess of the fish and faulty knowledge of the strength of their tackle, do not attempt to use all the power that is in their hands from the moment the fish is hooked. Then, generally rather suddenly, they discover that the fish actually is out of control; in this moment of excited or confused realisation they apply the full strength of rod and tackle too quickly—and there is a break.

From watching dozens, or perhaps hundreds, of fishermen, I am convinced that more than fifty per cent of the breaks that occur are due to this failure to take the upper hand and exert a maximum of pressure from the moment of hooking a fish. The Kamloops trout can run and jump and turn as swiftly and vigorously as any freshwater fish I know, and he is as likely as any to rid himself of an improperly set hook. But in the still, unobstructed waters of a lake any properly hooked fish of ten pounds or less should be controlled, turned and brought to the net easily enough by any of the four rods I have suggested.

Flies, even flies for the interior of British Columbia where fly fishermen have not had very long to work, are a big subject. The nature of the Kamloops trout and of the fauna of interior waters both contribute to make the wet fly more important than the dry fly—at least at the present stage of angling development—and it seems altogether probable that more fish are caught on "fancy" flies than on those which attempt to imitate natural insects.

Any wet-fly fisherman with a good collection of flies, tied on hooks varying in size from about No. 12 or 14 to No. 6, could go to the interior and catch plenty of fish without bothering to add to his collection. Conversely, an experienced wet-fly man who had no special knowledge of interior conditions should not find it difficult to buy himself a useful selection from any tackle dealer's assortment of flies tied especially for the interior. There is not much doubt that a fisherman generally does best with flies in which, for one reason or another, he has confidence. When searching a large water for fish that usually rise from a considerable depth and are therefore invisible, this confidence is a doubly important factor; seeking it, the average angler is likely to choose a fly that he feels will be easily seen by the fish from a distance. This is probably the principal reason for the great popularity of the rather gaudy "fancy" flies that are so much used in the interior and in lake fishing generally.

In the original edition of *The Western Angler* I went into a long discussion of the respective merits of "fancy" flies and those which are intended to represent natural insects. I even broke the thing down to include a third group, "intermediate" flies such as the March Brown, the Professor, the Grizzly King and the endless variations of coloured bodies with light and dark mallard wings. This discussion had its amusing points, but I am sure now that it was not really sound, if only because flies in both the "intermediate" and "fancy" groups are almost certainly taken by the fish at times as exact imitations—whether in spite of or because of the intentions of the fisherman. Similarly, it is rather ridiculous to accept a fly such as the wet green sedge as a natural imitation. This fly is usually tied on a No. 6 or No. 8 hook, with wings laid back as are those of the sedge fly and a heavy hackle tied ahead of them, presumably represent-

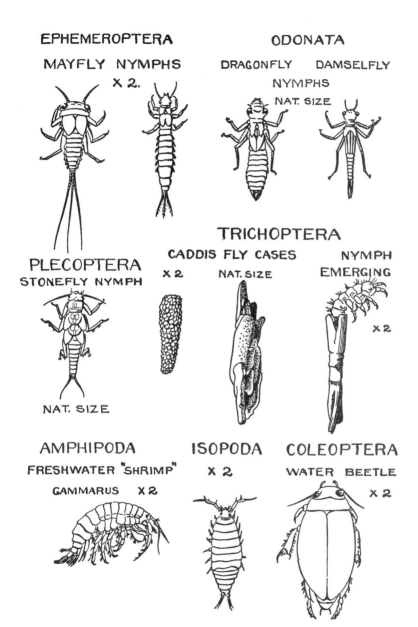

EPHEMEROPTERA

MAYFLY NYMPHS

X 2.

ODONATA

DRAGONFLY    DAMSELFLY

NYMPHS

NAT. SIZE

PLECOPTERA

STONEFLY NYMPH

NAT. SIZE

TRICHOPTERA

CADDIS FLY CASES

X 2    NAT. SIZE

NYMPH
EMERGING

X 2

AMPHIPODA

FRESHWATER "SHRIMP"

GAMMARUS    X 2

ISOPODA

X 2

COLEOPTERA

WATER BEETLE

X 2

SOME TYPICAL FAUNA OF BRITISH COLUMBIAN
TROUT WATERS

ing the legs and antennae of the sedge fly. It is then fished under water and with considerable artificial motion—a combination of appearance and behaviour that represents no stage of the sedge's sufficiently complicated life history between egg and death.

Interior fishermen have produced multitudes of wet fly patterns and new "special" patterns are being sent in every day to be copied by commercial tiers. The vast majority of these are nothing more than slight variations of existing patterns, and they probably contribute more to the vanity of the fisherman than to the discomfiture of the fish. Some worthwhile patterns have been developed and some fishermen have worked honestly and intelligently at the problems. But it is certainly safe to say that the interior has not yet produced its Ronalds, its Halford or its Skues.

So far as wet flies are concerned a really good imitation of the "freshwater shrimp" (*Gammarus limnaeus*) would seem most worth trying for. *Gammarus* and other crustacea make up something over 50% of the food eaten by trout in Paul, and probably most other interior lakes. Next in order of importance are the true insects—mayflies, stoneflies, sedges, craneflies, midges, dragonflies and others. These together make up another 25 to 30%, and perhaps even more, of Kamloops trout food. Their importance to the wetfly fisherman is during hatches, after the adult has broken out of its pupa and is swimming up towards the surface to dry off and unfold its wings.

Ants, bees and wasps, with certain land beetles and spiders, are important surface food at times, and the dryfly man probably does well to consider them in his selection of an artificial even when there is a good hatch of some natural water insect. The fish are very rarely feeding selectively to the point of rejecting an easy chance at a floating land insect.

Other creatures that may offer possibilities to the wetfly fisherman are the various water bugs—Notonectids and Corixids particularly—the leeches, the flatworms and the molluscs. This last group is made up chiefly of water snails and slugs, clams and mussels, and though all are important trout foods it is difficult to imagine successful imitation. The water bugs are a very promising group, though, and a fly with a thick, dull yellow body, a heavy dark mallard wing flat over it and a few bucktail hairs tied in the centre of the body, kills well.

This very bare outline of the entomology of the Kamloops lakes suggests two things. First, that here is a field where radical, but informed and intelligent experiment may very well produce some valuable imitations, particularly of underwater types. Secondly, that the fish are interested in such a diversity of feed that "fancy" flies will always have their place; and quality of materials and tying, especially of dry flies, may well be of greater importance than exact imitation.

I believe a dryfly fisherman, starting out for the Kamloops lakes on his first trip, will be sure to do well enough if he takes along his favorite fanwing, spent wing and sedge patterns, tied on hooks not larger than 10, nor smaller than 14. In addition he should have a few bi-visibles, possibly some deer hair patterns and certainly some proved imitation of the flying ant and of a bee or a yellow jacket. A few upright-winged mayflies may be worth taking, but the fanwings and spent wings will probably take care of any mayfly hatch that comes along.

To the wetfly fisherman going up for the first time I would say: take your four favourite patterns, no matter what they are, dressed on No. 6 and No. 8 hooks. You will fish them with confidence and they will almost certainly kill well. Back them up, if you like, with some of the local favourites—Nation's Special, Nation's Fancy, Green Sedge, Rhodes' Favorite and so on. Remember, as all good wetfly and nymph fishermen should, what Skues has written: "Representation or suggestion rather than exact imitation is what the dresser of nymphs should aim at," and: "That is one reason why dubbings outclass quills for bodies of nymphs." Dubbings, particularly seal's fur, also outclass silk or wool or raffia or any other body material in almost any case.

## REFERENCES

Dunne, J. W. *Sunshine and the Dry-fly*. London, 1924.

Halford, F. M. *Dry Fly Man's Handbook*. London, 1913.

Hardy's *Angler's Guide*. Hardy Brothers, Alnwick, England, 1937. Supplement of additions and alterations to same, 1938.

Jennings, P. J. *A Book of Trout Flies*. Derrydale Press, 1935.

La Branche, G. M. L. *The Dry Fly and Fast Water*. New York, 1926.

Moseley, M. E. *Dry-fly Fisherman's Entomology*. London, 1921.

Needham, J. G., Travers, J. R., and Hsu, Yin-chi. *Biology of Mayflies*. Ithaca, N. Y., 1935.

Needham, J. G., and Heywood, H. B. *Handbook of the Dragonflies of North America*. Baltimore, 1929.

Needham, J. G., and P. R. *Guide to the Study of Freshwater Biology*. 1927.

Pictet, F. J. *On Phryganidae*, 1834. *Histoire Naturelle des Insectes Neuropteres*, 1843-5.

Rawson, D. S. *Productivity Studies in Lakes of the Kamloops Region*, Biol. Bd. Can., Bull. 42, 1934.

Ronalds. *Fly-fisher's Entomology*. London, 1836.

Dates given are those of first publication. In many cases there have been subsequent editions.

# V

## On the Water
## & in the Mail

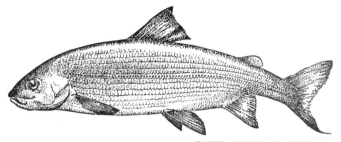

ROCKY MOUNTAIN WHITEFISH.

I T is not altogether difficult to make a list of certain essential things that help to make good fishing, but such a list would not be inevitably a description of good fishing, or even of fishing at all. The pleasures of angling are many, and they have many sources; both pleasures and sources are intermingled and interdependent, working together upon each other to produce the mood, the day, the ultimate satisfaction. Good fish, attractive water, the right tackle working smoothly, fair weather—one can have all these and the combination may produce a good bag of fish, yet the day may be forgotten while a day yielding fewer and smaller fish is remembered.

One remembers not merely the actual fishing, but all that led up to it and followed upon it—the journey, the country, the people, food, lodging, conversation, ideas and thoughts. Nothing wears better, for instance, than the journey up the Fraser valley to the interior; pulling out from Seattle or Vancouver and heading north, with all the dirt roads of British Columbia ahead, and Kamloops trout in a thousand lakes. I put rods and reels and flies in the car and started from Seattle that way in May of 1936. After crossing the border and getting over the last of the paved roads, hurry seemed to fall away from me. I drove lazily and stopped to eat sandwiches somewhere between Rosedale and Hope, where a little stream runs under the road and on through an alder thicket to the Fraser. Down along the stream a ruffed grouse drummed, and through the alders I could make out the end of the old rotten log on which he was standing. I walked down until I could see him and then, moving too clumsily, I flushed him. For a moment of time he was brown movement against the pale-green leaves.

Through the rest of that day I was with the Fraser, brown, turbulent, streaked always with the strength of its current, broken sometimes to white, a mighty river. The hard mountains were its banks, and down their steep sides running water sought the river—water in rushing streams, in tiny creeks, in mare's tail falls that made long lines of white against green and brown and grey or against the reds and yellows of mineral-stained rock. At dusk, a cold wind down the canyon and the beginning of the dry belt; and always that wonderful road, narrow, writhing its way through the hard country, having nothing to guard the sharp outer edge, nothing to hold back the slides that threaten it from above; not a scenic highway, but a road through a difficult place because people have to get through; by virtue of its function, its gravelled surface and its spareness, truly a part of the country it serves.

When it was quite dark I stopped at an inn that was perched on the outer edge of the road, where there seemed nothing but a straight five-hundred-foot drop to the river. There was a good bed there and good food, and the people talked untidily of Aberhart and Buchman and Marx; it was not yet fishing country, and the year was 1936.

Before noon the next day I was at my first lake. I stopped the car where the road crosses the outlet, and walked up until I could see the lake. It was a warm, pleasant day, full of spring; light clouds passed now and then across the face of the sun, and a little breeze scarcely moved the surface of the water. It was easy to stand there at the edge of the lake and look along the wooded hills; water that one is shortly to fish for the first time always seems abundantly full of promise, and I could see points and bays and could guess where the shoals ran out. A few small fish were rising near me, just above the outlet, and as I watched there was the quiet rise of a big fish just beyond them. It was a cruiser's rise, slow and smooth, showing a great part of the shoulder. He was a long cast out from shore, and for a moment I hesitated. Put up the rod and try for him? No, I thought, I'm too old for that; he'd be gone before I was ready, or I would find the cast just too long, with the scrub alders and little cottonwoods so close behind me. I went back to the car and drove on to the lodge.

But I knew as I drove that I should go back down to the outlet to look for the cruiser; he was not so very large and he certainly would not be there, but he was my fish—or I was his fisherman. I felt bound to him in some way, not free to try for other fish until I had at least looked for him. So I put up my rod, took one of the lodge boats and drifted back towards the outlet on the light breeze. Before I had time to get out the oars to hold the boat from drifting too far, the breeze had died away; the clouds were all gone and the sun shone hot and bright on the still surface of the lake; a few fish were rising, probably feeding on chironomid nymphs. I looked over a box of wet flies, but there was nothing that seemed to fit the big cruiser and his slow, easy rise. I remembered other Kamloops trout, feeding on chironomids, which had come to the brown and white bi-visible.

I tied a bi-visible to 3x gut and saw a small fish rise within easy reach. I hesitated, still waiting for my cruiser to show. The small fish rose again, and I set the bi-visible near him; he

came to it sloppily and missed it by two or three inches, so
widely that I was not even tempted to strike. A second later
he had turned and taken the fly quietly and gently. He made
one fast run and a noble jump, but he weighed barely a pound
and I netted him quickly. As I freed the hook and slipped the
fish into the box, my cruiser showed, almost exactly where I
had seen him before, and well within reach.

I dried my fly quickly, arguing with myself that it could not
be the same fish, though I knew it was. He rose again. I dropped
the fly ahead of him and waited, resolved not to strike to his
first rise unless I actually saw him take the fly under, in his
jaws. He came suddenly, right out of the water and down on
to the fly. In spite of my resolve the tip of my rod jerked up a
little, but the fly did not move. It lay there very flat on the
water, and he came back and took it with one of his great,
quiet, bulging rises. I struck, and he ran a little from the pull,
then turned sharply and came straight towards the boat. I kept
pace with him, hand-lining until he turned again and ran out
and down. I felt him start upwards at the end of his run, and
felt the line quivering as it was drawn suddenly against the
water instead of through it. A moment later he was high in the
air, shining in the sun, the broken water falling back all around
him. He jumped again and again, five times going away from
me, then I was able to work him back and draw him over the
net. He weighed an ounce less than two pounds—but he was
something I have learned not to expect too often in British
Columbia, a good fish, marked down, re-found and hooked
strictly according to plan.

On that same trip there was another day—a whole day, this
time—that I remember clearly. It was a day of mountain
weather on Paul Lake; there were strong winds, now from due
east, now from due west, scattering squalls of heavy rain; and,
once or twice, the sun shone through broken, racing clouds.
Jack Marsh and I were fishing together in one boat, the Doctor
and Bill Nation were in another. In the morning there were at

least a dozen boats out, scattered all over the lake, searching for fish. By lunch time our two boats had worked along the south shore of the lake to the Beaver House Shoal; Marsh and I had only one fish between us; the Doctor had about five.

We went ashore and began to collect wood to make a fire and boil coffee. Soon Bill Nation said: "No more wood; make a little fire and get up close."

We talked about mosquitoes and fish and the wind, and why the wind seemed to have discouraged the fish but not the mosquitoes. Bill said, "They'll come on early this afternoon."

"They ought to be on sometime on a lively day like this," I said.

"Hope so," said Marsh. "It was certainly pretty slow this morning."

The boats were still scattered when we got out on the water again. Marsh was fishing, and wanted to change his fly; he had been using Nation's Green Sedge all the morning. One nearly always did fish Bill's flies at Paul Lake in those days, and the Green Sedge had been doing well for several days, but Marsh wanted a change anyhow.

"To hell with Bill," he said; "what shall we try?"

I had some good Grizzly Kings, tied with olive seal's fur bodies, badger hackles and well-marked wings. They seemed not too far from the Green Sedge.

"What about these?" I asked him.

"Fine," Marsh said. "I like a Grizzly King."

Marsh is a good fisherman. He casts accurately and cleanly, with a strong arm and wrist. When he wants to, he can put out a long line, and he handles his fish quickly and smoothly. There was a sunken log, just visible through the shoal water, jutting out from the shore. He pointed to it. "Looks good to me," he said.

I held the boat so that his fly would cover the end of the log. He hooked a good fish at once, and I netted it for him, holding the boat in position against the wind. Still casting to the log, he hooked several more fish and landed three of them, all good, bright fish in perfect condition. By that time the boats were no longer scattered. They all closed in, the party of Scotsmen in two or three boats, trolling red and white plugs, the man from China who hadn't been doing so well, and the others. I held the boat where it was, and Marsh kept hooking fish all along his sunken log, losing some and landing others. The other boats were getting only an occasional fish.

"We'd better move out and let someone else in," I said.

"To hell with that. We don't crowd them when they're catching fish. I'm enjoying this."

So I held the boat where it was, and Marsh went on hooking fish. He was fishing beautifully and was very happy, laughing a lot. He urged me to fish while they were still taking, but I didn't want to, it was enough to be watching him and holding the boat, seeing the whole water and where the fish came from and how they came. When he had eight or ten fish in the boat I let the wind carry us away from the log and started slowly for home, following the shore line. Marsh soon picked up a couple more fish and wanted to keep the last few of his limit for the evening fishing, so I gave him the oars and began to fish myself, using the green sedge. Fish came easily and I had about a half dozen more in the boat by the time we were past Gibraltar Rock and within sight of the lodge. Then the wind shifted and began to blow really hard from the foot of the lake, dead against us. My fly dropped pleasantly on the waves and worked down into them in a lively way. One or two more fish took in the rough water, and I offered to spell Marsh with the oars.

"No," he said, "go on. I need the exercise and you're doing all right with that little rod."

Off Killkare Shoal the wind was very strong, and there were big whitecaps.

"Lord," I said, "I'd give a lot to hook a four-pounder now."

"You might," Marsh said.

The shoal was good, and I netted three nice fish as we

worked along it. Almost at the end of it a big fish rose well and began to take out line very fast; he jumped once, well clear of the water.

"It's him," I said; "a three-pounder, anyway."

The fish turned in his first run and came back fast towards the boat. I recovered line easily enough and kept in touch with him until he turned again and began to run out. He was a strong fish and ran deep against heavy pressure with thirty yards of fly line and some backing. I felt the angle of his run turn upwards a little, then the line was suddenly slack. The fly came back to me; and for the first time in several seasons I felt really sorry to have lost a fish. He had looked splendid in that first jump, and I wanted to see him again and again, silver and steel-grey, with the spray blowing from his jumps against the whitecaps. And there would have been difficult, anxious moments when he was ready for the net. In lake fishing one too seldom has the luck to hook a big fish when the conditions are all in his favour. As Marsh rowed the last two or three hundred yards to the float I counted the fish. There were twenty-two of them, all bright and in perfect condition, the largest just two and three-quarters pounds.

The Doctor stayed in after dinner, and Marsh and I went out with Bill Nation to try the water at the foot of the lake. The wind had gone down with the sun, and the lake was very calm. I was still fishing the Green Sedge, and hooked the first fish before we had gone very far. Marsh was after something really big to finish off the day, and had put on a tremendous Big Bertha; it was so big that it seemed likely to defeat its own purpose, but he had not used one before and wanted to see what it would do. Bill worked the boat gently across the still water, and big fish rose all around us. Marsh hooked a good fish and killed him. I was listening to Bill and enjoying the stillness of the evening after the windy day, fishing lazily. Marsh hooked another good fish and killed him. Most of the daylight was gone, and Bill told me to change to Nation's

Special; I began to fish hard, knowing that he wanted one of
his own flies to do as well as Big Bertha. But Bertha hooked
and lost three fish while I was losing one on the Special. She
hooked yet another and killed it. It was too dark to see the rises
and we both hooked and lost fish. Nation's Special killed the
last fish of the evening on the way back to the float, which
pleased Bill.

I don't think we realised how good that evening had been
until we really looked at the fish the next morning. Each of the
five was perfect, silver and clean as a salt-water steelhead, without the faintest trace of mature colouring. The largest just
shaded two pounds; the smallest weighed a bare three ounces
less than that. They might have been hatched from the eggs of
the same spawning pair and spent their whole lives within
casting distance of one another, though we had taken them one
by one all the way across the lake from the lodge to the north
shore.

It is some years now since Bill Nation died. I am quite sure
he brought to Kamloops trout fishing the most original mind
it has yet known. In a very real way he made the Kamloops
trout his own special fish and his active mind seemed never to
rest from thinking about them. Bill was a small, slender, soft-
voiced Englishman who talked almost incessantly from behind
a pair of big spectacles, yet listened well enough to seem almost
silent. He was a really good fly fisherman himself and as fine a
guide as a man could want—excellent company on the water
and tireless in searching for fish even on the worst days.

Bill was well read in the world's fishing literature and he was
a keen observer. But his mind had a happy, poetic slant that
must, I think, have developed through some Celtic strain in
him. He loved to theorise well up into the realms of fantasy
but always managed to come back down again with something
that had solid worth even though it still retained the incandes-
cence of fantasy. The frequent visits of good scientists like
Rawson and Mottley to Paul Lake helped Nation a lot both in

his ascents and descents—their sound and detailed natural history made fuel for his fantasy and guided the ideas he put into practice.

Nation will always be remembered for the series of wet flies he developed. In 1938 he sent me a list of the patterns he considered set, naming the natural prototypes as follows: *

| | |
|---|---|
| Nation's Blue | Coupled bluets (*Enallagma*) |
| Nation's Red | Coupled dragonflies (*Sympetrum*) |
| Green Sedge | Sedge nymph (*Glyphopsyche*) |
| Silvertip Sedge | Sedge nymph |
| Green Nymph | Dragonfly nymph ⎤ Species according to size |
| Grey Nymph | Dragonfly nymph ⎦ |
| Nation's Black | Chironomid nymph |
| Nation's Special ⎤ | |
| Nation's Fancy ⎬ General patterns | |
| Nation's Silvertip ⎦ | |

Few men who fish Kamloops trout waters do not carry at least one or two of these patterns and I imagine that Nation's Special alone has accounted for more Kamloops trout than any other half dozen flies together, if one leaves out the immensely popular Col. Kerry's Special. I often used to argue with Nation that most of his flies—except the two dragon nymphs and the chironomid nymphs—were fancy flies rather than true attempts at imitation, but he would never concede me anything at all on this and brought up beautifully involved arguments to support his views. For instance, he wrote me of Nation's Red: "One rather new fly I released the fall before last is an imitation of the coupled red dragon flies. You will see that the red front part of the body, with the red stripe on the wing, represents the strongly coloured red female in the lead, while the silver end of the body, with the light mallard tail, represents the lighter coloured male in tow."

Even allowing for the life that a wetfly fisherman can give his fly by artificial motion, I felt that this was a little far-

* Nation's own dressings of his flies are given in the Appendix.

fetched. So far as I know, the females of very few dragonflies descend below the surface to lay eggs, and even those that do so are rarely accompanied by males. I could find no record of any such activity for the two species of *Sympetrum* identified by Rawson from Paul Lake. Bill had a ready answer though. "The enormous gorge of dragons that the trout collect sometimes is composed practically entirely of adults taken on the wing. Therefore it is wrong to fish either the Red or the Blue as a floating still dry fly. For every natural floating red or blue there are 10,000 winged ones flying an inch or two above the water, therefore fish the Red or Blue artificial with a greased line and a vertical rod, work it fast enough to keep it no farther below the surface than the natural fly is above, say one inch. If you fish the fly slow and deep you will interest no trout."

I have quoted this discussion at some length to show Nation's bold and keen thinking and to give some idea of how closely he observed. His Red fly does take fish when the *Sympetrum* hatch is on and whether this is because of its appearance or because of the method of fishing it doesn't matter very much. The point is that he has departed a very long way from the flyfisherman's usual business of imitating mayflies and sedges, and has made something of it. He set great store by the motion of the wet fly at all times, and I am sure he was quite right. "Underwater life movements," he once wrote me, "might be classified into those that flick like a prawn, the large dragon nymphs; those that crawl like a snake on a boardwalk, in one plane, as the *Enallagma* nymphs; those that walk like a sheep, as many of the sedge nymphs. And the working of the fly that imitates these forms should also imitate the action of the particular nymph. Note that the nymph of the Green Sedge moves in a series of tiny jerks; these seem to be of great intensity, but each fierce, convulsive jerk only manages to move the nymph forward less than an eighth of an inch. This nymph moves on the shoals each evening from 10 o'clock on for a few days before hatching, and are in the chara weed, and the dyed seal's fur body of the sedge fly imitates the case more nearly than it does the actual body of the nymph. The fly is fished quite slowly under these conditions, and a very short, fierce jerk of one inch is sent through the line every ten seconds. This style of fishing works best during the four days preceding the full moon, so does not apply generally. For the Green Sedge it is advisable to carry peroxide of hydrogen to bleach the body to the desired shade of that of the sedge or nymph the fish are feeding on. I enclose some dyed seal's fur in various stages of sun bleach, and I pick the shade I want for my own tying."

Other men may solve more Kamloops trout problems than Bill did, make more ingenious imitations and develop more perfect ways of fishing them. But for me and for many another Bill will always be the true pioneer of the fishing, the man whose life was closer to those particular fish than any other man's had been or is likely to be. There is not space to write of the many things he did or attempted for his beloved Paul Lake fish—of how he tried repeatedly to bring the Traveller Sedge down from Knouff Lake, how he persuaded the government to introduce crayfish, of his suggestion that a proportion of Kamloops trout should be caponized by X-ray to ensure their continued growth without the interference of spawning. But nothing written of Kamloops trout could be reasonably complete without some account of him, and I hope there is enough of him in this chapter to show why that is so.

# PART THREE

*Coast Trout*

# Winter Steelhead

STEELHEAD.

THOROUGHLY sound information on the habits and life histories of coast trout is extremely scarce. The coast of the mainland of British Columbia and of Vancouver Island is a long stretch, and a tremendous number of rivers drain down to it, through an even greater number of lakes; both lakes and rivers present a fairly wide diversity of conditions, and it is not unreasonable to suppose that the habits of the fish vary more or less proportionately. Eventually, basic life histories will be fully understood, and detailed information about each major watershed will be available. When that time comes, some fortunate being will be able to sit down at his desk and work out the complete picture. In the present circumstances my only honest course is to give a detailed account of conditions in the waters I know best, and to indicate as far as possible how far these are likely to be applicable to other coast waters.

The watershed best suited to my purpose, both because it is well known and because I know it fairly well myself, is that of the Campbell on Vancouver Island. In many important respects it is typical of most coast watersheds; in one important respect it is not typical—salmon cannot ascend the main stream for more than a short distance, and fish have no access to the lower reaches of the river or to tidal water from the main chain of lakes. As a check on this difference, I am able to apply what I know of the Nimpkish watershed, also on Vancouver Island, up which migratory fish of all types can and do ascend for considerable distances and through several lakes.

In another sense, both these watersheds are atypical of coast streams. A great many of the rivers flowing down to the mainland coast are glacial, and their streams are cloudy with silt throughout the year, except possibly in the coldest months. This condition makes them difficult and comparatively unattractive from the angler's point of view, so I shall concern myself with them very little. The mainland streams which, though glacial, flow down through lakes and clear themselves by precipitation of the silt in still water are more important, but are probably sufficiently like the Campbell and the Nimpkish to be considered with them.

The Campbell watershed offers somewhere along its length an example of practically every type of game fishing to be found on the coast, and for that reason is perhaps preferable to more typical watersheds, for the present purpose. It heads in the several mountain streams tributary to the twenty miles of Buttle Lake, and runs from there about nine miles to Upper Campbell Lake. A short distance above Upper Campbell it is joined by its first major tributary, the Elk, which drains Elk Valley and Drum Lake. Between Upper and Lower Campbell Lakes the river runs strongly through several miles of good water, and is joined by one or two tributaries from small lakes. Several other lakes drain into Lower Campbell, and below this lake the river is really itself. It drops through one fall a little way below the lake, and wanders from there through a long reach that is for the most part slow and deep and holds—rather surprisingly—no fish over ten or eleven inches, so far as I know. This gentleness is drawn suddenly into the rush of Moose Falls, a forty- or fifty-foot drop through an angle of about forty-five degrees. From the foot of Moose Falls it is only a few turbulent minutes to the sheer hundred-and-fifty-foot drop of Elk Falls, which effectively landlocks all the water above it.

From the foot of the falls the river runs for about a mile through a deep canyon, and then spreads out suddenly into the Canyon Pool, about four miles from salt water and the first of the three main pools of the lower reaches. The Upper Island splits the river below the Canyon Pool and where the two streams join again is the Islands Pool, second of the main pools and one of the most attractive pieces of wet-fly water to be found anywhere in the world. The Lower Island divides the stream again below this pool, and a little beyond the new junction the Quinsam River runs in from its own chain of lakes. A few hundred yards below the mouth of the Quinsam is the third great pool, the Sandy Pool, and, from the foot of this rather less than half a mile of rapid runs down to the highway bridge and the approximate limit of tidal water. About a mile from the highway bridge the river runs out into Discovery Passage, on the east coast of Vancouver Island and almost exactly a hundred miles north of Vancouver. This lower four miles from the Canyon Pool to salt water, with a few miles of the Quinsam, is all the spawning area available to the runs of anadromous fish, but it supports an important run of spring salmon, a fair humpback run in alternate years, a fair cohoe run and a good run of winter steelhead. Some dog salmon also run to the river, and possibly in some years an insignificant number of sockeyes.

The run of winter steelhead * to the Campbell is about as

---

* It has been suggested that it might be well to drop the name "steelhead" and use only "rainbow trout," in order to strengthen public opinion against

good as can be found in a stream accessible by road, after all these years of indiscriminate commercial netting and almost equally indiscriminate angling. It is not easy to set reasonably exact time limits for the run; there can be little doubt that a few fish run to the river during every month in the year, and though there is a very sharp difference between the winter run and the spring or summer run in both size and age, the dates of arrival of the first and last fresh fish of the winter run vary a little from year to year. The earliest date on which I have caught winter-run fish in the Campbell is November 30th; the first good day is usually about December 20th. But it is quite possible that in some years there may be a very fair run of fish during November; it is difficult to check this by angling, because cohoe salmon are usually so numerous in November and take fly or minnow so freely that one cannot be certain that the steelhead have had a real chance.

The end of the run is more definite. After March 15th in any year the chances of hooking clean fish are so small, and the chances of hooking and injuring ripe fish and kelts is so great, that no experienced fisherman with any regard for the future would deliberately fish for winter steelhead in the Campbell after that date, even though there is occasionally a run of clean fish late in the month. In 1934 I could not catch a really clean fish after February 28th, and since then have always been prepared to avoid using anything but the fly during March if the proportion of stale fish is at all high.

The life history of the steelhead is not properly known, and it seems to me that there is little to be gained by any very positive statements at this point. I have read scales from a considerable number of steelhead caught in Vancouver Island streams during the past few years, and these readings have suggested to me certain conclusions. But scale reading unchecked by tagging

the commercial capture of these fish. While I believe the point is well taken, the name "steelhead" has so many associations for me and serves such a useful purpose in distinguishing migratory from non-migratory rainbow that I cannot bring myself to forget it.

and other more exact and concrete forms of research is of very questionable value; conditions of which the scale reader can have no exact knowledge may cause temporary slackening of growth and a resultant check on the scale that will be falsely read; a visit to fresh water while still immature may produce something like a spawning mark; and steelhead in salt water seem at times to make such even growth that their scales show little or no winter check, and it is really necessary to count the rings before committing oneself to a reading.

Bearing in mind these limitations of the method, I have read the scales of 100 winter steelhead caught in the Campbell between 1934 and 1937. The average weight of these fish was 11¼ pounds; thirty-nine were males and sixty-one were females. Nearly all were caught on the devon minnow, and the few that were not were taken on the fly. Apart from the method of capture the selection was a purely random one. The results were as follows:

> 78 fish had spent 2 years in fresh water and nearly 3 years in salt water.
> 10 fish had spent 1 year  in fresh water and nearly 3 years in salt water.
> 5 fish had spent 2 years in fresh water and nearly 4 years in salt water.
> 5 fish had spent 2 years in fresh water and nearly 2 years in salt water.
> 2 fish had spent 1 year  in fresh water and nearly 4 years in salt water.

Of the seven fish that had spent more than three years in salt water, all had spawned previously.

I have no figures that compare exactly with these, but it is worth noting that Long and Griffin, reading the scales of Columbia River steelhead, conclude that 12% of the winter run have spawned previously, and that 22% of the steelhead which have spent two years in fresh water (summer, fall and winter runs included) start their spawning migration in the second year of ocean life, 68% in the third, and 9% in the fourth year.

With this slight confirmation, it seems not too rash to assume that most of the winter-run fish of the Campbell have spent two years in fresh water and are returning to spawn as maiden fish after nearly three years of feeding in the sea, and that comparatively few, probably not much more than 10%, have spawned previously. This figure of 10% compares very closely with that given by most authorities for Atlantic salmon, and since the steelhead is likely to differ from the Atlantic salmon only in the possession of two or three more anal fin rays and three or four more vertebrae, it is perhaps legitimate to consider this a further confirmation.

Anglers, whether they fish for Atlantic salmon in the east or in Europe, or for steelhead on the Pacific Coast, are often disappointed when they find what a small percentage of the fish return to spawn a second time. Since comparatively few fish of either species are found dead in the rivers, and since well mended kelts are frequently caught, this is a natural reaction. In the case of Atlantic salmon the main cause of high mortality has been shown to be loss of weight before, during and after spawning, a total loss of 42% in males and 44% in females. The same loss is, in the case of most animals, including man, more than enough to cause death by starvation, and it seems probable that at least some Atlantic salmon and some steelhead do actually die of starvation. Possibly—I can find no figures— steelhead lose a smaller proportion of weight than this, but in any case the loss is very considerable and must materially reduce the chances a fish has of surviving the dangers of the sea during the first few weeks after its return.

In spite of the close relationship of the two fish, comparison of Atlantic salmon and steelhead is probably dangerous, from the scientific point of view, until more is known of the steelhead; but from the angler's point of view it is interesting and very profitable. Any man who can catch Atlantic salmon can catch steelhead, and any method that will take Atlantic salmon will also take steelhead. But there are some important differences.

The steelhead does not usually reach the size of the Atlantic salmon of the larger European streams. Cobb states that steelhead probably reach a maximum weight of 45 lbs. The world's record rod-caught steelhead weighed 29 lbs. The record for the Campbell is 24½ lbs.; the fish was caught by Reginald H. Pidcock. But a twenty-pound steelhead is extremely rare, as rare probably as a fifty-pound Atlantic salmon, and anything over 15 lbs. is a good fish, even in the Campbell which shows fish of a higher average weight than most streams. These maximum weights approximate much more closely those of the European sea trout than those of the Atlantic salmon. The record rod-caught European sea trout, from the river Em in Sweden, weighed just over 29 lbs. Sea trout up to 25 lbs. run to the Tweed in Scotland, and the rod-caught record in England is a fish of 21 lbs. from the Dorsetshire Frome—one that I am proud to mention, since the Frome is my parent stream. In concluding a discussion of large sea trout, Menzies, in *Sea Trout and Trout*, writes: "When we get down to sea trout of only 15 lbs., their number is so large as not to warrant mention in a short catalogue of outstanding examples." All these figures, from the record of 28 lbs. down to Menzies' final statement, apply so closely to the weights of steelhead that they suggest that a similarity in the sea-feeding habits of both species must have persisted in spite of a three-thousand-mile geographical separation.

In most seasons my own fish from the Campbell average just over 11 lbs.; the only exception to this so far is the 1937-1938 season, when the average was only 7¾ lbs. The average length in the normal years is a fraction over 30 inches, which gives an average condition factor of 41. Such an orthodox average as this is perhaps a little misleading; in the 1936-1937 season a 23½-pounder, 36 inches long, was caught in the Courtenay River, and a few days later I caught in the Campbell a 37-inch fish that weighed only 18 lbs., though it was uninjured and perfectly fresh-run; the average condition factor of these two fish is 44, but the actual figures were respectively 50 and 38. From such differences as this it seems quite possible that there are in British Columbia, as there apparently are down in Washington, two separate races of steelhead, one short and thick, the other long and slender. As yet no work on the study of this point has been attempted in British Columbia, but in Washington I have seen the progeny of both types artificially hatched and raised under identical conditions, with the thickness or slenderness of the parents persisting.

Broadly speaking, it is possible to say that the steelhead, like the Atlantic salmon, does not feed in fresh water. As far as I know, all salmonoid fish, including the Pacific salmon, are progressively less inclined to feed as they approach maturity. But I believe that the winter steelhead is a great deal more likely to take food in fresh water than is the Atlantic salmon. Of the hundred fish whose scale readings I have recorded, twelve had foreign matter of some sort in their stomachs. In several cases there was probably no question of feeding; two fish had parasitic worms, one had a small quantity of green algae, one had several clover leaves. Two had dragon-fly nymphs, one had a mayfly nymph, one had a single humpback alevin, and two, caught on the same day, had several breast feathers of the common goldeneye. The remaining two fish were undoubtedly feeding; the first, a 15-pounder caught on December 29th, 1936, had a solid mass of eyed cohoe salmon ova weighing over a pound. The second, a fifteen-pounder, caught six days later, had three eyed ova and the shells of more than forty others. In both cases there was ample evidence that digestion had taken place. The significance of all this is at least qualified by the fact that both these fish were caught during high freshet, when the eggs were probably rolling along the bottom past them and giving them the opportunity to pick up all they wanted without moving or making any considerable effort.

Partly, I believe, because of this tendency to feed, or at least to pick up trifles, the steelhead is an easier fish to catch than the Atlantic salmon. He is far less inclined to be dour, and in my experience he is not particularly sensitive to the state of the water. There are few days in the winter, between say December 20th and March 1st, when I cannot wander out of the house, rod in hand, at 2:30 P.M. and return at 3:30 P.M. with a couple of ten-pounders; high water or low, rising river or falling, it seems to make little difference so long as the current is not too slow to allow proper working of the devon or too fast to allow one to cover the water as it should be covered.

In the original edition of *The Western Angler* I said that it is not easy to catch winter steelhead on the fly. I have now completely changed that opinion. During the winter of 1938-1939 I began to use the fly at least as frequently as the minnow and found myself doing not too badly ·with it. Since then I have used the fly exclusively and, as nearly as I can judge, its effectiveness is at least seventy per cent that of the minnow. As time goes on I catch more and more fish on the fly in water that was unfishable or had seemed unproductive with the minnow; and I am inclined to believe that if I can continue to improve my techniques and my knowledge of the river I may find that the fly catches me just as many fish as the minnow ever did.

But spinning with the devon minnow is still the most popular method of fishing for winter steelhead on Vancouver Island, and it is probably as well to consider this fully before going into details about the fly fishing. Casting a minnow or any other type of artificial bait has in any case quite a lot to recommend it in really cold weather, when water is freezing on the line, and some men will always prefer it to fishing a big fly.

For winter minnow fishing in the Campbell I have always used a No. 2 Hardy Victor rod, 7' 9" long and weighing 7¼ oz. with a 3½" Silex reel. I used to use a light oiled-silk line spliced to a hundred yards of fine silk backing, but now prefer 100 yards of plain black silk or nylon casting line, about 18 lb. test. Of all the baits I have tried I still prefer the one that caught me my first steelhead in British Columbia, nearly twenty years ago—Allcock's Feathero devon minnow. This outfit, with a half-ounce lead at the head of a four-foot trace of Hardy's punjab wire, is just about perfect for comfortable side-swing casting up to forty yards or so under almost any conditions.

Many people, I know, distrust the devon minnow. Either it will not catch fish for them, or else they find the bottom of the river so frequently that the method becomes pretty expensive. Personally, I doubt if one need, at any time except perhaps in very muddy water, look for a more deadly bait than the devon. But it must be fished as slowly as possible and as close to the bottom as possible, and, as with the fly, every last inch of holding water must be searched. That is why it is such a satisfactory bait to fish. The casting is easy—a smooth swing of the shoulders and light fingering of the reel. Long casting seldom pays; a long cast once in a while may pick up an extra fish, but I find that many strikes are missed if one casts consistently farther than 35 or 40 yards—and a 35-yard cast is easy enough to make.

But the fishing of the water is difficult—more difficult actually than fishing the same water with a wet fly, because one must know the obstructions and currents of the bottom of the river as well as those of the surface and use them properly if every fish is to be offered a maximum of temptation.

The whole argument of my preference for the devon minnow over other types of bait, and for the Feathero in particular, is pretty involved. I know very well that I might use, with more deadly effect, worms, worms and spinner, prawn, perhaps even red sponge, fly and spinner, and plugs. But I feel no need for deadlier bait, for the devon has always caught fish for me at least as quickly and easily as I could wish. Worms and even prawns are less clean and less pleasant to handle, particularly in cold weather, and generally they must be replaced after each touch. The red sponge and the fly and spinner are cheaper baits than the devon and perhaps one dares to fish them closer to bottom, but this in itself is an argument against them; with eighty cents of devon on the end of the trace one must fish better, more accurately and carefully than when the loss will only be a few cents, so there is more virtue in the job well done. Then, too, these baits do not cast as pleasantly and smoothly as does the devon, and the working of them in the currents is not such a smooth, sweet thing; only the proper working of a prawn or of a fly on greased line calls for more skill and fineness of touch than does working of the devon.

So I like my devons because they are clean to handle, because they cast well, because they fish well and because there is an element of risk in fishing them properly. I like them, also, because the fish strike them hard and heavily, not with the gentle stop that comes so often with worms and the sponge and even with the prawn; and one's own strike in response to that of the fish is a clean, hard movement. And in nine cases out of ten the hooked fish throws the devon up the trace and jams it against the swivel of the lead, so that he is left free to do his best, with nothing more than a small hook in his mouth to confuse him and throw him off balance.

And why the Feathero in preference to other minnows? Because it is a pretty thing, most like a fly with its brown or blue feathers laid along the body under celluloid, and its silver or gold belly. And because it is exactly the right weight; heavy enough and compact enough to cast well and travel out ahead of the lead, yet light enough to ride through the water a few inches above the lead so that one can feel the lead touch before the hooks, and know in time to take in line a little faster. Rarely, in very heavy water, this is a fault and the Feathero will not work deep enough; then, perhaps once or twice each season, I used to change to one of the few metal devons in my box.

But it is a rich man's game, this risking of eighty cents time and again among the rocks and logs of the bottom. Or is it? I find that I lose or destroy one Feathero to every ten fish I catch. At the moment there are two in my box, each a little torn, each with one fin missing, but each likely to persuade another fish or two. The blue and silver has taken seventeen fish, the brown and gold fourteen. The risk is there, but the satisfaction is in taking the risk and keeping the devon. The surest way is to know the river well; but since the strength of the stream has as much to do with the conditions as the state of the bottom, it is seldom the same river two days running. One must fish with a hand sensitive to the bump of the lead on bottom and an eye quick to see check or change of angle in the line. And if the pull comes, one can avoid striking; it is so different from the hit of a fish. There will be a willow switch within reach; tie it in a circle, run it up the rod and down the line and work it against the current until it lifts the lead or the minnow clear. Unless the hooks have been driven firmly into a log or a branch, the minnow will come back.

For winter steelhead, as for Atlantic salmon, cover the water faithfully and well. Start with short casts, and gradually work up to the cast that covers the pool or the run from side to side. Swing the minnow across and across, slow and deep, letting it hang in the current where it will, casting at an angle upstream when the current is heavy, paying out line when the swing is too fast; search every corner and lie, cover them again and again and from different angles and at different speeds, if the fish will not take. A steelhead may take at the first cast or at the tenth or the fiftieth; he is never a hopeless fish.

I do not change my devons much for winter steelhead. I prefer the 2½-inch size, brown and gold for bright days, king-fisher blue and silver for dull days. Sometimes, late in the season, a smaller minnow does well, but it is never essential to good fishing. When I am fishing the devon I tell myself that the fish are stimulated to take it by the vibration set up in the water by the rapid revolution of its fins, which resembles that caused by the passage of a small fish through the water and is detected by the sensitive tube of the steelhead's lateral line. This is no more than a guess, but I cling to it because it makes me search my water well; try to bring the devon close enough to the fish for its vibration to be felt. Partly for this same reason,

I do not think the colours matter a great deal; one can use the brown on a dull day or the blue on a bright day, and still catch fish. Once I fished a pool from top to bottom with the brown and the blue and caught nothing, then changed to green and silver and caught a fish at the first cast. I went back to my blues and browns and caught nothing until I changed again to green. But it has not happened since, and I feel that there must have been some other factor than that simple change of colour.

The other baits that most anglers will continue to use in preference to the devon must also be fished carefully, slow and deep, for winter steelhead. There are some days in every winter, usually when the temperature of the air is noticeably warmer than that of the water, when steelhead will come well to a bait or a fly fished high and fast. The angler will find these days quickly enough for himself—a fish will take as he reels up quickly at the end of the cast, or as the bait hits the water—but the secret of catching steelhead is in deep fishing and above all in slow fishing, in the hanging, hovering holding of the bait in the current. Fish the prawn if possible more slowly and caressingly even than the devon. Fish the worms bumping along the bottom, catching, slipping, rolling down and twisting with the current. Worm and spinner or fly and spinner should be fished very much as the devon is, but they must be given more time to sink well down. Plugs I have never been able to use with any satisfaction. Most of them have far too many hooks, and because of their erratic movement I never feel comfortably sure that they are fishing right or just where they are in the water, how near or how far from bottom. This is a serious disadvantage in steelhead fishing, and the erratic movement probably accounts for a tendency in the fish to show at a plug without taking. I have frequently taken fish that have shown to the plug in this way, by covering them with the devon a few moments later. Plugs have recently come into favour among salmon fishermen in Great Britain, and it may be argued from this that they should be good for steelhead. But even if they were proved a dozen times more deadly than the devon, I should not care to use them; the few fish I have hooked on plugs were so gagged by the clumsy mouthful that they came in like half-dead kelts; I freed them and returned them to the water, ashamed to have inflicted such indignity upon them.

The red sponge, which really is a small cube of sponge dyed red, will take fish when worked as one works a hookful of worms—or a cluster of salmon eggs. And that last point, apart from the rather unattractive method of fishing it, is my only objection to the red sponge; it was originally produced as an imitation of salmon roe, and I believe that its success owes everything to the fact that it is a very fair imitation. The use of salmon roe, fortunately, is illegal on Vancouver Island and in many parts of the mainland, and to use an imitation seems, however illogically, a shade undesirable; but that is purely a personal feeling, and I hope will not dissuade any angler who enjoys the method.

Now, having been as fair as I can to the devon minnow and most other baits, let me consider the fly again. The first objection to it, and one that held me from using it extensively for so long, is that winter fly fishing is excessively cold work because it means handling a lot of wet line. I can only say that I no longer notice this trouble—in fact I think I must have imagined it or taken it over from someone else in the first place. The absolutely overwhelming advantage of the fly is in the way the fish takes it. With the minnow and any other bait I have fished there is nearly always a perceptible pause between the strike and the fish's first run—a pause that lets the angler collect himself, and so gives him a very strong advantage. With the fly, nine times out of ten, there is no pause—the strike comes right back to the reel and the fish on his way, out in the air in his first jump as often as not, before the fisherman knows just what has hit him. That I find exciting, and the business of regaining control is nearly always prolonged by this abruptness of the fish. I am satisfied also that, on the average, fish run faster and further and jump much more frequently when hooked on the fly.

A sensible man, fishing a large fly in a river like the Campbell, would use a twelve- or thirteen-foot double-handed rod. It is easier, more comfortable and less tiring than fishing a single-handed rod heavy enough to cast a 2/0 fly. I do sometimes take out a double-handed rod, if the river is particularly high. But nearly always I use an eleven-foot, single-handed Hardy Wye rod with a No. 5 King Eider double-tapered line. My flies vary in size from 2/0 to No. 6 or 8, my gut from 3/5 to 2x, but in winter fishing I usually stay with flies from 2/0 to No. 2 and gut somewhere between 3/5 and 9/5.

I doubt very much if fly patterns make a great deal of difference. On the whole I prefer full-dressed, built-wing flies of the type used for Atlantic salmon, but I could not possibly defend the preference unless on traditional grounds. I believe, but am by no means sure, that there is generally some advantage in a body of gold or silver tinsel, and a good orange feather somewhere in the wing. The two flies that have caught me most fish have been Preston Jennings' Lord Iris, in sizes from 2/0 to No. 2, and the Silver Grey, tied on a 2/0 hook. Both these are complicated and elegant dressings and I may as well admit that I have fished them far more frequently than any other patterns. One very simple pattern that has caught fish for me on all sizes down to No. 6 is the light mallard and silver—yellow swan tail, silver body, blue hackle, light mallard wing. It would probably kill just as well without the tail, though I don't believe I would go so far as to leave out the hackle.

As with the minnow and all the baits, the way of fishing the fly is all-important. On nine days out of ten it is essential to work it slow and deep, hung and hovered, rolled and held. On the tenth day, when the air is appreciably warmer than the water, fish will come to it high and fast and the wise fisherman will turn to a greased line and a small fly fished without artificial movement. For the deep-sunk fly, use a line that has never been near grease or other floatant since leaving the factory, preferably one with the dressing worn away a little so that water soaks in more quickly. Cast the fly well across on a slack line, lift the slack immediately and throw it in a belly upstream. Then do everything possible to keep the fly working slowly—follow it with the rod top, use any slack water there may be to delay the pull of the line, pay out line if the lay of the water allows it. Fishing in this way it is by no means impossible to hook bottom with a 2/o fly in six feet of really fast water.

I find that most fish take hold in that favourite resting spot of steelheads, about two-thirds of the way down a run or pool, where the fast water begins to spread and smooth out. I prefer, if possible, to be wading almost directly upstream of such a place, so that I can hang the fly there as long as possible, fishing it back and forth across the lie by the swing of my rod, drawing it back to me sometimes and letting it drift down again. It may be that many of the fish that take hold in such places have followed the fly around. But I have several times hooked fish after hanging my fly for a full minute or more.

It would be easy to go on at length about fly fishing for winter steelhead, but this outline covers most of the essential details and any competent fly fisherman who follows it fairly closely will, I am pretty sure, find himself catching fish. There are few forms of fishing that come near it for pleasure and excitement.

One commonly used steelhead bait for which I care less than nothing is salmon roe. There is some feeling that its use should be permitted again in waters where it is now prohibited. It is argued that the poor man is denied the use of a cheap and effective bait. The proper answer to that is that worms are just as cheap and extremely effective—really too effective for the good of the fish. But the answer I wish to give, very positively and dogmatically, is that if the use of salmon roe is permitted there will soon be no steelhead fishing for any man, rich or poor, and perhaps no cutthroat fishing, either. Without having

seen and heard something of the difficulties that face those who
would perpetuate the steelhead runs of Washington, I should
not dare to be so positive. Even that objection, perhaps, would
not be enough to yield a clear-cut conclusion; there are so
many other factors, such as density of population and accessibility of rivers, to be considered. But, a few years ago, finding
myself working and arguing strongly against the use of salmon
roe, I suddenly had the grace to ask myself: "What in hell do
you know about it? Did you ever use the stuff? Or see it used
in British Columbia?"

Two or three days after that—it was in February—I took my
rod, my devons, some extra leads and some hooks to gut, and
went up the river. The water was high, but the Canyon Pool
was fishing well enough from the north side, and I stayed there.
After nearly an hour of fishing with the devon I hooked and
killed a twelve-pound female fish. I cleaned her, mounted one
of my single hooks and draped a cluster of eggs tastefully
upon it.

The conditions for an experiment of this type were as right
as they could be. I am a fair devon minnow fisherman, and it
had taken me nearly an hour to kill a fish with the minnow.
Until that moment I had never in my life fished with salmon
roe, though I had watched others once or twice, and also knew
something of fishing a worm. I felt that if I could pick up two
or three steelhead in the next hour I should feel thoroughly
justified in fighting the use of salmon roe.

It was about eleven o'clock, a cold, clean day; the river
rolled dully in front of me, the main current on the far side. I
laid a neat row of tags on the rock beside me, with the tagging
pliers and my notebook and pencil ready, and took a quick
look around for lurking game wardens or a possible witness.
I was breaking the law, I supposed, even though I did intend
to return the fish and make them serve a useful purpose by
carrying tags in their tails. I made a cast, and saw the line stop
before the lead had reached bottom. I struck, and quickly

landed an immature steelhead of about fourteen inches. In the next ten casts I hooked ten more of these fish, striking quickly to prevent them from getting the hook too far down. In February there is often a run of small fish of this type, obviously immature steelhead that have been to salt water and returned after a short while of feeding probably in or near the estuary. Usually, they are only in the river for a few days, and it seems probable that they follow the mature fish in schools.

My next three casts brought me three fine spawning cut-throats. A little disgusted with the success of the experiment, I tagged them and returned them. The pool was evidently full of small fish, and it seemed as though I must catch each one of them before whatever steelhead were there would get a chance. In fifteen or twenty more casts I hooked, tagged and returned eight more small steelheads and three more spawning cut-throats. I looked at my watch about then; twenty-five fish in an hour and a half. I mounted a fresh cluster of eggs and wiped my fingers again on my reeking handkerchief; I had not realised what an oily job it would be, or I should have brought a pack-ful of rags. I cast again, and the lead went down to the rocks; I felt it bump, and kept the bait rolling gently along the bot-tom. There was a stop and I struck—a steelhead of about nine pounds. I resolved to limit myself to ten more casts. It took me over an hour to make them, because they hooked me seven more steelhead, the smallest seven or eight pounds, the largest perhaps fifteen. A little over three hours of fishing—trout tags 1700-1724 and salmon tags 16908 to 16915 safely swimming about in the depths of the pool; no fish had taken twice and no small fish had taken after the first mature steelhead. I took my single minnow-caught female and went home.

That is why I feel now that I can be dogmatic, that I can say definitely and positively, without qualification or reserva-tion, that if the general public chooses to insist upon using salmon roe, then it must not expect to have decent fishing of any sort for many more years. No cultural effort could possibly keep pace with the drain on the public streams that this bait would cause; I doubt very much if it could be done at anything approaching reasonable cost even in privately owned water. By limiting the angler to one fish in a day's fishing, the drain on the run of spawning steelhead actually in the river in any one season might be kept to a reasonable proportion; but no legislation could adequately protect the spawning cutthroats or prevent destruction of the immature steelhead that would make the spawning runs of the future.

Another threat to the runs that should be swiftly met is the law by which a trout of over 3 lbs. may be sold; fresh-water fishing on the coast cannot possibly stand any commercial drain. The steelhead runs cannot stand much longer the drain upon them by commercial fishermen in salt water. The commercial value of the fish is extremely small, but its value as a sporting fish is potentially tremendous, and to allow the commercial net fishermen to treat the run more or less as a by-product of the salmon runs is utterly wasteful.

Many anglers feel that there is a significant drain on future spawning runs from the slaughter of kelts by rod fishermen in March and April. Naturally enough, it is unpleasant for an experienced fishermen to have to contemplate the slaughter, in the name of sport, of fish that are valueless as food, ugly to look upon, too weak to fight properly and very much inclined to take anything offered. But whether this actually is a significant factor in reducing the numbers of future runs is very doubtful in the light of such evidence of survival as is available. And there is also some room for doubt as to whether a veteran produces eggs as satisfactory as those of a maiden fish; it has been suggested that the percentage of deformity and infertility is high. But while these points are as debatable as they still are, the sportsman interested in the future of his sport will do everything in his power to avoid killing kelts; the argument of slow recovery and inefficient use of time and feed that applies to Kamloops kelts in a lake producing a maximum

weight of fish per acre obviously does not apply when the
recovery is to take place in the sea. Something could be done
to protect the kelts by legislation—at least in the rivers of the
east coast of Vancouver Island, where the spring and summer
runs of steelhead are not very important. Though it is true that
steelhead run to these rivers in every month of the year, they
do so in such small quantities between March and December
that no angler really goes out to catch them, except perhaps in
late April and in May; and I believe the bulk of the kelts are
usually well down the streams, if not actually out in salt water,
by the end of the second week in April. By prohibiting the
taking of any steelhead from these streams between March
15th and April 15th they would receive a great measure of
protection, and fishermen would be very little, if at all, incon-
venienced. It would, of course, be far better to prohibit the use
of any bait or lure other than the artificial fly in streams open
to salt water after March 15th, since a great many kelts are
certain to be caught and injured by worm and spinner fishermen, but this would not be acceptable to the majority of
anglers.

Another serious drain on the runs is caused by the killing of
steelhead parr, barely over the legal size limit of eight inches,
in the spring months. This could be prevented by raising the
legal size limit of trout to ten inches in streams open to salt
water, but again it is probable that such a move would not yet
be acceptable. The better course would be to show anglers the
difference between these fish and cutthroat trout of the same
size, by means of coloured posters, and suggest that they be
returned unharmed to the water. This method has been successfully used by local authorities in Great Britain, where some
anglers have found it difficult to differentiate between brown
trout and Atlantic salmon parr.

All these are comparatively insignificant measures that would
not in any way touch the question of development or constructive conservation. Constructive work can only come after

proper research and in the light of full knowledge of the winter steelhead's life history. But in order to preserve a sufficient breeding stock to make constructive work reasonably economical when the time comes, restrictive legislation, more or less along these lines, must be put into effect quite soon.

I have not written of the winter steelhead in those moments between the strike and the net. He is good and very often spectacular, but I do not think he is quick enough or vigorous enough to catch an experienced fisherman off balance in the way that Atlantic salmon, summer steelhead, Kamloops and cohoes can and do. Even a big fish in very heavy water will seldom take out more than sixty yards of line under a proper pressure, and I find that I play most of my hooked fish on my forty yards of casting line, with the backing still on the reel. The smaller fish sometimes jump really well; fish of over ten pounds are often slow and give in very easily if one puts pressure on them from the moment of the strike, but every once in a while one hooks a big fish that is full of fireworks; nearly every one of the dozen fish of sixteen pounds or more that I have killed has put up a strong and spectacular fight. Generally even the vigorous fish are easy to control and easy to lead, and I have never had much difficulty in holding the fish to the pool in which he is hooked. The lift of a No. 2 Victor or even an eight-ounce fly rod, properly used, is quite enough to keep any steelhead from sulking or to bring him to the surface somewhere within the bounds of a fair-sized pool. A fish hooked near the tail of a pool, and apparently determined to break down over the rapid below, will nearly always turn and swim quietly back up into the pool if the strain on him is slackened. He has, after all, climbed the river to the pool for a definite purpose, and he will leave it only in panic fright. In much the same way, he can often be led quietly past a dangerous rock or root if he is not driven to fight the terrifying strain; but the full strain must be applied again immediately he is in open water.

I do not think a more satisfactory or more valuable fish than the winter steelhead swims in British Columbian waters. He frequents beautiful streams and splendid water. He runs at a time when other fishing is slack. He is big enough to be an exciting opponent, and his strike to the right bait is something to send a thrill up the most experienced arm. Above all, he demands of the angler skilful, careful, thorough searching of the water, extreme concentration and a nice knowledge of things below the surface. And fresh out of the water, with the sea lice above his ventral fin, he is of a quality and a beauty that are enough.

## REFERENCES

Belding, David L. The Cause of High Mortality in Atlantic Salmon After Spawning. Trans. Amer. Fish. Soc., Vol. 64, 1934.

Cobb, John N. Pacific Salmon Fisheries. U.S. B.F., Doc. 1092, 1921.

Long, John B., and Griffin, L. E. Spawning and Migratory Habits of the Columbia River Steelhead Trout as Determined by Scale Readings. Copeia, 1937, No. 1, April 10th, 1937.

Menzies, W. J. M. Sea Trout and Trout. Arnold. London, 1936.

# 11

## *Summer Steelhead*

THE summer runs of steelhead to Pacific Coast streams offer fishing comparable in quality to that of the best of Atlantic salmon rivers, even though the fish are generally of smaller average and far smaller maximum size. Unfortunately, really good summer steelhead streams are few and far between. For some reason, the streams of the east coast of Vancouver Island, with the exception of the Nimpkish and to a lesser degree the Campbell, have no important summer runs. Some of the lower mainland rivers have fairly good runs. The rivers of the west coast of Vancouver Island are likely to have good runs; one or two streams in the Queen Charlotte Islands have runs, and there are runs in some of the rivers and streams that feed the great inlets of the northern coast. But with the exception of the lower mainland rivers and the Stamp River, which flows out to the west coast of Vancouver Island near Alberni, these streams are accessible by boat only and have not yet been much fished. Largely because good summer steelhead rivers are hard to find and reach, the interest of the average angler in this type of fishing is not nearly so great as the quality of the sport would suggest, and very little research work has been done. I think it is fair to say that neither the life history of the summer steelhead nor the relation of summer fish to winter fish is even nearly understood.

One factor which makes valueless any casual study of the fish is the difficulty of distinguishing, by any method short of scale reading, between migratory and non-migratory rainbows. Size is an indication, though in a stream with an accessible lake somewhere along its length a big fish—a five- or ten-pounder—may always be one that has made his growth in the lake and has dropped down to the stream from there. But in case of a coast stream with no accessible lake, it is fairly safe to assume that any trout, cutthroat or rainbow, of over two pounds has had some salt-water feeding—in fact, I doubt that the majority of coast streams have sufficient feed in them to produce even one-pound trout.

It is known that there is no structural difference between, say, a ten-inch land-locked rainbow trout of Buttle Lake and a ten-pound winter steelhead of the Campbell or any other stream open to salt water. It is known also that rainbows of land-locked lakes are likely to be migratory in that they ascend to tributary streams to spawn and drop down from those same streams, as fry or yearlings, to feed in the lake; and, more fundamentally, that any trout, even the brown trout which may appear season after season at the same feeding post, or the cutthroat locked in a lake with no accessible tributary or draining stream, will tend to move at spawning time from a feeding area to one more suitable for spawning and to return when spawning has been completed. So it is necessary to define what is meant by "migratory." When speaking of the winter steelhead the word means, as it does in the case of the Pacific salmon or the Atlantic salmon, a fish that spends the first period of life in fresh water, then descends to the sea and makes by far the greater proportion of his growth in salt water, usually feeding at some considerable distance from the parent stream and returning to it only at full maturity, to run up and spawn.

Such a fish is in the full sense not only migratory but anadromous—having made nearly all his growth in the sea he runs up the river to spawn. A cutthroat trout in an open stream is also fairly certain to be migratory; that is to say, he will move down to the estuary or out into the salt water near his river to find food that he cannot find in the fresh-water pools. And he is anadromous in that he will certainly return to fresh water to spawn. But he differs from the strongly migratory fish such as winter steelhead and Atlantic and Pacific salmon in that he probably does not move out into the sea very far beyond the influence of his river, and he is likely to return to the estuary daily at certain stages of the tide. And he differs from the strictly anadromous fish in that he returns to fresh water not only to spawn but quite often to find food; he will move up into fresh water to pick up humpback alevins in the spring, caddis in July and humpback eggs in the fall.

Fish are individuals, and the individuals of some species differ more widely in habit from one another than do the individuals of other species. It is possible to set an outline of what the general life history, feeding habits and structural characteristics of a certain species will be, but only with the mental reservation that a larger or smaller number of individuals will depart at some point or other from this programme. The quantity and degree of departure varies with the species; it is possible, for instance, to set harder and faster rules of migration for the humpback salmon than for the spring salmon, narrower limits to the feeding habits of the sockeye than to those of most other fish. It seems fairly safe to conclude that evolution has drawn these species, of more predictable habits, into a greater degree of specialisation, and while it is not necessarily true that less specialised species are at a lower stage of evolution, it is altogether possible that they are at present more actively evolving—that is to say, their imperceptible tendency, through a rather wide degree of individualism, is towards greater specialisation.

Most ichthyologists agree that all trout, all char, all Pacific salmon and the Atlantic salmon have been evolved from a common ancestor within what is, geologically speaking, a comparatively short period of time. It is not known exactly whether this common ancestor was originally a fresh-water fish or a salt-water fish. Many scientists believe that it was a salt-water fish and that the habit of migrating to shallow water to spawn and of working along the shore to get as far in as possible, led the fish to the heads of inlets and bays and so inevitably up into the streams. Another opinion is that fresh-water fish, driven by the search for food, gradually worked farther and farther out to the sea. Though the former opinion is probably more generally held I am inclined to believe that the second theory has a good deal to support it; the search for food certainly has an important influence in modifying the habits of fish at the present time. If we accept, for the sake of this present argument, that the common ancestor was strictly a fresh-water fish then the alteration of the humpback, which spends almost ninety per cent of its two-year life in salt water, is the most complete; and that of the non-migratory trout is the least complete. The alteration of the other species touches nearly every degree between these extremes.

While the degree of alteration varies with the species, it also varies within the species so that a sockeye may descend to salt water in its fry year, as a yearling, a two-year-old, or even five-year-old and a spring salmon may return to spawn after a year in salt water or after as long as seven or eight years. The factors influencing such variations are not easy to measure, but since the major part of the run of any species to a given river is likely to fall into one, or at the most two age-groups, it is not unreasonable to suppose that the habits of the species are still in evolution and that eventually all members of the species will more nearly conform to the general habit.

Somewhere in the line of descent from their common ancestor with the Pacific salmon and Western trout, the European species—Atlantic salmon, brown trout and sea trout—must have had an ancestor common to themselves alone from which they evolved to their present state. At the present time the brown trout and the European sea trout, though each has a different life history and both are separated structurally from the Atlantic salmon, are themselves structurally identical. Perhaps it is not too much to assume that their species is the common ancestor of two fish that will one day be structurally different from each other.

Of all the native fish of the North American continent, the closest, structurally, to the Atlantic salmon is *Salmo gairdneri gairdneri*, which is the coast rainbow, the summer steelhead and the winter steelhead—structurally and scientifically one and the same fish, yet in practice sufficiently different from each other to require separate consideration. Drawing a dangerous parallel, match the non-migratory rainbow to the brown trout, the winter steelhead to the Atlantic salmon, the summer steelhead to the European sea trout. The inference then is that *Salmo gairdneri gairdneri* is the common ancestor of three future separate subspecies and perhaps eventually of three separate species.

The controlling factor in this evolutionary process is food. In New Zealand, where the rivers hold plenty of food for him, the rainbow trout has little inclination to move down to salt water; more remarkable still, in those waters the Pacific spring salmon, a strictly anadromous fish in his native waters, has shown a strong inclination to live out his life in the rivers. British Columbia's coastal lakes and streams are generally so poor in feed that they have almost exactly the opposite effect; brown trout of non-migratory stock show an immediate tendency to adopt migratory habits. The steelhead or coast rainbow, then, is adapting himself to this scarcity, and the adaption is so plainly a current process that one reasonably expects to find, between the full migratory habit of the winter steelhead and the non-migratory habit of some rainbows in streams open to the sea, a full range of variation.

It seems certain that this range does exist and that many of its degrees are evident in the fish of the summer runs. There can be no doubt that the bulk of the winter run is composed of fish which have spent two or three full years in the sea and have travelled long distances from the mouths of their rivers in this feeding migration; whether or no they are the progeny of truly migratory fish, these fish are themselves truly migratory, and the extreme rarity of immature fish in the winter runs suggests that they need the stimulus of maturity to guide them back to the parent streams. The same is probably true of the larger fish of the summer runs, though it is possible that even these make a less definite migration than most winter fish. But the smaller mature fish and the considerable proportion of immature fish to be found with the runs in some streams may well have grown to their size without travelling more than a few miles from the parent stream or perhaps without leaving the estuary; if estuarial feeding will produce a four-pound cutthroat one may expect it to do the same for steelhead.

I am well aware that this is an outrageous piece of theorising and that I am drawing inferences from experience on a stream that has a patchy rather than a good summer run of steelhead, but nothing could show more clearly how complicated the problem is. And it is not altogether unreasonable to assume that a stream with a varied and patchy run may have shown things that would have been harder to learn from a more orthodox water. The Campbell has a run of summer—or rather, spring —steelhead that is certainly not typical, but which seems to me strongly indicative of what I have suggested.

Though one has a very fair chance of picking up a fresh-run summer steelhead in the Campbell at any time between March and early October, the main run is generally to be found in the Canyon Pool and the Islands Pool between April 10th and June 1st.* The fish that make up this run vary a great deal in size and in degree of maturity, so much so that an account of averages and percentages does not present a very clear picture, and the figures certainly should not be applied to rivers which have a more orthodox summer run. The point of difference, I believe, is that the proportion of truly migratory fish—that is to say, fish which travel well beyond the influence of the river in sea feeding and return only to spawn—is much smaller than in the case of more typical rivers. The average size of a hundred fish from this run was 2½ lbs., with a maximum of 8 lbs. and a minimum of 13 ounces. In spite of this variation in size, the scales of every fish showed very clearly the change from river to sea feeding; ninety-five had left fresh water at two years of age and the remaining five at three years.

Sixty of the fish were returning to the river for the first time at four years of age, after two full years in salt water, but twenty of the others were veterans, between five and seven years old, which had also made their first return at four years. The remainder were back in the river after a very short migration and were all below the average weight. These and ten of the four-year-olds were quite obviously immature, and their return to the river was in no sense a spawning migration. Thus, the composition of the run differs sharply on several points

* It should be emphasized that this is in strong contrast to more orthodox summer steelhead streams. In these the summer run usually starts in the last half of May and makes good fishing in June, July and September. In August the rivers are generally too low, but the greased line method opens up new possibilities in this month.

from that of the winter run. It is composed chiefly of maiden fish returning for the first time at four, instead of five years. The proportion of immature fish is very much higher, and includes at least some fish as large as the smaller spawners. And, finally, 20% of the run is composed of fish returning to the river for the second or third time, while only about 10% of the winter run are veterans. Incidentally, this figure of 20% compares with a figure of 3.4% given by Long and Griffin for veteran spawners in the summer run of the Columbia.

Of the mature fish in the run, typical specimens were between 3½ and 4½ lbs., clean, bright, well-conditioned fish with firm scales and some spawning colouration. Of the immature fish, a majority weighed between two and three pounds and were very bright, with loose, silvery scales. Milt sacs or ovaries almost invariably showed some development, and it seems likely that these fish, running as true grilse, would have gone back to salt water almost at once and returned as mature fish in the following winter; in other words, this part of the run is probably not sharply separate from the winter run.

A broad theory would suggest that the run is composed of a nucleus of mature and truly migratory fish, accompanied by a certain number of slightly smaller immature fish, and drawing after them in their migration a certain number of mature and immature fish of a less strongly migratory type—fish feeding near the river or in the estuary. These last may account for the high percentage of previously spawned fish, since their shorter migration would give them a better chance for survival. Of the few kelts taken, it is notable that those under five pounds were in fairly good condition and had firm, red flesh instead of the white, flabby flesh of winter kelts.

Another peculiarity of this run is the high proportion of feeding fish. Over sixty per cent had food of some sort in them, and about twenty per cent had evidently been feeding fairly freely. This is probably due in some measure to the greater availability of feed during the warm months, and perhaps helps to account for the high survival; but I feel that it is also another indication of partial rather than complete migration.

The Campbell run suggests that a certain proportion of summer steelhead are not much more definitely migratory than sea-run cutthroat, and therefore that their progeny will not necessarily be migratory at all, though scarcity of feed will probably make them so. It also suggests that there may be an extremely close connection with the winter-run fish—that an immature fish running up with the summer spawners may be going to spawn with the winter run, and so, by rather remote inference, that summer-run fish do not necessarily produce summer-run fish. From the cultural point of view this is of vital importance. It may well be that examination of a more typical run—that of the Stamp, for instance, or the July and September runs of the Nimpkish—would show a sharp and clear separation—or the inferences I have drawn might very well fail to stand up under a proper examination of even the Campbell runs. But before anything of value can be done, the exact truth must be known. The present runs, even in good streams, are not large enough to stand the drain of heavy fishing and occur in only a small proportion of the streams that seem to be suitable; nor are they sufficiently good to be a really strong attraction to the anglers of other countries. But a complete understanding of the life history of the fish might very well show ways of building up the runs in those streams which already have them, and perhaps of establishing them in streams which at present have only winter runs.

The summer steelhead, like the winter steelhead, is probably an easier fish to catch than the Atlantic salmon, though one may well go about trying to catch him with almost exactly the methods that are used for Atlantic salmon. The larger mature fish of the orthodox runs are not likely to be feeding seriously, if at all, and in the low water of late summer and early fall the steelhead can be quite dour; but they are always, at any time of the season and any stage of water, essentially fish that deserve to be caught by the fly only, and fishermen are better advised to turn, in the difficult times, to low-water fly-fishing methods than to spinning and bait-fishing.

One of the most important items of equipment for summer steelhead fishing is a pair of felt-soled or well-nailed waist waders, and with them a belt or shoulder-strap to which a good wading staff may be attached. There is plenty of wading to be done, sometimes in heavy water and nearly always over round and slippery rocks.

As to the rod—well, the streams are of a fair size, particularly early in the year, and spey or roll-casting is the only way of getting out line in many places; so a double-handed thirteen- or fourteen-foot split-cane is not out of place for fishing an honest wet fly. I belong to a young and cocksure generation, and prefer for myself a single-handed eleven- or twelve-foot rod of the Wye or Wood type; dry-fly habit and early training have taught me to prefer keeping my left hand free for the line, and if the fish seem to suggest at any time that I change over to the dry fly or to greased-line fishing, my rod is right for the work. It is perfectly possible to use effectively a lighter and shorter single-handed rod than these; for several years I used a 10-foot Crown Houghton which weighed eight ounces, and before that a six-ounce rod; but with such small rods one is often reaching, and it is not nearly so easy to keep full control of the line on the water. A six- or eight-ounce rod will handle the fish, though an eight-pounder in heavy water is a strain on everything and is likely to have fairly full charge of the proceedings for several minutes. I do not think it is possible to match the fishing more exactly than with an eleven- or twelve-foot single-handed rod, and if the angler finds this too tiring he will be well advised to turn to a double-handed rod unless he is fishing a small stream or in very low water.

Hardy's No. 2 St. John is a reel that matches almost any of the powerful 11–12-foot single-handed rods; it will carry 35 yards of IBI fly line with 100 yards of backing, or 42 yards of

No. 5 line with 60 or 70 yards of backing. The makers generally recommend the IBI line for these rods, but I believe this line more nearly fits a 10-foot trout rod, and though it is good enough for low-water conditions it does not develop the full possibilities of a powerful 11-foot rod. The less amount of backing may seem too little, but it should be enough for summer steelhead, though they are strong fish and far more active than the larger winter fish. The strongest summer-run fish I have ever hooked was a 4½-pounder, lying in a pool so tiny that it is almost lost in the rapid below the Lower Island in the Campbell. This pool, which extends out into the rapid only ten or fifteen yards from the left bank of the river and is not more than twice as long as its width, lies a little way upstream of a similar but rather larger pool under the right bank of the river, just above the mouth of the Quinsam. The fish took a No. 8 Lady Caroline and started to run almost as he touched the fly. The pool was too small to interest him and in a moment he was out of it and half way across the rapids. I held him hard, trying to turn him with the current and bring him in a semi-circle back to my own bank. The pressure made him jump several times, right in the white water but always downstream and across towards the Quinsam Pool; each jump took out line and I felt that Ox gut, for once, was not enough. He reached the pool and I found that I had 40 yards of fly line and a little over 50 yards of backing out, with the width of the river of fast, broken water between me and the fish. As he held in the pool I released the pressure a little and he began to swim upstream. I moved down along my own bank until I was below him, then tightened again, and he ran at once upstream and out of the pool. I turned him when he had travelled a little way and brought him diagonally down and across the rapid to the beach.

Before and since that time I have had to give as much as 30 or 40 yards of backing to a summer steelhead, but it happens rarely and nearly always in heavy water. No fish I have ever

hooked has shown the confidence and watermanship in ma-
noeuvring across a really strong rapid that this good four-
pounder showed me. He went free, with a tag in his tail, but I
have not met him since.

Good wet flies for summer steelhead are, as are good wet
flies for Atlantic salmon, dependent upon the fancy of the
angler rather than upon the preferences of the fish. One could
fish satisfactorily through a season with a range of full-dressed
Jock Scotts, on hook sizes from 1 or slightly larger up to 12.
Most of the trout flies in the boxes of the average British
Columbian fisherman, especially the Kamloops flies, will catch
fish. Most of the flies tied for Atlantic salmon will catch fish.
European sea-trout flies and lures, such as terrors and demons,
will take fish well. And to add to this wide choice there is a
great variety of flies tied especially for the purpose—most of
them rather bright flies and a good proportion of them winged
with bucktail or bear-hair.

Generally speaking, I believe the fairly bright flies are likely
to catch more fish. Over several seasons on the Nimpkish I
fished two flies on a cast, one of them a dark fly such as Greenwell's Glory, the other a bright, full-dressed salmon fly, Tor-
rish, Silver Doctor or Durham Ranger. I found that the bright
fly took the steelhead and the dark fly the cutthroats, with
surprising regularity. What I have seen since has persuaded me
that I should probably have caught just as many fish had I not
offered them a choice, but the division of the catch was quite
definite enough to suggest that there is likely to be some degree
of preference.

Like most fishermen, I generally carry with me a tremendous
diversity of flies; but if some unkind realist ordered me to confine myself to three wet flies only I should choose without
hesitation the Silver Lady,* Jock Scott, and the low-water
Lady Caroline. In these I should have a sufficient variety to

* For dressing, see Appendix.

please myself, and more than enough to please the fish. I should regret most the loss of one or two favourite bear-hair patterns that have often done well for me.

For greased-line fishing, I think only two flies are necessary, the Blue Charm and the Lady Caroline; even the Blue Charm is probably superfluous, but on a really dark day it is possibly a little more effective than the Lady Caroline. Steelhead like the Lady Caroline surprisingly well, whether she is fished as a simple wet fly or by the greased-line method.

Of all dry flies I have tried I prefer the bi-visibles, though La Branche's Pink Lady and the regular Palmers are good at times. Generally, dry flies should be large, tied on 8 or 10 hooks, and frequently sedges will do well on these sizes. There is rather an important advantage in using sedges if, as many people believe, the hackles of flies tied palmerwise tend to shield the point of the hook and so make striking difficult.

No other fish chooses a better meeting ground for himself and the angler than does the summer steelhead. The young streams of Vancouver Island and the mainland coast are incomparably, heroically beautiful, in the mould of the wet-fly man's ideal. Clear water between tall trees, lost from sight at a little distance, yet world filling when one is by its side. White rapids with resting places lodged and hidden here and there about them; deep pools and shallow pools, smooth, slow pools and wide, broken pools; current to pull at a man's legs and test his footing, to carry his fly and give it life; the breath of a breeze and sunlight in the time of the run; the problems of high water in the first months of the run, calling for the long cast and strong searching; the more intricate problems of low water later, summoning the delicate and subtle method, the difficult thing faithfully accomplished.

The beauties are those of the rough mountain streams, magnified a hundred times, lost in the magnification yet drawn to a full and broader perfection of their own, with room for the doing and a setting for the deed. But such water, fast and clear over clean rocks and gravel, is not of a type to produce fish to scale. The still waters of a lake, the trailing weeds and quiet reaches of older streams, are the places where trout grow large and difficult. Only a migratory run, grown bright and strong in the plenty of salt water, could put proportionate fish into the setting.

It is unquestionably a fly fisherman's setting, and the fly fisherman is free to enjoy it; when the summer steelhead are in, the fly will take them. Everything else, spinners and devons and lures, phantoms and plugs and worms, can be laid aside and forgotten. There need be no anxious wondering about the light spinning rod or the advisability of taking along one or two small spinners, just in case they make all the difference between a few fish and a blank day. If the fly fisherman is versatile and knows the variations of his method, he can depend upon the fish to respond to it—if they will respond to anything at all on that particular day. Real summer steelhead fishing—that is to say, fishing for mature, truly migratory steelhead—is essentially Atlantic salmon fishing, though the fish be a thousand times a trout. As in fishing for winter steelhead, the slow, thorough searching of all the holding water, and a good knowledge of favourite lies and the currents over them, will catch fish. Match the size of fly to the height of the water and the brightness of the day; in high water and cloudy weather a big fly between No. 2/0 and No. 4. On a bright day, unless it is a great, wide water you are searching and you feel you need confidence, do not be afraid to go down to No. 6. In low water and sunny weather, small flies—No. 10 is often not too small.

It is straightforward, satisfying fishing when the river is still holding from the stored-up snow in the high hills. A good holding pool in July, with a strong rapid at the head but an even flow of water over a wide part of the pool's surface; some big rocks in deep water near the tail of the pool. The river has fallen a lot, but is not yet down to summer level; the day is sunny, but somehow not too bright on the water. Starting at

the head with a No. 4 Jock Scott. A few short casts to cover
the water immediately below the rapid, then across the current
and around, slowly and easily, to the side. Another cast, delay-
ing the fly for a moment in the slack water of the far side with
an upstream "mend," as in greased-line fishing. Following
round with the rod point, holding a little at the edge of the
strongest current. A fish shows well behind the fly. Fish out
the cast. Rest him. Change to a No. 6. Cover again, hanging it
where he took; this time he has it and is into a run without
waiting for the strike. An upstream run and across towards the
far side, unwisely checked a little too soon. The second run is
downstream, with two clean jumps. He comes back from that
unwillingly against the current, but there is no point in following him down all that new water so early in the day. He runs
straight across and the strain of the rod lifts him very near the
surface in the fast water. Time to get out, on to the gravel bar.
It is easier from there—the rod is suddenly longer and one is
suddenly taller; but the fish works in short runs, trying for the
current each time, rolling and twisting jerkily as the pressure
draws him up and stops him. He is quiet at last, and slides easily
on to the gravel.

The rest of the pool fishes blank, but it is a good holding
pool and there are more fish in it. A short rest and start back
with the same fly, casting across and a few degrees upstream,
covering the best spots with short casts as well as long ones, to
vary the angle. A fish comes from behind the rocks to a short
cast, but the fly is suddenly free as he turns at the end of his
first run. But the day is very young, and there are other fish
and other pools.

Those are the good wet-fly days, when a run is fresh from
the sea and conditions are right. There are others. And later in
the season, with fewer and staler fish, the wise angler will not
be content with the wet fly, unless it happens to do well for
him. There is always the dry fly, which may take fish, and
there is greased-line fishing, probably the most delicate and

worthwhile method of taking dour non-feeders under difficult conditions that man has yet thought out. The essential principle of greased-line fishing is a small, lightly dressed fly fished right up in the surface film and without drag. The normal cast, in straightforward water, is across and slightly downstream, with a slack line. As the current pulls the slack into a belly that threatens to draw the fly, the fisherman makes an upstream "mend"—lifts the belly of the line without moving the fly and places it upstream—and the fly continues to fish down and slightly across at the speed of the current, instead of being drawn against it by the pull of the line. But it is not necessary to go into the details of the method here; that has been well and fully done in "Jock Scott's" book, *Greased-Line Fishing for Salmon*. It is enough to say that summer steelhead will respond to the method and that the streams of the country lend themselves to it almost perfectly.

The feel of fishing a run of less strongly migratory fish, such as the spring run in the Campbell, is altogether different. The non-feeding fish are there, five- and six-pounders generally, and one searches for them diligently and carefully, tempts them from every angle and with every trick of the trade. But because many of the fish are feeding, one works over the water more easily and confidently once they are found. It is trout fishing again, and very good trout fishing. On the best days— there are not more than one or two a year, and they are generally between April 11th and May 24th—one finds the fish in the Islands Pool, most of them towards the tail and to one side of the main run of current, in about four or five feet of rippled, flowing water. Sometimes they are rising and will come to a dry fly, but the wet fly is usually better; the Silver Lady always does well, particularly with the larger fish, but I think Lady Caroline is better; the feeding fish like her well, and unless the run is very freshly in from salt water, they are the better fish. On these days it would not be difficult to pick up fifteen fish of two to five pounds, if one chose to and felt prepared to

argue with a game warden that the fish were rainbow trout, not
steelhead. But it is easy to break the barb of the hook so that
it is nothing more than a little hump and, standing there in the
water, let the fish shake the hook from him, after the rise and
strike and a few moments of running and jumping. It is not
too difficult, even with a barbless hook, to net the two or three
especially fat and silver ones that deserve a place on the table.

Other days are less easy. When the fish get up into the
Canyon Pool it is difficult to wade deep enough to reach them
properly with the fly, and they take less freely. Often the
Islands Pool seems empty of fish, or rain in the hills and melt-
ing snow have brought the water too high for one to wade out
to the bar. But the few great days come every year, and there
are many times in the season when two or three fish, hardly
found and tempted only by stern persistence or wild ingenuity,
seem worth all the great days of a dozen seasons.

## REFERENCE

"Jock Scott." *Greased-Line Fishing for Salmon.* Seeley Service
    Co., London.

# | | |

## *Migratory Cutthroat Trout*

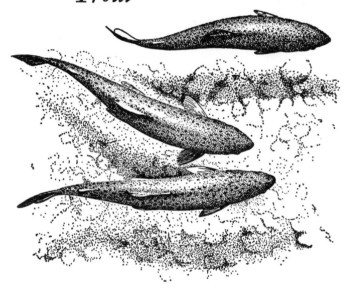

THERE is not much doubt that the cutthroat trout of the lower reaches of nearly all coast streams move down to tidal water from time to time. They are not a truly migratory fish in the sense that the winter steelhead and the Atlantic and Pacific salmon are. They move down and often out to sea in search of food; they make by far the major proportion of their growth in salt or brackish water; but when there is food for them in fresh water they move up to find it, whether or no they are driven at the same time by the urge of maturity.

But the first movement to salt or brackish water seems to

mark a definite stage in the fish's life history, and, from the time it is made until the approach of maturity, the salt water, in spite of shorter or longer visits to fresh water, is the real home of the migratory cutthroat. Over 98 per cent of the scales I have read from Campbell River cutthroats show this very clearly in a sudden and marked increase of growth rate at the end of the first or second year, an increase which is maintained until the occurrence of a spawning mark. The few fish whose scales do not show this sharp change are always quite small— under three-quarters of a pound—though they are either maturing to spawn at four years or have already spawned at that age. Their small size at maturity is an interesting confirmation of the belief that coast streams do not produce enough feed to permit non-migratory trout to make rapid growth.

The normal life history, shown in about fifty per cent of the scales read, appears to be two years in fresh water followed by two years of sea feeding—undoubtedly with more or less frequent movements to fresh water and the river mouth—and then the first spawning at four years. This coincides fairly well with the normal life history of the non-migratory cutthroat, though it would not have been surprising to find the division of the years rather different—one year in fresh water and three years in salt—and it is quite possible that in many rivers this is the case.

A considerable number of the Campbell River fish, perhaps as many as thirty-five per cent, spawn for the first time at three years, after either one or two years of fresh-water life. Of the remainder (about fifteen per cent) nearly all spawn after three years in salt water preceded by either one or two years in fresh water. These, naturally, are the largest and best fish, though the fish maturing to spawn at three years, after one year in the river and two in salt water, are usually well grown and in exceptionally fine condition.

Though some other streams may have, even in their lower reaches, a higher proportion of non-migratory fish, these broad life histories are likely to be fairly representative; only an extensive tagging programme could yield really satisfactory information on this point. The proportion of Campbell River fish showing spawning marks and either spawning or maturing to spawn a second time is not more than five per cent, a surprisingly low figure in view of the number of fairly well mended kelts one catches. Most of the fish have made rapid growth during the years of salt-water feeding and this may shorten their lives, but it seems likely that there is a heavy loss of kelts when they first reach salt water after spawning.

The maximum size normally reached by sea-run cutthroats is about four pounds. A fair number of fish reach this weight, or within a few ounces of it, after three years of sea life; although I have heard many reports of fish of six or seven pounds, I have never handled such fish or been able to obtain the particulars of one.* Yet cutthroat in lakes attain a maximum of at least eleven pounds, and it might reasonably be supposed that the same fish, with all the delights of the sea to tempt them to overfeeding, would attain tremendous weights. The fact that they do not do so suggests a circumscribed migration and something less, through lack of opportunity and a less selective feeding habit, than the really savage gorging of the spring salmon and the third-year cohoe.

I do not think the cutthroat ranges in salt water beyond the influence of his river. I have seen them picked up by purse seiners, setting close to shore, about four miles north of the Nimpkish; and I believe they are caught by anglers in Puget Sound at favourite points even farther than this from the mouth of a stream. But the normal range is probably very little beyond the extent of the river channel into salt water, out on the ebb tide and back with the flood.

* A cutthroat of 6½ lbs. was caught on the minnow by a steelhead fisherman in the Campbell during February 1940. But I still feel that four pounds should be considered about the normal maximum for sea-run cutthroats in this river.

From the point of view of the average angler, this movement with the tides is the most important of all the cutthroat's habits. The movement outward, with the ebb, is probably a very natural movement, within the current rather than with it, in pursuit of feed that is unresistant to the current. It is not at all a complete movement, and frequently many fish are left, still feeding, in the river channel proper as the tide drains away from its banks. Other fish are carried out at least far enough to come across the schools of needlefish and small herring off the mouth of the river, and undoubtedly much of their good growth is made from this feed. The return is more definite and brings the fish up, often high in the water and swimming against the river current rather than down in the tidal flow, as soon as the tide has made a foot or two in the lowest reaches. Its extent varies; sometimes the fish stop to feed in certain favourite places until the tide has left them far behind, sometimes they pass through quickly and follow the tide up to its limits, or else spread out to feed over the newly flooded flats.

The Campbell is a sizeable river with a wide estuary at high tide, so that the angler who would fish from his feet and find his fish concentrated within a reasonably small area must fish the extreme low tides, for about two hours on either side of low-water slack. The fish do not seem to respond well to the intermediate tides and are nearly always hard to find on them, either because they are spread over the flats or because they have not been drawn in from salt water.

As soon as the tide has left the main channel of the river well exposed, it is worth starting to search for fish. There are sure to be some hanging in the favourite places and ready to take. But the best of the fishing, if it is to be a good day, should be at certain pools and eddies in the channel and in one of the sloughs, during the last two hours of the ebb. If it is a bad day and all the fish have gone out with the tide, those two hours may be dull, with only an occasional fish showing. At some time in the first two hours of the flood they will pass, visibly or invisibly, on their way up; they may stop and feed gently as the tide makes, and it will be a good but difficult hour; they may pass on in fifteen or twenty minutes, feeding actively and taking, with slashing rises, what they are offered; they may pass through in a flurried two minutes, leaving perhaps one of their number behind, perhaps only the memory of a half dozen casts, each successively wilder, through confidence to anxiety to flustered pursuit and final pleading, in the angler's mind.

Sometimes, still on one's feet, it is possible to cut in higher up the stream and find them again, but when the big tides start to make they make fast, and the flats are soon flooded; and when the fish pass swiftly through the favourite places they are generally late on the tide, and nothing but a boat will put the angler within casting distance again.

Fishing from a boat is very often productive, particularly in July when the fish sometimes feed well in the river mouth until the flood is half in. There are places, above the mouth of the second slough and in the big bend, for instance, that are always unapproachable by wading, but make good fishing at times. And from a boat the early stages of the ebb and the late stages of the flood are fishable, and one can take fish as they work with the tide into the flooded grass of the island at the mouth of the slough or as they draw down past the log dump. In all the larger streams, an angler who would make full use of his opportunities must be prepared at times to fish from a boat, no matter how much he prefers wading.

Even in the lower reaches of the Campbell, where it is safe to say that every cutthroat worth the angler's while has run to sea at some time or other, there are always occasional fish in the fresh-water pools. But there are one or two important movements, from salt to fresh water, that have counterparts in all coast streams. There are spawning fish in fresh water during the winter months, and one catches—and returns—them rather frequently when fishing for steelhead. But at this time the majority of the immature and many maturing fish are in tidal

water, particularly in the upper slough, where they are caught
in large numbers because the present laws place no close season
on trout fishing in tidal waters. In April or early May—de-
pending on the average temperature of the stream during the
winter—the humpback fry hatch out, large numbers in the odd
years, smaller numbers in the even years, and the trout move
up to find them. In the big years this is a very strong movement, and makes excellent fishing for two or three weeks. Even
after the bulk of the fry have moved seaward, many cutthroats
remain in the pools, and the fishing is often good until well on
in June; the fish that remain pick up a few late fry and alevins
but also feed on caddis, bullheads and terrestrial insects such
as beetles and caterpillars that drop into the water from trees
and bushes; and occasionally they will rise well to the excellent
hatches of duns and craneflies that are often on the water at
this time. By the middle of June at the latest, and often by the
end of May, most of the fish have dropped back to the estuary
again, and for big bags one must study the tide books.

But even after the middle of June and all through July, there
are a few fish in fresh water. Some of these stay in the pools
after the migration of fry is over, and a few others run up from
time to time to join them. These last are not more than occasional fish and probably drop back to the estuary again almost
at once, but if one can find them they are worth catching;
many of them are maiden fish in their second or third summer
of sea feeding and the two-pounders are a bare sixteen inches
long; which means a condition factor of nearly 49 and a fat,
perfect fish, beautifully coloured and ready to run and jump
like a Kamloops from the moment he touches the fly. Even in
July, the quietest of all fresh-water months in the Campbell,
I have caught such fish far above tide water yet straight from
the sea, with needlefish undigested in their stomachs.

The next strong movement to fresh water comes usually in
the second or third week of August. It is for the most part a
movement of maturing fish, but it is not, strictly speaking, a

spawning run, since most of the fish that make it up will not be spawning until February or March of the following year. Nor is it strictly a feeding run, though it appears to follow the first of the humpback salmon. The humpbacks run into the river and lie in the pools a full month before they spawn. The cutthroats, generally with empty stomachs, lie behind them and wait. It seems too much to believe that they are anticipating the feast; how should they know, how should even an inherited instinct tell them to forsake the plenty of salt water for the promise of plenty in fresh water much later? It seems more likely that the explanation is in the degree of maturity of the waiting fish; that the riper maturity of the humpbacks communicates itself to the cutthroats and draws them to follow and wait.

From the angler's point of view it is a fortunate accident, because it gives him a perfect chance at the biggest fish in the river when they have reached their maximum size, and before full maturity has begun to spoil their colour and freshness. They are hard to catch as they lie in the pools behind the humpbacks, but they will take if the gut is fine and the fly is offered properly, even on a bright day; and on the rare dull or windy days they come freely.

When they are first up there, in the Islands Pool or the Canyon Pool, many of the biggest fish weigh 4 pounds or a little over, but they lose weight rather quickly, and it is not easy to get a four-pounder much after the first week in September, though 3¾ pounds or 3 lbs. 14 oz. is likely to be a common top weight as long as the fish will take at all. Many of the fish are considerably smaller, between 1½ and 3 pounds, and there are always a few smaller than this, down to about ¾ lb., but even these are almost certain to have well developed milt sacs or ovaries.

This run is really over, from the angler's point of view, when the first salmon begin to spawn. True, fish can be caught even then on flies—of a sort—but it is unattractive fishing, and the fish themselves have deteriorated very noticeably; by that time, too, the cohoes are in the river and it is often difficult to make a cast without hooking an old red cock. When the spawning is well under way, many of the immature fish come up to feed, and drop back to tidal water again as soon as the main spawning period is over. The mature cutthroats stay up through the winter, shed their eggs in February or March, and are still in fresh water to start their mend by feeding on the hatching humpback alevins. Later one catches them in tidal water—still partly mended fish, some of them twenty or twenty-one inches long and weighing perhaps a bare three pounds.

These more especial movements of the fish do not necessarily apply at all to other streams than the Campbell. Their main controlling factor is the quality of feed available in fresh water at any given time, and this in its turn is chiefly controlled by the movements of the salmon. A stream such as the Nimpkish, for instance, which has an important sockeye run in late May and June, will draw cutthroats up into fresh water all through the summer, and the angler will find good sport as soon as the water is low enough to be safe for wading; all too often not until late July. In the same way it is the emergence of the dog-salmon alevins that draws the attention of the Nimpkish cut-throats in the spring rather than, as in the Campbell, the emer-gence of humpback. Another stream, with a really strong run of cohoes, may hold cutthroats all through the year, since cohoe fry usually spend a full year in fresh water before migrating. The possible variations are numerous, and nothing short of close and fairly intelligent local observation will find them properly.

The cutthroat runs of British Columbian streams are not even nearly so good as they were at one time or as they probably could be again. One afternoon in 1911, two rods—not won-derfully good rods, either—took from Big Qualicum River 125 fish, some of them up to twenty inches long. At that time one could probably have made a comparable catch in any of a dozen streams on the east coast of Vancouver Island, to say nothing of the west-coast and mainland streams. Much of the damage has been done by just such catches, and it is still being done by more intensive fishing and larger bags than the runs can stand. But often the angler has had efficient assistance in his work. The runs of the Campbell and the Nimpkish were reduced to small fractions of what they had been, by the practice of drag-seining for salmon inside the mouths of the rivers, a practice continued at Nimpkish as recently as 1933. Dozens of cutthroats were taken in the sets for sockeye or spring salmon and thrown out to rot on the beaches.

The logging methods at present in use, and the lack of adequate fire prevention, also seriously threaten the future of the Vancouver Island streams. The practice of clear logging leaves the banks of the streams without cover, and at the same time causes a rapid run-off of the rainfall, with resulting extremes of high and low water. Extensive forest fires follow inevitably in the path of clear logging, destroying whatever ground cover may have grown up after the logging, and burning the soil to a fine powder. The resulting erosion produces silting of spawning beds and heavy losses of fish of all kinds. There are more or less serious forest fires on Vancouver Island every year, and undoubtedly they have reduced the productivity of many of the east-coast streams.

Loggers and miners, handy with dynamite and salmon roe, have done their share. I believe the reduction of the Big Qualicum run is traced partly to dynamiting during the building of the E. & N. Railway bridge and partly to a big freshet which followed soon after, washing out log jams and shifting channels. The Oyster, one of the finest of the island trout streams, was seriously affected by the intentional removal of log jams—presumably with some vague idea of giving the salmon runs easier access to spawning water—but no doubt had suffered from illegal fishing before this.

There is not much doubt that the runs of accessible rivers

are still being depleted. There are three main contributory causes: The bag limit of fifteen fish per day is too high; the size limit of eight inches is too low; and the drain of year-round fishing in tidal waters is too great. It is difficult to under-stand why it should be supposed that rivers in a country where the water is publicly owned and exposed to all types of anglers and all types of angling should be able to stand the drain of a seven-and-a-half-brace limit. Highly preserved trout streams in other countries, with all the benefits of artificial stocking and artificial encouragement of weed and feed growth, are asked to stand the drain of a three- or four-brace limit taken by a strictly limited number of anglers on the fly only. It is not logical to expect these publicly owned rivers to be able to yield their eight-inch innocents when preserved streams have size limits of twelve or fourteen inches. And they cannot reasonably be expected to produce fish in every month of the year, including the spawning months, when the preserved streams are usually closed for at least six months.

There is, then, a clear opportunity for restrictive legislation that would work hardship to no one. A three-brace limit with a 10-inch size limit would leave plenty of scope for a full day's sport, and a season from April 1st to September 30th would be quite long enough. Possibly these regulations would not exactly fit the needs of all streams, but the existing regulations do not fit the needs of any streams. As a matter of fact, blanket regulations can never be satisfactory; they are at present justified by the authorities on the grounds that it is almost impossible to enforce local regulations, and while these grounds exist it is perhaps best to look upon the perfection of local regulations as a distant dream.

Protected by some such regulations as those suggested above, existing stocks should be able to maintain themselves—without increase—until the time comes for constructive measures. Research work on migratory cutthroat is not yet at all advanced, but it seems likely that it will be found possible to increase the runs by hatchery work; it should also be possible to increase the feed and the holding qualities of streams by general improvement work. The smaller streams, especially, offer excellent opportunity for improvement work. Many creeks which at present attract few if any cutthroats could be made good holding water by the construction of a few small dams, or even by the introduction and proper protection of beaver. Such stream control might prove its value not merely by producing better fishing, but also during the forest-fire season. The larger coast streams are not easy to control and do not lend themselves to cheap improvement work, but the building of wing dams, even if these were only piles of boulders, would improve many stretches of barren water. It is not too difficult to create log jams by placing obstructions at chosen points in certain streams, and all existing log jams should be protected with as much care as the fish themselves, unless it can be shown very clearly that they hinder the ascent of spawning fish.

For most sea-run cutthroat fishing, a 9½-foot, 6½-ounce rod, powerful enough to handle an IBI line, is ideal. Any good and reasonably powerful rod will do the work, but too light and short a rod is a handicap on many streams. There is often a stiff wind on the tide flats, and when the flood tide is making the fish are sometimes feeding well out. Up the river, in the heavy water of some of the pools, one may strain a light rod in lifting the line, and long casting is usually essential on those burnished days when the big trout are lying behind the humpbacks. A fairly strong man who fishes much may even prefer, on most days, a 10-foot rod weighing anything up to 8 ounces.

It pays to fish fairly fine gut. In strong spring water with a large fly ox may be fine enough, but unless the fly is very large 2x is always better; and there are times when 3x or 4x and small flies will take noticeably more fish than anything coarser.

The fish in tidal water are usually feeding either on amphipods ("shrimps," very often *Gammarus cenfervicolus*) or on fry, and on the good days an imitation of one or other will nearly always do well. It is not at all easy to find good shrimp imitations; a decent March Brown or Hare's Ear is far better than the stiff creatures produced by the tackle shops in effort at imitation. Generally I prefer the fly I have called Gammarus * to either of these, and when Gammarus will not do the work, the low-water Lady Caroline will. Generally speaking, shrimp flies should be tied on a No. 8 hook. Fry imitations are numerous. Many anglers use teal and silver, and silver-bodied flies winged with bucktail or polar-bear hair are very popular. I prefer a browner wing and generally use the Tinsel * or my own Silver Brown,* both of which catch fish. The demons and terrors, tied with two or three hooks in tandem by English tackle makers, are very good; Hardy's "Dandy," a double-hooked fly with silver body, red hackle and light mallard wing, is especially good, but I believe that all these creatures are rather too deadly for the average fly fisherman to be able to use them with a really clear conscience.

There is often a difficult time in sea-run cutthroat fishing, quite soon after the tide has started to make on a good day. All through the last hour or more of the ebb, and perhaps on the very start of the flood, one has been catching fish fairly easily on the wet fly. Quite suddenly the fish stop taking. They are there, rising gently, probably more in evidence than before, and others have come up with the tide to join them. But they will not look at Lady Caroline or whatever it was that was taking them before, no matter how it is fished. Often at such times they will take a dry bi-visible really well, fish after fish as each is covered, with good, solid rises. There is an almost infinite variety of bi-visibles—any two hackles of different colours will make one—and some anglers do well on such combinations as orange and white or purple and grey, but I believe the best of all for cutthroats, under these conditions, is the old brown and white. Dry flies other than bi-visibles seldom seem to do well in tidal water, and the fishing is not particularly easy

* Dressing in the Appendix.

even when the fish are taking the bi-visible. Usually by the time the rise has started and one has changed from the wet fly, the tide has made quite a bit and it is already necessary to cast a longish line. The rises are not frequent, and if the water is at all slack, as it generally is, the fish are probably cruising and must be covered almost as they rise. But a quick and accurate cast is generally rewarded, and sometimes there are fish out in the current that are rising fairly steadily. On a good rise one has time to land three or four fish, with a proportionate number of missed rises, late casts and other mishaps, before the tide is touching the tops of boots or waders; but the fish that come in this way are usually large, and the chance to see an honest rise to a dry fly, even though it is more like a piece of thistle-down than a fly, is not one to be missed.

In fresh water the same flies do well. On the start of the humpback hatch a silver-bodied fly is almost essential, and the Tinsel is the deadliest of them all; but as the fry work down to salt water, some cutthroats always stay up in the river. These spread over the pools, instead of collecting to wait for the fry at favourite spots, and begin to feed on whatever the river has to offer. One can still catch them on silver-bodied flies—probably better on silver-bodied flies than anything else—but they will take shrimp flies or a large Greenwell's Glory or a Western Bee or almost anything one cares to tie for them out of seal's fur and feathers.

This is far more attractive fishing than that of even the best days of the fry run; in fact, the keen wet-fly fisherman could scarcely ask for better conditions of water and fish and weather. Some morning or afternoon of late May one wades in at the head of the Sandy Pool, knowing that most of the fry have gone and many of the trout are still there. 2x gut and a No. 8 low-water Lady Caroline. A few casts to get out line, and one is reaching well out into the edge of the fast water. Trees and banks fade far into the background; there is only the good, known water, the fly searching, and one's two feet solidly on the bottom. A step downstream, a short cast and a long cast; the rhythm grows. A step downstream, a short cast, work to the last of it, recover; false cast at half the angle, letting out line, recover; the long cast, curving out past the limit of the last holding water; and bring it round, working, working, working. Forward again, taking in line, short cast, work, recover; false cast, long cast, work and work. A minor break where the current changes a little. A more significant break to fish a special place, when the line shoots three or four extra yards and the fly curls over a rock and is sucked gently into fishing. These are a part of the large pattern, still rhythm. Even a rise and the strike, a fish jumping, are part of it. Check him, hold him, bring him to the net without changing position, without breaking it. Cast again and work on. Another rise will come to balance the first, and a third to match that. And if they don't, it is all still there, rhythm and movement, the smoothness of the difficult thing easily done.

It breaks and renews itself as you change from overhead to roll cast where the bushes come down to the water's edge, breaks again as you work round some rocks, as each new stretch of water, wider or narrower, faster or slower, comes up to you. But the whole is a prolonged, quiet absorption, something beyond the mere casting of the fly and the killing of the fish.

Or on another day, starting far down the pool, one finds a hatch of duns on the water. A few fish are rising. It seems worth while trying 3x gut and a No. 16 Iron Blue. A quiet cast, quite short, and a fish comes up from the bottom through three or four feet of fast water. If it is a good day they will do it for you all the way along the shallows, from the mouth of the creek to the big rock.

Somewhere about the first of June—this year it was on May 19th—there is a hot, bright day, and the flying ants are suddenly everywhere. It is like the mayfly hatch on a chalk stream, and the fish can be almost as difficult. They rise well to the hatch, either in the tidal water or up in the pools, but they are particular about artificials, probably because the natural is so abundant. Most of the ants on the water are drowned or half drowned; they do not float serenely down with their feet on the surface as do aquatic flies, so it is not strictly a dry-fly time. Many fishermen use a dry Black Gnat tied on a No. 8 or 10 hook and it will catch fish, though I have never found it really good. A wet Black Gnat is better, but still not good. A black and brown bi-visible will catch fish as a dry fly, and in a ragged, half drowned state can be deadly. Brown hackle with a peacock herl body, wet or dry, will catch fish. But the deadliest fly I have found is an untidy creature,* best tide by an amateur's clumsiest hand, on a No. 8 hook with a black seal's fur body, ribs of gold tinsel and bronze peacock herl, and a ragged black or metallic green feather stripped on one side and wound palmerwise up the body. Worked as a wet fly—for this, the hook may be as large as No. 6—or drifted down half submerged, it is liked by the fish, and they will go for it in the midst of a swarm of naturals. On the Campbell, the main hatch is over in a single day, but there are a few ants on the water for several days after that, and the fish still take the bedraggled black fly better than anything else.

Late June and July days in the fresh-water pools are pleasant, even though often unproductive. There is always the chance of a summer steelhead and there are a few cutthroats up there, generally good fish, often fresh from salt water. For the most part they are feeding on caddis larvae, but they are strictly open minded and will take what comes in the way of drowned terrestrial insects. Big, black caterpillars with yellow spots along their sides are popular; so are the cedar borer and a host of other beetles; there may or may not be an occasional response to floating ephemeridae, or a rise to sedges at dusk. The river is low and easy to travel, and it is wholly pleasant to search the revealed places. It is worth taking many flies; perhaps the changes do not make a great deal of difference, but

* See Black caterpillar, Appendix.

they give one fresh hope, and occasionally there is a fish that will only come to the last of a half dozen offerings.

The big fish that follow the humpback run in August are the most difficult of all. Sometimes one can catch them in the Islands Pool, on their way up; they are easy there, fresh from the sea, and in the good, broken fly water of the pool. Often there are three- or four-pound steelhead with them. But they do not rest there long, and in their last waiting place, the Canyon Pool, there are times when they really test a fisherman's control and accuracy. The Canyon Pool is hard to wade; quickly deep from the shore and with steep, brush-covered banks. And in low summer water the tail of the Pool is a long, glassy glide, about sixty yards wide where the fish lie. The late August and early September days are still and hot, with a tall, glaring sun that throws hard shadows and pierces to the darkest rocks of the deepest water.

The fish lie deep, near the bottom, in five or six feet of water, and often cruise slowly in schools of three or four. Occasionally one rises or breaks water and goes down to the bottom again. If the light is right, one can wade the shallows at the tail of the pool, look down at their wide backs and try to guess which of them will be over four pounds. It looks easy to float a dry fly down and rise them one by one. But even 4x gut throws a shadow that looks like quarter-inch rope at the bottom of six feet of still water; as it passes over them the fish move gently to one side—and let the fly pass too. The curved cast, with the fly coming over the fish before the gut, has the same effect, partly because of the depth of the water and partly because the fish are in groups and all are sensitive to the movement of one. For the same reasons, a dry fly floated down from above usually fails, though both methods would be successful if the fish were hanging, as brown trout do, only an inch or two below the surface.

On such days I find that I can catch them best by wading out as far as I can from the north bank of the river and waiting

quietly until I find where most of the fish are lying. Sometimes one can catch a glimpse of them between two patches of
light, and a few always show themselves by breaking water.
Then, if possible, I wait still longer, for a breath of breeze to
come down the canyon. As it comes, I get out enough line to
swim the fly across two or three feet upstream of the nearest
fish. Generally, the breeze has failed before the cast is made,
and one waits again and perhaps fails again. When the cast is
timed right with the ripple a fish will rise, and there will be a
long, sullen fight; the water is too deep for much change of
position, and the fish must be kept quiet until he is ready for
the net. But the breaths of breeze from the canyon are few and
far between; on some days there are none at all, and at last the
waiting, with water so nearly over boot tops, is too strained.
Very quietly, taking always the nearest fish, one swings the
fly across. It must sink as it touches the water, and draw at
least two-thirds of the cast down with it. If it is all gently done
and the shadow of the gut is kept well upstream, fish will come.
They rise on the swing of the fly, swimming a little upstream
to meet it, and each strike is true and hard. They are strong
and big, even though not fast and active, and the moments of
the fight are strong moments, yet delicate; a hard, quiet holding
of the fish from the draw of fast water at the tail of the pool,
the long, gentle humouring to persuade him to work his way
upstream, the release of pressure as he works too near the surface and threatens to break water and frighten himself—there
is something in all this more subtly exciting than the wildest
rushing and leaping of the rainbow. And the strength is never
out of your four-pounder when he is close enough for the net;
there must always be long minutes of reaching and watching,
holding against his outward boring, attempts to lift and draw
quietly that fail again and again; and a careless movement, an
untidy plunge of the net or an attempt to hurry him may
destroy the whole thing and send him off downstream again in
a strong, boring run.

Now that I have learned, I use only one fly up there on those days, the Silver Brown tied on a No. 8 low-water hook, which is just small enough to be carried by 3x gut. I don't know why the fly is so good, unless it is because it sinks swiftly and swims through the water with only the slightest disturbance; but when it is presented properly even the largest and best of them take it gladly. Of the scores of other flies I have tried, none has been nearly so good.

There are rare days in late August and early September when a grey sky or a heavy wind makes the fish in the Canyon Pool easy. I have only tried for them once on such a day, and shall not do so again. The pleasures of the hard, still, bright days are too intense and too precious to be wasted on days when conditions reduce their quality by even the smallest fraction.

# IV

## Non-migratory Cut-throat & Rainbows

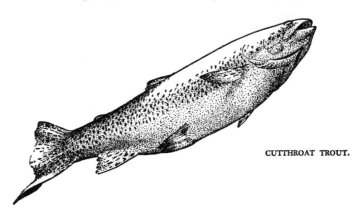

CUTTHROAT TROUT.

To avoid having to decide whether a cutthroat is or is not migratory and whether *gairdneri* is steelhead or rainbow, it seems best to write in this chapter chiefly of the fish of the Campbell watershed above Elk Falls, which really do settle any question of identity rather satisfactorily.

There are at least five species of fish land-locked above the Falls: Cutthroat and rainbow trout, Dolly Varden char, sculpins (rather generally known as bullheads; *Cottus asper*) and sticklebacks. There may be some kokanee in one or other of the lakes, but if so I have not seen any specimens. A fair number of Kamloops trout have been planted in lower Campbell Lake from time to time, but I understand that no one planting has been larger than 30,000 fry which, in a 2,500-acre lake already carrying a stock of fish too large for the available food supply, is an unimportant number. Even allowing for a survival of three per cent, which is an improbable figure, such a planting would not yield more than one fish of legal size to every two and a half acres. Though I have examined a fair number of rainbow trout from the lake, I have not seen any specimens with a Kamloops scale count; but since the count might well change to that of the coast rainbow in one or two generations, this does not mean very much. There is no reason whatsoever to suppose, as many anglers do, that Kamloops trout would grow to a larger size or thrive better than the native rainbows do in coast lakes.

Of the five species that are native to this part of the watershed, the sticklebacks and sculpins are important as forage fish; the sculpin is also a voracious predator, but it is difficult to judge whether or no his destructiveness matches his usefulness. The Dolly Varden char are competitors of the trout and also to some extent predators, but are not so numerous as might be expected. The only important game fish are the cutthroats and the rainbows.

Of the two, the cutthroat is the more important, in my opinion, even though he is probably not so good a fish as the rainbow. He seems to have achieved for himself a wider distribution through the watershed, and when the two fish are together under identical conditions the cutthroat are generally of a noticeably larger average size and are likely to attain a very considerably larger maximum. These facts argue that they are more adaptable to the conditions and superior in competition for the available feed: probably the two species have somewhat different feeding habits and are not always in competition, but they do unquestionably compete for most types of feed.

The normal life history of both species appears to be a four-year period of lake feeding closed by spawning at the end of the fourth year. Very few scales, even of rainbows taken near the mouths of streams, show a period of creek feeding; some fish, both rainbows and cutthroats, show as many as five or six years of growth with spawning marks at the end of the fourth year and each subsequent year, separated by very limited growth.

The normal fly-caught fourth-summer fish of Buttle Lake is ten or eleven inches long and weighs about a half pound or a little less. Individuals up to 14 inches or a little larger are not uncommon, but it usually takes a 15-inch fish to weigh a pound. Fishing with the fly and returning anything under 10 inches, one can expect to get one fish of over a pound in every ten killed.

The general average in Upper and Lower Campbell, the two other principal lakes of the watershed, is somewhat smaller, but in all three lakes there are also very much larger fish. Buttle Lake, especially, holds some exceptionally large fish; a spawning cutthroat 31 inches long, which should have weighed over ten pounds in good condition, was killed there two or three winters ago by a prospector, and fish of three, four and five pounds are commonly caught by trollers. This is not at all unusual in the large Vancouver Island lakes; I have seen an 11½-pound cutthroat taken by trolling at the outlet of Nimpkish Lake, and have myself taken a 5½-pounder on the fly a little farther down the river. Such lakes as Cowichan, Sproat and Great Central all produce a few very large fish. Normally, these big fish are quite deep, and the fly fisherman does not see them or get a chance at them, but some years ago three or four fish averaging over six pounds were taken on a fly with a small spinner ahead of it, near the mouth of Wolf Creek on Buttle Lake. Apparently, the fish took in quite shallow water and were caught by casting from the shore; the deed was done in October, and seems hard to explain unless the fish were running up to spawn in the creek. The spawning time of cutthroats variest greatly, though early spring is the normal time throughout most of the Campbell watershed.

An important question is whether these large fish are of a

distinct type or are simply individuals that have adapted themselves early in life to predatory feeding. I think there can be little doubt that they are all primarily predators or that sculpins are their chief diet; one rarely catches a fish of over 1¼ lbs. in any of the lakes without finding one or more sculpins in him. And there is not much doubt that they must have turned to predatory feeding in the second or third year, since trout that turn to predatory feeding only after their first spawning seldom seem to make really good recovery or growth. But for one incident I should feel perfectly prepared to accept the idea that they are individuals that have learned the business of scooping up bullheads. One July evening in 1936 I was fishing the Northeast Shoal at Buttle with Edward, who shares my affection and respect for the lake. We were catching the usual run of ten-, twelve- and fourteen-inch fish on medium-sized wet flies, when I hooked a fish that seemed a great deal stronger and more active than the others. I landed him finally, and we looked at him. About eleven inches long, very bright and clean, very fat and with distinct parr marks along his side.

"That's a grand second-summer fish," I said ponderously. "He'll be really big one day. Better put him back to grow."

Like an idiot I did put him back, and Edward encouraged me. We caught four others that evening, all fat, strong, full-bellied, eleven-inchers, and all with distinct parr marks. It was not until we were back in camp drinking coffee by the fire that I realised what a thorough examination of the fish might have proved. The normal Buttle Lake second-summer fish is about six inches long in July and weighs about three ounces instead of nearly three-quarters of a pound. I haven't been able since then to find those good little fish again, and I still don't know if that is the way the five-pounders look in their second summer. A few scales from them, and a list of what was in their bulging stomachs, might have explained a lot.

But although there are big fish down on the bottom, the typical fish of this land-locked part of the watershed is quite small. Lower Campbell Lake produces each year hundreds of fish, averaging about three to the pound. Upper Campbell does the same, though it is less intensively fished, and Buttle, which is very little fished, probably could produce a slightly higher average. They are unquestionably low-productivity lakes, capable of yielding perhaps two pounds of trout per acre each year. In the case of Lower Campbell, for instance, this means about six fish to the acre, which is a decent plenty in numbers. But 8- to 10-inch trout are not wholly satisfactory; even an abundance of them will not draw visiting anglers from very great distances.

A fifty per cent reduction in numbers would raise the average size to nearly ¾ lbs.—still not large; but an abundance of only three fish to the acre is probably not enough to make satisfactory fishing. There will always be plenty of anglers willing to search all day for a brace or a leash of 3-pounders, but they are not so likely to do so for the same number of ¾-pounders. So it is obvious that the present productivity is unsatisfactory.

The lake lacks the necessary food supply to make it a high producer. Attempts to introduce valuable fauna to a water already carrying a heavy stock of fish are seldom likely to be successful, and in lakes in which bottom cover is thin and scattered—as is the case with most Vancouver Island lakes—the chances of success are still further reduced. But it is just possible that some improvement might be made by the introduction of *Gammarus limnaeus*. This is very locally distributed on Vancouver Island, and experiments carried out by the Fisheries Research Board suggest that this is not due, as had been supposed, to a preference of the species for alkaline waters.

But though *G. limnaeus* is apparently not present in Lower Campbell Lake, many other valuable forms of aquatic life are present. *Daphnia longispina* and other small plankton forms are fairly abundant. *Hyalella azteci* and the water snails *Lymnea* and *Physa*, as well as some of the univalve molluscs, are in the lake; dragon-flies and damsel-flies of many different species; water-boatmen and back swimmers and leeches; some mayflies, stoneflies and caddis, and the chironomids are there. Besides these, there are the two forage fish, sculpins and sticklebacks. But all of them, especially the valuable aquatic insects, are present in wretchedly small quantities. This seems rather a strong argument against the possibility of successful introduction of non-indigenous species such as G. *limnaeus*. It is obviously impossible to introduce and keep on introducing a sufficiency to feed the fish; and if the breeding stocks of indigenous insects are not well enough protected to be able to multiply to a decent abundance, there is no reason to suppose that the introduction of what might be, under reasonably favourable conditions, an adequate breeding stock of G. *limnaeus* would yield results of any importance at all.

The better course is to account for the failure of the present stock of fauna to increase. The most apparent reason for this failure in Lower Campbell Lake is the lack of bottom cover, which is a deficiency common to nearly all coast lakes. As a general rule, waters of high productivity have good weed growth in which forage animals can breed and multiply in comparative safety from the attacks of trout. The interior lakes, such as Paul, have their wonderful evergreen shelter of chara; the English chalk streams have their fabulous banks of trailing weed that would choke their flow every summer were it not for the scythe. But the Campbell Lakes and most Vancouver Island lakes have only inadequate patches of pond weed here and there, a few water lilies in the sloughs, and perhaps a small area of varied weed growth near the mouth of a slow-flowing creek.

Once again, the remedy is quite obvious—plant weeds. But, as is always the case in fish culture, there are complications; many weeds make such rank growth that they may easily choke and ruin a valuable water; some weeds such as hornwort (*Ceratophyllum*) actually compete with aquatic insects instead of aiding them; and the most valuable weeds are not always easy to establish. Many of them—and chief among these is the best of them all, chara-weed—are lime lovers. It has even been shown that in really soft water, which is water low in lime content, it is impossible to obtain a permanent growth of useful vegetation of any kind. Many attempts have been made to introduce chara and other weeds to Vancouver Island waters, always without success, and the explanation is not far to seek: Lower Campbell Lake is fairly typical of the majority of island waters, and its alkalinity is only 21 parts per million of lime ($CaCO_3$) as against the 300 to 350 parts in those interior lakes where the chara does really well.

It may yet be possible to find a valuable weed that will thrive sufficiently in water of such low alkalinity. Some of the milfoils are fairly tolerant and are good producers, though far inferior to chara. But it is extremely doubtful that any way will be found of reproducing in coast waters the dense, matted, protective jungles of lakes like Paul, and without them a really high productivity probably cannot be obtained. The most promising suggestion at the moment seems to be that of building great brush shelters from intertwined branches and treetops and other lumbering waste, lashed together with galvanised wire and framed with small logs; these could be towed into position and sunk by piling rocks on the corners. To do this on a large enough scale would be costly, but once in place the piles would provide excellent shelter and would be for all practical purposes permanent, since wood decays very slowly when completely submerged.

The other alternative is to introduce lime to the water. This again would be a considerable undertaking, but not necessarily impossible or prohibitively expensive. At the present moment, Dr. G. C. Carl of the Fisheries Research Board is conducting experiments with lime in a small lake on Vancouver Island, and his results will indicate what should be attempted. A few tons of crushed limestone, introduced to a lake at strategic points, should make an improvement lasting several years. In some cases, it might be possible to find veins of good limestone within easy reach of the water, and a few sticks of dynamite would be all that would be needed.

The best hope of increasing the productivity of Vancouver Island lakes is probably in judicious application of both these principles, the sinking of brush shelters and the placing of lime. The brush shelters would be immediately effective in providing protection and would justify experimental introductions of valuable forage animals, if it were felt that the native species were insufficient. In some waters the introduction of lime might be cheaper than the planting of brush piles, and it is altogether possible that some of the important forage animals will not do really well if the water is below a certain degree of alkalinity. Even though it has been shown that *G. limnaeus* will live and grow in soft water and perhaps breed and multiply to the same extent as in alkaline water, it seems logical to suppose that most crustaceans and molluscs need a fair quantity of lime if they are to grow and reproduce with maximum efficiency.

So much talk of low productivity should not convey the impression that there is not really good fishing to be found in both the upper waters of the Campbell watershed and in many other parts of Vancouver Island. A cold-blooded examination of the possibilities deals with generalities; the angler in search of sport looks for the exceptions, and in a country that is not overrun with anglers he is certain to be able to find them.

In the three main lakes of the watershed there is exceptional fishing to be found, in the sloughs, in favoured bays, off the mouths of creeks, in all the special places that experience has taught anglers to examine. The same thing is true of the twenty or more smaller lakes tributary to the chain; in a few of them there is such wide individual variation that they actually differ markedly in character from the rest of the chain. There are the three shallow lakes lying just north of the foot of Buttle, for instance; tiny lakes full of plankton and with a bloom of algae all over their surfaces in midsummer, but holding trout up to 20 inches long, trout that will come to the fly. In the hot months their water is far too warm, and most of the fish are lazy and in wretched condition; but in spring or fall they can provide excellent fishing.

And there is Unknown Lake, just off the Buttle trail, fed and drained chiefly by seepage. It is only a small lake, but it is the most productive I have ever seen on Vancouver Island and probably capable of a yield in every way comparable to those of the good interior lakes. One can go there almost any day in the spring before June 1st or any day in the fall after the first week or two of September, and raise to the fly a hundred or more trout in a couple of hours' fishing. They are nearly all fair sized fish from ten or twelve inches up to a pound and a half or more, clean and in good condition. The lake is full of every kind of feed and shows hatches of dragon and damselflies that I have never seen equalled. I do not know the secret of this plenty, but the fact that there is such a lake in the watershed gives reasonable hope that research might reveal some factor that could be reproduced in the other waters. And the fishing, if you are in the mood for a barbless hook and some gentle experimenting with plenty, can be fascinating.

Besides the lakes, there are in this country plenty of streams which offer good, and sometimes very good, fishing. They are really of two quite different characters. The first are those joining the main lakes—the Campbell between Upper and Lower Campbell, and the Buttle River between Buttle and Upper Campbell. These are large streams with strong rapids and good pools and some extensive log jams. As soon as they are low enough for comfortable wading they hold a fair number of good trout, up to 1½ or 2 lbs., which come quite well to the fly. Most of the water is real wet-fly water, somehow simpler and better for being inaccessible to migratory fish, more truly a trout fisherman's own water.

But the most satisfactory fishing of the whole watershed is in the mountain streams, streams that head in some high, small lake or stem directly from the slopes of the great mountains and feed one or other of the big lakes. The first and perhaps greatest of these is the Elk River, which flows down Elk Valley from Drum Lake to join the Buttle River a few hundred yards above Upper Campbell Lake. But flowing into Buttle Lake are at least a half dozen others, all good—Wolf and Phillips and Myra, Shepherd's and Price and the others, all crystal clear and sparkling, beautiful between green woods, and snow-cold even in July and August.

Any good fly rod will do the work in these streams and lakes; it is not too difficult or exacting. But there is a considerable variety of conditions, and one rod cannot meet them all with equal satisfaction and comfort to the user. I think two rods are necessary, and never go off for more than a day with less than two. A 9½- to 10-foot, 6- to 8-ounce rod is often a comfortable thing to have when fishing a big lake on a windy day or when working a wet fly in the larger streams; and very often it will send a dry fly across one of the wider pools of the mountain streams when a lighter rod would not. But for calm days on the lakes one needs a light rod to get the most out of the small fish, and for most of the dry-fly work in the sloughs and mountain streams a 9-foot 5-ounce rod is quite enough. I use an 8¾-foot Davy, and have yet to handle a rod that fits the purpose better.

Two reels and two lines to match these rods, the St. John and an IBI line for the big rod, a Uniqua or a St. George with an ICI line for the Davy. Gut casts of all sizes from 1x to 4x. And flies.

If one does not wish to experiment, there is no need to carry a tremendous selection of flies. Of those I have suggested for migratory cutthroat it is worth taking Gammarus and Lady Caroline, both of which will do well on No. 6 and No. 8 hooks; Gammarus can be fished on sizes down to 13 or 14 with effect.

For general lake fishing, take also Teal and red, Teal and green, Teal and yellow, and Dark Mallard with the same three bodies. Add a series of Jock Scotts in sizes from 4 to 10 or 12, and this range of larger wet flies will be sufficiently complete.

But it is also well worth taking a few small wet flies on 14 or 15 hooks; Light and Dark Olive, Wickham, Tup, Greenwell and Red Quill are enough. Any or all of them will catch fish really well again and again during the hatches of chironomid nymphs that are common in many of the lakes and off the mouths of the mountain streams all through the summer. It is really pleasant to handle such flies for a change after the clumsy No. 6's.

Dry flies are important. A few brown and white bi-visibles on 10-12 hooks should be in the box of every fisherman who wanders about British Columbia, no matter where he is going. Some of the tested American favourites are very good—fanwing Royal Coachman, Professor, Western Bee, Black Gnat, Cahill, Hendrickson, Quill Gordon would be a useful group, tied on hook sizes anywhere from No. 10 to No. 14. The McKenzie River deer hair patterns are effective, though they are usually tied on unnecessarily large hooks. Some of the standard English chalk-stream patterns—Ginger Quill, Iron Blue, the Olives, Blue Upright and so on—are often taken with complete faith and occasionally in preference to most other artificials.

And finally, the sedges. I used to swear by the Williams grey-bodied sedge as the deadliest fly of any sort, wet or dry, on these mountain streams. I still think it a useful fly and one that will kill under most conditions, whether or not there is a hatch of sedges on the water. But I have known it to fail quite badly at times and have been able to persuade fish that had previously refused it by changing to something that matched more closely the fly on the water. There are some good sedge hatches on these mountain streams and perhaps it is as well to have light and dark imitations as well as the Williams sedge. Lee Wulff very kindly sent me some of his Grey Wulff and

White Wulff patterns a few years ago and during this last season I found fish taking the White Wulff with complete confidence towards dusk. There is an important advantage in this because it is a large fly and easily seen, even on broken water in a bad light; and I suspect that sooner or later a five- or ten-pounder, lurking near the mouth of Myra or Phillips or Wolf or Henshaw Creek, will roll up and fasten himself solidly to it.

I have purposely avoided mention of silver-bodied flies. It is probably an axiom that cutthroat trout will take them—such flies as the Silver Doctor, Teal and Silver, Silver Brown and all the others—better than they will any other wet flies. But when it is possible to catch plenty of fish without them it seems like murder to use them.

In all of British Columbia there is no gentler, grander or more beautiful lake than Buttle, or one that offers pleasanter fishing; it would be a comfortable fate to have to spend every summer there for the rest of one's life. I have seen and known others of the great Vancouver Island lakes; Nimpkish I knew and loved many years before I first saw Buttle and I still know it better than I shall ever know Buttle—combing its shores for logs, hunting its timber for game and fur, searching its streams for fish showed me the last secret hollow in the limestone, the last hidden bay, the last creek bed draining the last gully. But Nimpkish, with its monotonous north wind in the summer and its grey, hungry southeasters in winter, is a cold, hard, work-man's lake compared to Buttle. It is open to the sea and the harder for that, with the seals and the salmon running up into it. Its shore line is cold and grey and rocky, with few beaches and few tributary streams.

Buttle smiles, while Nimpkish has thin, firm lips—not less beautiful, or less desirable, or less worth knowing, but less friendly. Even in bad weather Buttle is friendly; you must not take liberties with her, but if you do she will not punish you with the cold, majestic cruelty that Nimpkish would use. The mountains lean back from Buttle and they themselves have room to smile; they crowd over Nimpkish and frown—Karmutsen, Table and the Hankins.

It is not a fair comparison; to have worked on one lake and only played on the other is not to have known both. But the perfections of Buttle are enough to stand by themselves, without a foil to set them off. More than twenty miles of deep water, draining from south to north, bordered by timber that slopes up to scrub and bare rock and snow, plainly visible from the easy surface of the water. A hundred beaches, a dozen tributary streams, deep valleys that invite the imagination, if not the feet, to travel through the woods.

I am not a fanatical camper; a real roof pleases me better than all the stars or all the canvas in the world, a real bed better than all the scented balsam boughs, a real meal better than a dozen cooked in the frying pan. But I am humbly glad to camp at Buttle, if only because it is so easy to get there that one can take everything necessary for a comfortable camp. From Campbell River, twenty miles of road—most of it very bad road—runs in to the foot of Upper Campbell Lake. Generally we load ourselves and all our stuff into a boat there, and Walter Sutherland runs us up to the head, where Bill, his brother, is waiting to load the pack horses. Nine miles of easy pack trail, along the Buttle River, past the junction with the Elk, past Unknown Lake, up through green timber and along through alders beside the river, then green timber again, and finally Buttle Lake, just above the outlet.*

The last time we went in that way was in 1937. We loaded the stuff into the boat, Ann and Edward and I, and rowed on up the narrow finger of lake that runs nearly a mile from the outlet before it spreads and becomes the real lake. The foot of the lake is the quiet end, wide and with gentler mountains sloping up from its shores. We camp always in the edge of the

* They've logged above the trail now and one has to find a different way in. But it can still be done—through slash and burn and logging débris.

woods behind a big root stranded on a shingle beach, and stay there for a night or two to break the journey. That night we went back down to the outlet with our rods and played with the nine- or ten-inch rainbows that rise there every evening in their hundreds. There are always larger cutthroats among them, and one always hopes to rise a five-pounder. On this night we found two or three cutthroats of over a pound, and killed three of the little red-fleshed rainbows for the next morning's breakfast. One that Edward hooked was taken across the middle by a big cutthroat and for a few moments it seemed that both fish would come to the net. But the cutthroat let go, and while Edward was trying to tempt him again I found a big cohoe fly in my box. He took it at once, and started down into the current like a good fish. But he turned almost before I had put a real strain on him, and he fought the rest of it sullenly and deep. The 3x gut was far too light for the big fly and might have broken easily if he had really tested it with a strong run, but he came to the net still sullen and slow; exactly two pounds.

The next morning we fished the Northeast Shoal, which is a good, wide stretch of shallow water running out from the east shore for a long mile up the lake. A good ripple from the south made it real lake fishing with Teal and red, Mallard and green and Jock Scott. The fish take freely there, all along the shoal, and one little bay whose whole mouth is guarded by a reef of rock two or three feet under the water always suggests big fish. We found none that day, though there were plenty of rises to keep us busy, in near the tops of fallen cedar trees, straight out from shore in twenty or thirty feet of water, off the points and in the bays; most of them fish from ten to fifteen inches long, but in that part of the lake a fourteen-inch fish weighs barely fourteen ounces and a fifteen-incher may be just a pound.

That day at the foot of the lake was no more than a renewal of acquaintances, an appreciation of freedom. Bill would be there to pack us out in ten days' time; until then there was nothing to worry about, except perhaps keeping count of the days so that Bill would not be kept waiting while we idled half our lives away up at Myra Creek. We rowed quietly up to Harry Rogers's cabin the next morning, and it felt like a return to things lost in a distant childhood with a better, sparkling future stretching far ahead. With Harry we went across to see Con at Titus's camp. Con, in breeches and wool stockings and light shoes, grey-haired and smiling, speaking in his soft whisper, holding out his welcoming hand, remembering last year— and many years before that on the lake. We stayed there too long, talking with Con and Harry about how it was last winter in the big snow, and how Con's dog Barney held a cougar at the foot of the bluff behind the camp, and how Harry hunts from his boat, with his big dog standing up in the bow and sniffing the breezes for the scent of a cougar on shore. But there was a north wind blowing when we left, and we put the sail up and were idle, sure of reaching Myra in time to make camp before supper.

From Buttle one can see most of the high mountains that are the real heart of Vancouver Island. There is the Rooster's Comb for a few minutes as one passes Wolf Creek, and Mount McBride, towering and close, the upper slopes open so that, comfortable there in the boat, one feels it would be easy and pleasant to travel over them and find heather and ptarmigan and alpine plants. Beyond McBride there is Marble Mountain, its veins of marble, good marble, plain in the sunlight. Looking back, one sees a distant snowcap that might be Elkhorn, and another that might be Crown Mountain.

Past Phillips Creek on the right, past Shepherd's in the deep bay on the left, and into the Narrows, fifteen miles from the foot of the lake, with the wind still fair. Henshaw's long, smooth valley opens up on the left, with The Dome over it. Myra Mountain high on the right, at the head of the lake. Price Creek valley cutting far into the hills, and Thelwood running off from it to the West; these last six miles were all our own.

At Myra last year's bench and table were still standing, just back from the edge of the little bay that faces up the lake. We made our camp once more on the narrow spit between the bay and Myra Creek, with a sandy beach for the boat and the fire, and the tents beside the creek. It is such a tiny spit of land, little more than wide enough for a small camp, yet there grow on it cedars and pines, alder and barbary, yew and balsam; the lightest breeze blows through it, so there are no flies. The lake brings firewood; the fishing is close at hand. There is nothing left to need.

Just before sunset we took the boat up the creek to the Falls, so that we could see them on the first evening. They grow up from the dark pool, white in their groove in the rock channel they do not use in July, and the green timber is spaced well back from them by the broad bare rock. Above the first pool is a rock bench, with a second pool fed by a second fall; and above that another and yet another on back into the timber. Water falling and spraying and pouring, always there, always waiting to be watched and admired, yet seldom seen.

One does not fish vigorously on Buttle Lake. There is nothing to do with the fish except turn them back into the water, and there are enough of them, rising freely enough, to make that a chore if one is vigorous. It is better to seek new places where the trout are feeding, and more satisfying ways of catching a few fish. The water of the mountain streams like Myra is clearer than clearest air, lighting even the tiniest pebble of the bottom to brilliance. Move upstream slowly in a boat, or wade if the water is low enough. Here and there will be a trout, rainbow or cutthroat, holding gently in the smooth, soft current. Drop the Grey Sedge above him, and he will rise easily to it through the clearness, perhaps follow it down a little way, his nose almost pressed against it, and take it. You can watch him as he dives for the sweeper near the bank, see the curve and flash of his body as you turn him, see his sudden run up from the depths before he breaks the smooth surface and throws shining drops from his body into the air. Then, when you have freed him, you can watch while he readjusts himself to freedom, turning a little uncertainly this way and that as he works upstream, perhaps to bury himself out of sight under the bank, perhaps to lie quietly out in the open, perhaps even to take up his old place and be ready to feed again. In the brilliant morning sunshine this is rare fishing.

For the afternoon there is Price Creek, at the very head of the lake, or the slough to the right of it. We went to the slough that first afternoon, following its windings, searching for fish among the lily pads. We found a school of yearlings, and I killed one to take the scales and measurements. At the next cast a great dark cutthroat jumped clear out of the water and fell back on the fly. He hooked himself and fought with savage head slashings like a pike, but he came in like a pike, gasping and quickly tired. Eighteen inches long and barely a pound and a half. A spent male trying to regain condition quickly on a diet of his offspring.

Up at the head of the slough the beaver were still working. We frightened good fish as we took the boat up to the dam but, watching, we saw them work back into position again, and within five minutes of the boat's passing they took the flies we offered them.

It was a still evening when we got back to Myra, and the twelve-inch rainbows and cutthroats were rising where the creek mouth breaks down into the deep lake. We went out there and began to catch fish on the Grey Sedge or anything we offered them. Once or twice a strong little rainbow fought deep and something took him and stripped line off the reel, running fast out into the lake, then let go and sent him back with the marks of teeth on him. Nothing to troll with, not a spinner, or a devon, or a phantom; not even a swivel or a lead or a bare hook in the whole outfit; too damned pure.

"What about the yearling?" Edward said.

I mounted a big bucktail on the strongest cast we had, and

hooked the yearling through the back of the head. We let him go down to the bottom at the break off, in twenty or thirty feet of water.

"You go on fishing," Edward said. "I'll hold the rod."

I fished, and caught one or two more of the little ones. Nothing happened to the yearling. I moved the boat a little to cover some fresh rises, and something took the yearling. He held on tight and took a lot of line, but when Edward tried to bring him up he let go, and only three-quarters of the yearling came back. It happened again the next time I moved the boat.

"Give him to me," I said. "I'll fix him properly."

I took the gut off the line and threaded it through the yearling's vent and up through his mouth, then fixed the hook where his tail should have been. I held him up, and Edward admired him and Ann admired him. I put him overboard, and we all three leaned over the side to watch him go shining down and down into the depths. It was almost dark, and everything was very still. He disappeared at last, and we leaned back again.

"Now," said Ann.

"Yes, now," Edward said. "We might get something if you had tied my gut on the line again." He held up his rod with the end of the fly line hanging free in the air. I still haven't handled one of those big fish from Buttle Lake.

The full moon, behind us and still hidden below The Dome, was lighting the tip of the mountain in front of us, while the whole lake and all its shores were still dark. The curved shadow of The Dome crept down and down the mountainside, and the trees above the shadow were lighted up and the rocks stood out. The shadow came down, almost to our feet, and we could look behind us and see the trees on the crest of The Dome clear and sharp against the face of the moon. Clear and pale and perfectly round, a part of the earth while the trees still touched her, the moon climbed until she was free of the last of them and lighting the whole still lake. A loon cried instead of sleeping and another answered; the sound whiplashed back and forth across the lake, from mountainside to mountainside. We knew we should see them, seven black and white birds, huge on the still water, off Myra Creek in the next day's dawn.

## REFERENCES

Carl, G. C. Report of Preliminary Survey of Campbell Lake, Sept. 15th, 1937.

Saunders, L. G. Freshwater Amphipods of Vancouver Island. Contr. Can. Biol. Fish., Vol. VIII, No. 19, 1933.

Titcomb, John W. Aquatic Plants in Pond Culture. U.S. B.F., Doc. 948, 2nd edition, 1923.

# PART FOUR

*The Pacific Salmon*

# *Tyee Salmon*

TYEE SALMON.

THE run of large spring salmon off the mouth of Campbell River during August provides what is probably the best known game fishing in British Columbia. In this fishery the angler's chief—in fact, his only—concern appears to be with fish of over thirty pounds. As a fisherman at Campbell River once bitterly remarked: "You've got to get a thirty-pounder here or nobody will look at it. And then they'll only glance at it."

The run is composed entirely of almost mature spring salmon, a considerable proportion of which are running to the Campbell. The first individuals usually appear late in July, and between August 10th and 20th in a normal year the run should reach its peak. Though no exact check has been made, the abundance appears to vary from time to time throughout the season, and there can be little doubt that it is very much influenced by the temporary pause of schools of fish bound for rivers other than the Campbell. The fishing grounds lie in

Discovery Passage, a few miles south of Seymour Narrows, and so are on one of the main routes of southward migration to the Fraser. There are strong tides throughout this area, and the bars off the mouth of the Campbell are sometimes partly shielded, sometimes in a natural eddy from the main flow of tide. The general contours of the bottom give even better shelter than the surface flow would indicate, and the whole forms a very natural resting place for migrating fish, particularly since there is always a body of Campbell River fish in the pools and along the bar to decoy them.

Since fish weighing less than thirty pounds are not entered in the official record of the Tyee Club, and since no other record is kept, the figures available are of a highly selective fishery, and it is difficult to learn much from them. But it would appear that a very high proportion of the fish on the grounds at any time are between the weights of thirty and fifty pounds, with a smaller but still significant proportion of equally mature fish weighing between fifteen and thirty pounds. A relatively small number of fish weigh over fifty pounds and probably up to at least seventy pounds, and there are always in the run some individuals, usually maturing early, which weigh less than fifteen pounds and as little as two or three pounds.

From year to year the proportion of fish at different weights may vary somewhat; in some years there are a considerable number of fish weighing between twenty-five and thirty pounds, and in other years the average weight may be noticeably high, with a fair number of fish in the high forties and low fifties. Such variations are almost certainly due to feeding conditions during the salt-water life of the fish, since the vast majority, probably at least ninety per cent, of those weighing more than twenty-five pounds appear to be in the same type and age group; ocean-type fish returning to spawn at five years of age. Of the remaining ten per cent of these large fish, rather more than half are stream-type, returning to spawn at six years of age, and the remainder, usually fish under thirty-five pounds, may be ocean-type four-year-olds. The majority, probably seventy per cent, of the fish weighing between fifteen and twenty-five pounds are likely to be ocean-type four-year-olds, while the remainder are poorly grown ocean-type five-year-olds or stream-type six-year-olds.

The fish are structurally identical with the king, quinnat or chinook salmon of Washington, Oregon and Alaska waters and the spring salmon of British Columbian waters, and the name tyee is arbitrarily applied usually only to those fish that weigh over thirty pounds. Owing to this condition and others, such as the normal time and place of capture, the tyee is likely to be an ocean-type five-year-old, a non-feeding fish within one or two months of full sexual maturity. From somewhat haphazard observation I believe that the great proportion of fish that actually enter the Campbell have usually finished spawning by the end of October, and that the bulk of the fry migrate to salt water in June of the following year. Scale examination suggests that the fish are normally three to seven inches long at the end of the first year, eleven to twenty-one inches long at the end of the second, twenty to thirty-one at the end of the third, and twenty-nine to forty or more at the end of the fourth; during the fifth summer they may add a further four to ten inches. Unusually large fish have generally made extremely rapid growth during the second and third years of salt-water feeding. I have seen no scale that suggested a previous spawning, and have never seen a spring salmon in any river that showed signs of recovery after spawning.*

* Details and scale-reading of two sixty-pounders are as follows:

No. 1. Caught by Mrs. W. C. Butler, of Everett, Aug. 25th, 1935. Weight, 60½ lbs., length, 46½ inches. Condition factor 60. Very thick fish. bright. Male. Ocean-type. Almost 5 years old when caught. 18 inches at 2 years, 30 at 3, 42 at 4 years.

No. 2. Caught by J. C. Agnew, Seattle, Aug. 31st, 1934. Weight, 64 lbs. Length, 49½ inches. Condition factor 53. Male. Stream-type. Almost 6 years old when caught. Good growth second year, exceptional third and fourth, falling off slightly in fifth and sixth.

The abundance of fish lying off the Campbell during the season is, according to local opinion, very much less than it was twenty or more years ago. At that time the resting pools near the mouth of the river were so crowded that large numbers of fish lay off Gowlland Harbour, on the other side of Discovery Passage, and a great many fish lay in the river, between the Spit and the first pool below the Highway Bridge. There can be little doubt that this account is substantially correct. Local drag seining, purse seining throughout the coastal area, south as well as north of the Campbell, and local and northern trolling have been factors in the reduction; and the log dump of the Elk River Timber Company in the Campbell itself has affected much valuable resting water in which some fish may have spawned. The tremendous reduction of the humpback run to the river by drag seining may also have had an effect; it seems probable that the rotting carcasses of a large run of spawned salmon are an important factor in the fertility of a coast stream, and that young salmon, even those which migrate to sea in the first summer, are dependent upon this fertility for their early growth.

The Tyee Club records are not an altogether satisfactory means of checking the yearly run, for several reasons—they deal only with fish over 30 pounds, they give no estimate of the fishing intensity and they do not by any means include all fish of over 30 pounds that are caught at Campbell River, since many are not registered. But they are records that have been kept consistently, even as to their omissions, and so may be given some value. It would appear from the records that in a normal year somewhere between 130 and 170 fish are weighed in. It is a poor year when the number drops below 120. In only two seasons has it exceeded 200—in 1929 when 246 fish were weighed in, and in 1945 when 319 were weighed in. 1944 was a normal year with 154 fish, 1943 a poor year with 116. The years 1927 and 1928 yielded respectively 71 and 60 fish.

While it is obvious that the intensity of the fishing has

increased very greatly since the club was founded in 1924, these figures suggest that there has not been any really serious reduction of the run; there may have been a temporary depletion by the very intense commercial troll fishery of the thirties, which reached its peak in 1934, but if so this has righted itself.

In spite of this I do not think it can or should be said that the fishery is in no danger. There seems very real danger that the steadily increasing numbers of sport fishermen alone may be enough to cause serious depletion and I believe it is far past time for a thorough investigation of the fishery with a view to finding sure means of perpetuating it.

A new factor that makes this investigation very much overdue is the Elk Falls power development. There is no apparent danger from the dam itself, which will be well above the limit of spawning water. But unfortunately the water will have to be piped down to a powerhouse at the foot of the canyon, which means that very little water will be going through the canyon itself during the months of the spawning run. I do not know how many fish spawn inside the canyon normally, nor, I am quite sure, does anyone else; but some fish do spawn there and any reduction at all of the available spawning area is obviously a serious thing, since the whole run has always had to find spawning room within some two miles of river. Whether or not the loss of the canyon's length will make a serious difference, I am quite sure that proper location of the powerhouse outlet and a proper method of returning the water are all-important. There is heavy spawning right in the Canyon Pool, where the powerhouse is being built, and all the way from there down. The outlet must be designed, then, to ensure a full natural spread of water over the bed of the river in the Canyon Pool itself and through the whole length of spawning water below. And it should be carried back as far as possible up river from the powerhouse itself.

That the government should have gone ahead with a project of this kind, on a stream as important as the Campbell, without thorough investigation is a shocking example of the carelessness with which game fish resources are handled in British Columbia. If the project turns out to have a seriously adverse effect, it will be very difficult to put things right. Since the power-house is supposed to be operating sometime in 1947 there obviously is not time for anything like a thorough research program now; but I believe such a program should be undertaken in any case, because there are many questions to be answered, quite apart from those raised by the power development, if the future of the run is to be made secure.

One question of obvious importance is: what proportion of the yearly catch made by rod fishermen would have spawned in the Campbell? There is undoubtedly heavy spawning in the Campbell, but it is also quite possible that good numbers of fish from other runs pause long enough to be exposed to the spoons and plugs of the tyee fishermen. Another point of considerable interest is the relationship between the total catch and the total spawning escapement. And it is essential to have the answer to several life history questions before, for instance, artificial propagation could be intelligently attempted.

Members of the Tyee Club and their guides, with no outside assistance beyond limited scientific advice, could carry out quite important parts of this research. One of the first essentials is an exact record of all fish caught during the season, including salmon of other species as well as the smaller mature spring salmon. This should not be at all difficult to achieve if its purpose is made clear. In the same way it should be quite simple to record the intensity of the fishery, if only in terms of the total number of boats fishing and the number of hours per boat per day.

A limited, but certainly useful tagging program could also be carried out by the club. Many members already have bronze, silver and gold buttons and so do not really need to weigh in any more thirty- or forty- or fifty-pounders. It is difficult to believe that these men would not very willingly tag and return at least a proportion of the fish they catch. By doing so they would not only discover, within a few seasons, whether the run has other parent streams than the Campbell, but they would ensure a number of additional spawners. I can assure them, from a good deal of personal experience, that there is at least as much satisfaction in tagging and returning a fish as there is in knocking him on the head and weighing him. When the tag happens to be picked up elsewhere later on, the satisfaction is very much greater.

Generally speaking there is little to be said for artificial propagation of Pacific salmon to the fry stage—natural spawning has been demonstrated to be at least equally efficient under normal conditions and it is certainly much cheaper. But in the case of the Campbell, where natural spawning areas are very limited and where the exceptionally high dollars and cents value of each fish caught would justify rearing beyond the fry stage, artificial propagation may well be a sound answer. Artificial propagation suggests also the possibility of lengthening the Campbell River season by introducing fish from, say, the Phillips River, which has a July run, and the Nimpkish which has a September run. An experiment of this sort might be a complete failure, but would be justifiable because success or failure would have bearing on the problems of many other streams.

Tyee fishing, as practised at Campbell River, is not every man's sport. It is a matter of salt-water trolling with a large spoon or plug and several ounces of lead. And it is often slow fishing because the fish are not feeding. On the other hand the fish are big and strong, they fight well and they are salmon. Most of the fishing is done in beautiful weather and in beautiful surroundings. And there are the Tyee Club buttons—bronze for a thirty-pounder, silver for a forty, gold for a fifty, diamond for a sixty.

Award of the Club buttons is conditional upon the use of tackle that falls within certain specifications. These are approxi-

mately the same as those of the Catalina Tuna Club's "Light
Tackle" and "Three-six Tackle" classes. There are no specifications as to the type of reel or the type of bait for either
class, though the bait must not have more than one hook. The
line for Light Tackle class must have a dry breaking strain of
not more than 25 pounds by actual test. Rods must show a
certain deflection when held at a point 12 inches from the butt
with a one-pound weight attached to the top ring—a 6-foot rod
must deflect six inches, 6½-foot, 8 inches, 7-foot, 10 inches and
from there on an additional three-inch deflection for each six
inches of length.

Three-six specifications, as most saltwater anglers know, are
somewhat simpler—rod not less than six feet over all, weighing
not more than six ounces, used with a standard six-thread line.

The first tyees are usually weighed in at Campbell River
during the last week of July. The fishing should be at its best
by August 10th or soon after and by the first week in September the fish are usually getting dark. The fish lie for the most
part along the edge of a bar that extends for some distance on
either side of the mouth of the river, and they usually take the
spoon or plug at a depth of less than thirty feet.

The tyees lying off Campbell River in August are as essentially non-feeding fish as Atlantic salmon are. They must be
tempted, irritated, tormented or otherwise persuaded into
taking and it is only possible to say that in certain sets of conditions they are more likely to succumb to temptation or respond to torment than in others. The conditions that affect
them most strongly are tides and light. The biggest tides of the
season are always the best; early morning and late evening are
nearly always the best times of day; and when high or low slack
tide coincides with first or last daylight the fishing is more
nearly certain to be good than at any other time. Apart from
this combination of favourable circumstances the best fishing
time is likely to be one hour after flood or ebb on the big tides.

Remembering that maturing salmon are stimulated to activ-

ity by a flow of current and that practically all ocean fish are
conditioned, by movement of plankton and other dependent
organisms, to respond to changes of light, it is not too hard to
find some sense in all this. My own conviction is that when
non-feeding fish, be they Atlantic salmon or Pacific salmon or
steelhead, do take hold, the action is purely reflex—the movement and proximity of the lure trips something in the brain
and the body responds from long habit by pursuing and seiz-
ing. Returning for a moment to the tides, the big tides stimulate the maturing fish to travel and so bring them down from
the north to their resting places off the Campbell. Here they
find shelter from the main force of the heavy tides of Discovery
Passage along the bars. Even here there is tide, though, and it
stands to reason that shortly after each turn of tide most of the
sheltered spots will become exposed. The fish feel the fresh
current and almost certainly respond to it by movement—
either movement to new shelter or simply the restless movement of maturity, possibly both. Under these circumstances
they are at once more likely to see the lures and more likely to
respond to them. First or last daylight is simply an added stimulus, probably sufficient in itself to cause restlessness and movement after the long years of ocean feeding and certain to do so
when combined with the stimulus of changing tide. The whole
inference, then, is that it is easier at such times to trip the brain
mechanism that produces the reflex action of the strike.

This is not to suggest that fish are not taken at all times of
day and at almost all stages of tide. There is often fair fishing
for at least two hours on either side of slack water, but at such
times the fisherman is probably dependent almost entirely upon
the fact that the condition of the water allows proper working
of his bait or upon the recent arrival of a new run of fish.
There may be some variation, too, in the length of time it takes
for a change of tide to affect different resting places along the
bars.

This rather involved discussion gives some idea of how large a part local knowledge plays in the catching of Campbell River Tyees. True, luck is involved, as it must always be in trolling, and complete strangers do occasionally go out by themselves and come in with big fish on the first evening. But most visiting anglers hire guides to row them and an overwhelming proportion of the catch is brought in by local guides.

The guides at Campbell River know the bars and the tides, and they understand the business of keeping a spoon or plug working at the right speed and for as long as possible in the right places to catch fish. There have been, and there still are, some outstandingly good guides at Campbell River—men who have made good catches season after season for many years. Probably the greatest of them all was the late Herbert Pidcock, who had known the waters from boyhood and who was almost miraculously consistent in catching fish. He once told me: "The man who will get most fish out there is the one who can keep his spoon working right, in the good places, for the greatest proportion of time." I asked what proportion of the time he thought his own spoon was working right. "Probably thirty per cent," he said. "And that's not much when you figure the fish may be taking for only fifteen minutes or half and hour on an average tide. Come through one of the good holes a little too fast, or with a piece of weed on the spoon or fishing too deep or too shallow, and you may have wasted your one real chance of the whole day."

Herbert had a lot more than that though. His watermanship was excellent and he knew the tides intimately; he could read perfectly from the beat of the rod-top what his spoon was doing twenty feet below the surface. Fishing certain places he would read his position, not from marks on the shore, but from changes in the resistance of the current to his oar-blades— which is bringing local knowledge down to a pretty fine point. His calm, unruffled temperament was another factor and an important one in fishing as strongly competitive as the Campbell River fishing is. But his greatest asset was probably his ability in using his tremendous fund of experience. As every hunter and fisherman does, Herbert played what he called "hunches." In his case the hunches were sound a great deal more often than is usually the case, and if one persuaded him to analyse a hunch it usually turned out to be something much more like an effortless, almost instinctive, use of past experience.

I think its unpredictable quality must be a good part of the attraction of Campbell River fishing. It is also comfortable fishing, apart from the fearsome hours—the weather is nearly always good and the favourite places like Painter's wonderful lodge and Len Idiens' new cabins make perfect holiday living. But the big thing is the salmon fisherman's everlasting dream of a fish up in the next ten-pound range—the thirty- or forty- or fifty- or sixty-pounder that tops his previous best.

The chance of realising the dream is very good at Campbell River. The average of the fish weighed in by the Club is approximately forty pounds, year in, year out; in the twenty-one year history of the Club about twenty sixty-pounders have been caught. The present Club record is 66½ lbs., caught by Mrs. T. B. Randall in 1941. It is safe to say that there is no other place in the world where so many really large salmon are caught by rod-and-line every year.

Campbell River is accessible, it is very well equipped to cater to visiting fishermen, it has an excellent run of fish that can be caught in shallow water and it has a Tyee Club that has become world-famous. For all these reasons the name of the place has become practically synonymous with the sport. But tyees are caught elsewhere, notably at Brentwood Bay, near Victoria, at Port Alberni on the west coast of Vancouver Island, at Comox and Nimpkish on the east coast of the Island, and at Phillips Arm on the mainland. Brentwood, Comox and Alberni, like Campbell River, are accessible by road and make excellent provision for fishermen—good accommodations, boats and guides are available. Nimpkish and Phillips Arm are beyond roads and the fisherman will have his troubles in finding boats, guides or accommodations at either place, though nowadays some sort of arrangements can usually be made at Painter's Lodge or, I understand, through the recently formed Malibu Club at Princess Louise Inlet. There is outstandingly good fishing at both places—at Phillips Arm in July and early August, at the Nimpkish during September—and the fishing has, for me at any rate, one advantage that puts it in an entirely differ- ent class from that of the more accessible centers: the fish can be caught by casting.

I was lucky enough to fish the Nimpkish for several seasons between 1927 and 1933 and I had fishing there that was in many ways the most breathlessly exciting I have ever known. For the most part I used a Hardy Murdoch side-swing casting rod with a 4-inch Silex reel and a light casting line. It was never necessary to use more than one ounce of lead and that was necessary only to carry out a No. 6 or 7 spoon to a respectable distance in casting and to hold it from riding the surface in fishing. I saw my spoon taken many times within a foot of the surface.

We caught fish in this way out in the salt water, in the mouth of the river and in every pool up to the head of tidewater. The most consistently good fishing was out in the salt water just beyond the edge of the tide flats, and a few hundred yards inside the mouth of the river. But the most exciting fishing was in the pool at the head of tide water, by the Lansdowne farm. On most days of the season one can expect to hook a fish there just as the sun goes off the water in the evening, but on one memorable afternoon we started catching fish at 3:30 and went on hooking them with practically every cast until dark. With the current to help them they fought splendidly and several times from that pool we have had fish run forty or fifty yards up into the white water of the rapid at the head.

The biggest fish we killed at Nimpkish weighed 58½ lbs., but a fish of 66 pounds was killed by a handline well inside the mouth of the river and I have seen ninety-pounders weighed from the drag-seine nets. Casting from a boat anchored by Sachem Island as the schools came up the river we used often to see a really big fish turn for the spoon, only to have a twenty or thirty-pounder dart in ahead of him and take it; but I am quite certain that the law of averages allows the big one to arrive first sooner or later. It did so once for us, but the spoon came away after three uncontrollable runs each of which took more line than I have ever had to give a fish before or since.

Even with Phillips Arm and the Nimpkish the possibilities of tyee fishing in British Columbia are not nearly exhausted. I believe that the right sort of effort would find good rod-fishing on the commercial trolling grounds, where the fish are still feeding. There are huge fish off Milbanke Sound and Bull Harbor and Egg Island and I have been told of a run of great white spring salmon in Gardiner Canal. Wherever the fish are to be found near the surface in salt water they can be caught by rod and line. In most places away from the crowded centres I believe they can be caught by casting. I like to remember that a commercial troller caught a fish of 109 pounds off Egg Island in 1937, and when I have time I am going north again with the Murdoch rod and a new Silex reel to look for another like him.

# 11

## *Cohoe Salmon*

SINCE cohoe salmon are willing to run up and spawn in even the smallest creeks, they are extremely well distributed all up and down the coast. A large proportion of them make only a comparatively limited migration in their sea-feeding years, and many grow from yearlings to full maturity within the limits of the Strait of Georgia, so they are in some degree available to anglers and commercial fishermen at all stages of growth and development. This is unfortunate, as it leads to significant depletion during the immature stages; anglers catch them in some numbers at all weights from half a pound upwards, often calling them "sea trout"; commercial trollers go to work on them early in their third summer, when they weigh little more than a pound or two, and kill great numbers; purse seiners catch them at all stages, very often when setting for other fish, and cause a considerable wastage.

It is a great pity that the immature cohoe, in what is known as the blueback stage, at the start of the third summer, is a valuable commercial fish. The value is due to the red flesh of the fish, which holds its colour through canning operations and produces a pack comparable in quality to the sockeye pack. The very red flesh changes to a slightly paler colour as the change of diet from crustacea to needlefish and herrings begins to have its effect, and by August and September the fish is slightly less valuable to the canners; it is, however, considerably more valuable to the commercial fishermen and to the angler, because by September a fish that weighed only four pounds in June will weigh at least seven or eight pounds. Taking into consideration also the fact that the blueback will keep for only a very few hours after it is caught, so that quite large quantities of the catch are frequently wasted, it seems reasonably certain that the commercial capture of the cohoe at any stage of immaturity represents an economic loss to the country as a whole.

As in the case of the spring salmon, the intensity of the fishery for the mature cohoes has increased tremendously since 1933. This is undoubtedly due largely to the depletion of the sockeye runs, which has made the cohoe a fish much sought after by canners; but the sharp difference between the catch of 1934 and that of all previous years was caused mainly by the tremendously increased catch of the trollers, and lack of other employment must have had a good deal to do with this. From 1920 until 1933 the average annual catch of cohoes by all commercial methods was about 1,300,000; in 1934 it was over 3,500,000 and it held at over three million during 1935 and

1936. The trollers' average catch from 1920 until 1933 was well under 400,000. In 1934 it jumped to over 2,500,000 and held fairly close to the two million mark in 1935 and 1936. In 1937 there was a sharp drop. The total catch fell to less than 1½ millions and the trollers' catch was about three-quarters of a million. This drop was due to overfishing in 1934, and heavy floods early in 1935 which caused destruction of redds and loss of eggs.

Besides the wastage of immature fish and the excessive intensity of the legitimate fishery, deliberate poaching causes serious reduction of the spawning escapement at times. In most years, great numbers of mature cohoes may be found waiting off the mouths of creeks for the fall rains in September and October. A few unscrupulous purse-seine captains often work within the limits set by the fisheries department off the mouths of such creeks, and make heavy catches by doing so. Usually an old, small boat of little value is used for the purpose, and about half the normal length of shallow purse net, so that in the case of capture and confiscation of gear the loss will be comparatively small, easily covered by one or two successful ventures. The majority of captains commanding full-sized purse seiners never stoop to illegal fishing, and the fishermen mark and despise these small boats and their crews as "creek robbers." But the practice persists, though it has been reduced in the last few years by aeroplane patrols and by the canneries' refusal of overmature fish. Its effect is really serious, because one or two successful sets near the mouth of a good creek in the fall may easily clean out practically the whole spawning run of that year. An effective remedy that might not meet with general approval would be to issue purse-seine licenses only to owners who could prove an investment of not less than eight or ten thousand dollars in boat and gear. Few captains would care to risk the loss of such an investment for a holdful of creek fish.

Actually it seems very doubtful that the capture of cohoes

by purse seiners at all is economically sound. These fish are extremely important to the commercial troller—even more so, perhaps, than the spring salmon, the only other fish that the commercial troller takes in significant quantities—and there is no type of employment much more valuable to the country than that provided by commercial trolling. A man with a few hundred dollars to invest in a boat and a small quantity of gear can go out and make a living year after year, provided he gets a fair price for the fish and learns to understand the fishing. The purse seiners have the sockeyes, pinks and dogs, all of which are far more important to them than cohoes and springs and which should, if the runs were maintained at a proper peak, be quite sufficient to keep them employed.

Though anglers are not generally willing to realise it, those who fish for cohoes are themselves at present doing their share towards endangering the future of their sport. Until recently rod fishermen were limited to five Pacific salmon per day, with a provision that ten might be taken in any boat from which two or more anglers were fishing. In practice this meant usually a limit of ten fish per day, since many rod fishermen were content to abide by the letter rather than the spirit of the law and considered a guide or a non-fishing friend as the second rod. But this was not enough, and two or three years ago, in response to pressure from rod fishermen, the limit was entirely removed. Efforts to have it replaced since then have met with the strongest resistance.

This is especially astonishing, since the angler is usually a good conservationist, little concerned with killing more fish than he can use. His sport is not in any way dependent upon the death of his quarry; it is entirely in the hooking, playing and netting of the fish, and the blow of the club that ends a fish's life is no part of it at all; rather it is a necessary but unpleasant preparation for supper or a slightly less defensible precaution against the doubts of friends. Unfortunately for the cohoes, British Columbian anglers are inclined to argue that such tremendous numbers of them are killed by purse seining and other commercial methods that the angler's best efforts at wholesale slaughter can only be insignificant in comparison.

The logic of this argument seems to be that out of slaughter added to slaughter will come adequate survival. From the point of view of conservation it can have nothing to recommend it, even if the angler's efforts at slaughter are comparatively ineffective. Actually, they are by no means as ineffective as might be supposed; fly fishermen at times kill as many as thirty-five cohoes in one day's fishing, and fairly frequently manage to get ten or fifteen or twenty. Bags of from five to ten fly-caught fish are common. This means that one day's fishing in one small bay where the cohoes are feeding especially well may yield (and has yielded) more than 200 fish to ten or a dozen boats. Even a purse seiner would not sniff at such a haul. And, to add to the trouble, the rod-caught fish are likely to be very considerably more important to the future of the runs than those caught by purse seiners, because they are taken directly from the spawning escapement, usually in waters closed to commercial nets. Practically one hundred per cent of the fish caught, for instance, in Duncan Bay or Cowichan Bay, would ascend their parent streams and spawn, having survived the natural hazards of fresh- and salt-water life and all threats of purse seiners, gill nets and commercial trollers—were it not for the rod fisherman.

This fact should be enough to warn the rod fisherman of the danger to his sport. It is sufficiently obvious that the runs are decreasing rather than increasing, so that it is quite useless to hope that from the five thousand or so eggs shed and fertilised by a pair of spawning cohoes in (let us say) the Campbell, more than two fish will return to spawn at the end of three years. It is equally logical to argue that by killing two fish in Duncan Bay today one makes it extremely probable that there will be two less fish in their place three years from now. Actually, a vast multitude of incalculable factors may influence this effect, so that perhaps twenty or two hundred or perhaps no fish at all might have resulted from the spawning of the two fish killed. But, just the same, there is more than a germ of essential truth in the idea.

Another argument put forward by those who would have no limit is that catches of as many as twenty or twenty-five salmon in a day are made in some English and Scottish salmon rivers, and that no limit is enforced. Such catches are made on strictly preserved private water by very limited numbers of fishermen. They are still further removed from comparison by the fact that the owners of such waters have bought up the rights of the commercial net fishermen on the stream, and the run is therefore subjected to little or no other drain than rod fishing. The rod fisherman in British Columbia cannot reasonably expect to obtain for his one-dollar license fee the same unlimited freedom.

A more important argument is that rod fishermen who have come long distances and spent much money should be given their money's worth. They may, it is argued, fish for two or three weeks and happen upon only one or two good days; allow them, therefore, to kill all the fish they possibly can on those days—and, incidentally, on any other days that may happen to be good. The question is, What makes a good day? I do not think there would be found many fishermen to argue that a day which yielded five very game fish, averaging six or eight pounds apiece, to the fly, is not a good day, especially if it happens to come in the middle or at the end of two or three weeks of quiet days. And if a limit of five or ten fish is not enough to allow an angler to have a good day, what is there to prevent him from becoming a little selective? Killing less than ten fish because he hooks, plays and returns to the water unharmed all fish in excess of that number; after all, his pleasure is not in killing, and sportsmen have used this way out of the difficulty for a great number of years.

Against this it is argued that fish returned to the water will not live. But they will; they do; tagged fish are being recovered all the time, and they must have been caught to be tagged. Then, more subtly, it is said that netting cuts the slime and removes scales from a fish so that when it enters the river to spawn it will be attacked by the fungus disease and will infect the eggs it deposits. This can be prevented very simply by removing the hook from the fish's jaw without taking him into the boat; seldom a difficult task for a man who knows his job, especially if he is using a hook that is barbless or has a reduced barb. But to meet the issue more squarely: The fungus disease presumably is *Saprolegnia parasitica*. A good deal is known about *Saprolegnia*. It is a "parasitic disease" caused by the development of water molds; there is not much doubt that it is always present in all coast streams and that it gets its hold upon practically all Pacific salmon either before or shortly after death. It is also recognised as the cause, but only the secondary cause, of a high percentage of the mortality of fertile eggs; it cannot attack live, healthy eggs, only those already dead or having some foreign organic matter adhering to the surface. If it could do more than this, the tremendous prevalence of the disease in spawning waters at spawning time would long ago have killed off all the runs; it is always present in sufficient quantities to infect dead, dirty or improperly buried eggs, but these are losses in any case, and a few net-marked fish cannot contribute significantly to the spread. Actually, there are always considerable numbers of fish in the rivers bearing the scars of escape from commercial nets or predators, and there is evidence to suggest that by no means all of these are attacked by *Saprolegnia*. Hobbs, writing of quinnats spawning in the Broken River, New Zealand, notes that: "In one instance *Saprolegnia* had attacked the gills of a live fish, though it was not noted to occur on any open sores of any fish."

These last half dozen paragraphs were written in 1938 and I have not changed them at all. It is now 1946 and through September of this year I listened to the doleful stories of anglers who were coming in from Duncan Bay and Poverty Point, even from as far away as Cape Mudge, with perhaps one or two fish to show for a day's effort, rarely more than five or six. It would seem that the golden goose is already mighty exhausted, and there is no shadow of doubt in my mind that British Columbian rod fishermen should be content to submit to a limit of not more than five fish per rod, per day. Such a limit would serve several useful purposes. It would remind the angler that he has a responsibility to himself and other people. It would aid in providing an adequate escape of spawning fish. It might be used to encourage a widespread tagging programme. And it would give the angler some grounds on which to ask for the reservation of certain waters to rod-fishing only; at present, conducting his sport on a commercial scale, he cannot ask such reservation on good grounds, and certainly cannot do so without legitimate protest from commercial fishermen. And the preservation of good relations between the commercial man and the sportsman is of first importance in all steps towards conservation.

The building up of cohoe runs by other means than restrictive measures may be possible and may very easily become necessary. Some improvements could be made in the accessibility and in the spawning conditions of many small creeks. Where a fair proportion of the mature fish are likely to fall to the angler, some hatchery work might be economically justifiable, and the losses of ova, alevins and fry that presumably occur in creeks of uncertain flow might be considerably reduced. But extensive tagging programmes would be necessary in order to ascertain which creeks or rivers produce the fishing of such areas as Duncan Bay, and the angler could render valuable service in this. He could also do much to provide an accurate check of the situation by keeping full records of his catches and by urging resort keepers to keep full records of all fish caught by their visitors. Only by such records can a constant decline of the run be instantly separated from annual fluctuations.

Just before the war rod-fishing for cohoes was moving well up towards the top of all sporting attractions as a money maker for the province. There seems to be rather less interest now, partly because the novelty has worn off a little, I suppose, but mainly because the size of the runs to the really good spots has fallen off. It is the sort of fishing that calls for lots of fish—half the attraction and excitement of it is in seeing the heavy, fierce break of feeding fish near the surface, the quick wheeling of gulls, the showers of needlefish or herrings leaping out of the water ahead of pursuing salmon. But as long as there are cohoes around at all, the chance of catching them on the fly in salt water will draw anglers just about as powerfully as any other form of their sport. The cohoe is extremely active and fast, often a spectacular fish when hooked, and the excellent chance of hooking a half dozen of any fish as game as he is on a trout rod or light salmon rod, with a fly and no lead, is something to attract most keen fishermen.

Cohoes have probably been caught on the fly for over forty years. In a letter dated December 31st, 1905, and quoted in Hodgson's *Salmon Fishing,* Sir Bryan Leighton wrote: "Of salmon on the Pacific Coast we find six varieties—the king or spring salmon, the cohoe, the steelhead, the humpback, the dog salmon, and the sockeye. Only the first three will take a lure, and I have caught the cohoe on the fly only." And farther on in the same letter: "The cohoe I have many times caught on a fly in the estuary of a river." And again: "I found that the cohoe took any silver-bodied fly and that No. 4 or No. 5 was the best."

The development of the sport since those early days has been quite slow. Though there are quite a few keen fishermen who can claim an eight- or ten-year-old habit of spending September and October with a fly rod in some bay where the cohoes school and feed, it is only since 1935 that the sport has become widely known and really popular. Even now there is still a great deal to be learned about flies and tackle and methods, and about times and places when the fish may be expected.

There is quite good fly fishing for large bluebacks or small cohoes in June and July in some years, but the best of the fishing is usually in late August and September. In these months the mature fish are tending towards the rivers, but the spawning urge is not yet stronge enough to send them straight on to the end of the journey, and they stop here and there to feed with only slightly diminished voracity. In October, unless the fall rains have come early, the fish are usually waiting more directly off the mouths of the rivers, and often still come well to the fly.

The best known places for this fishing at present are probably Cowichan Bay, about 35 miles north of Victoria, and Duncan Bay, about a mile north of the mouth of Campbell River. The two places are about a hundred and forty miles apart, both on the east coast of Vancouver Island, and both accessible by road. Duncan Bay has the advantage of a somewhat earlier run of fish, and Cowichan is rather closer to large centres of population, so both are about equally well known.

Bays of this type are well sheltered from the tides, and schools of needlefish and herrings collect in them much as they collect in the eddies behind the banks off the west coast. Finding them there, the fish feed well, and give the angler his chance. The needlefish or sand-launce (*Ammodytes personatus*) is the natural feed that provides most of the fly fishing. It is a slender, eel-like fish of from one to six or more inches in length, with a silver belly and a darker back; it is closely related to the sand eels of Great Britain and is probably identical with the candlefish of Puget Sound. When the cohoes are really feeding well on these fish, they take the fly better than any other lure, and big catches of ten or more fish to the boat become readily possible.

Unfortunately, the fish take a trolled fly very much better

than a cast fly, as a general rule. There are the exceptional days and the exceptional times when the cast fly comes into its own, but even these are fewer now that so many boats crowd into the favourite places. In Duncan Bay most of the fishing is done from fourteen-foot boats, with a guide rowing and the angler, seated facing the stern of the boat, fishing two rods. Usually he handles one rod only, making occasional casts with it, and allowing the fly to swing in behind the boat, while the second rod is beside the guide, its fly trailing steadily some sixty feet astern. Even this can be exciting work, though, with six- or eight-ounce trout rods or light, single-handed salmon rods. The guide keeps the boat moving fast through the water. A fish breaks within casting distance and is covered. He does not take, and both flies swing back behind the boat. Feeding fish show again, working towards the flies. The guide turns the boat quickly, to bring the flies still closer to the fish. Two ripples are following, one behind each fly—eight- or ten-pound fish, remember, strong and lively as fish can be, and nothing between them and the hand but a light rod, a length of fly line and a grilse cast. The first fish takes in a swirl, and almost as he starts his run the reel beside the guide goes away as though the heart were being torn out of it. There is very little hesitation, very little sulking or boring about a cohoe. Even when he is free, migrating or feeding, his jump is the cleanest of all Pacific salmon jumps—twice, along the line of his movement, straight out, far clear of the water and landing back on his tail. The resistance of the line may make him come down on his head when he is hooked, but the jump is still clean, far out of the water, beautiful to watch, and splendidly exciting. He will run a hundred yards straight or with a half dozen jumps, come back and go almost as far again. If it is all over quickly, in two or three runs and a quiet sinking of the net, that is as it should be. The fish that fights best rarely fights long, and the intensity is greater for being over quickly, with a calm close on either side of it.

Perhaps the guide's fish is waiting quietly, sixty or seventy yards out, as the first fish is netted, perhaps he has made his run and gone free. It doesn't matter very much in cohoe fishing, because there are always more fish around when you've found a feeding school. And it doesn't matter much if there is no guide and no second rod. It is not like rowing for tyees; the fish are there in plain sight, breaking water, feeding with the needlefish jumping out and shining in the sun ahead of them. Turn the boat to cover that school, turn again to cover this one. They'll see it sooner or later. Or if there are few boats out and the fish are showing well, let the boat drift, and cast to cover them as they show within reach.

When the exceptional time does come it can be very, very good. Back in the distant days of 1933 and 1934 one thought little of it. Quite often I have rowed to Duncan Bay and turned back almost without wetting a line because they did not seem to be coming well enough for casting. And at other times, when they were showing well, it was simple to tie to the kelp and kill five fish in an hour or two, without moving the boat. To cover the slash of two or three feeding fish, work the fly a foot or two, feel the take and strike into that noble first run is fishing at its best.

It still happens often enough to make one ever hopeful of a good day. It is no longer possible to tie to the kelp unless the bay happens to be very empty of boats—to do so would be to hold a good position too long. But sometimes they are feeding well in the rip that makes out towards the channel from the point of the kelp and sometimes one can find them farther up, away from the other boats. And simply to drift, casting from time to time and rowing enough to keep out of the way of the trollers, is enough. The best way of all is to have an enthusiastic fisherman at the oars, quick to spot feeding fish and move within casting distance of them; an hour or two of such work, even without a fish to show for it at the end, can pass like a moment of time.

It is not altogether easy to account for the effectiveness of the trolled fly. It is possible that the fish are often widely scattered and that trolling covers more water, but this seems hardly likely since the cast fly is effective for trout in wider waters with fewer fish. Possibly the trolled fly fishes generally a little deeper, yet it is often taken when only an inch or two below the surface. Certainly, it travels through the water more smoothly and generally more swiftly, but these are not, normally, qualities of movement that attract a predatory fish to an imitation of his prey. The most probable explanation seems to be in the cohoe's frequent habit of following the fly before making up his mind to take and, less frequently, of coming a long distance to a moving fly. When either of these things happens, the caster sees the surge of the fish moving towards his fly; he works the fly on its way, as cunningly as he knows how, drawing it fast or slowly, smoothly or jerkily; the surge of water follows and follows and follows—then ends in a swirl as the fish sees boat or fisherman. The course of the trolled fly is calm, even and endless; it draws on, and the fish can follow, turn away, come back again, follow again and at last, perhaps, make up his mind to take.

Yet when they drive into a school of needlefish the cohoes turn quickly this way and that, grabbing what they can in the shortest possible space of time. And on the days when casting is best, they often take the fly almost as it touches the water. So it is probably sound to conclude that the fault is in the flies used; that for some reason their appearance usually fails to reproduce in the fish's brain the instantaneous reaction that is produced by the appearance of the needlefish. Within the past two or three years cohoe flies have been tremendously improved. Until 1935 most fishermen were content to use a standard fly, dressed with a silver body and white, red and brown bucktail hairs about 2 inches long, on a 2/0 hook. In 1935, flies tied with hairs up to three or more inches long, still on the 2/0 hook, came into general use, and often green hairs were used in place of the red. The long flies proved themselves very quickly, and several times green flies caught fish when the red would not.

This was enough to arouse an intense interest in any and every fly that differed from others before it. Yellow flies appeared, scarlet flies, blue flies, purple flies, mauve flies—flies of every shade and colour were towed through the water, and nearly all of them took fish at times. Some of the new colours were genuinely useful and should have a place in every cohoe fisherman's box; but the greatest advance was the substitution of polar-bear hair for bucktail. The old bucktail fly was a dead, ugly creature, dull of colour, without lustre or any illusion of translucency. Polar-bear hair is superior in every way; it takes dyes much better, it has a brilliant lustre, and it is far less brittle than bucktail. There is very little doubt that in nearly all conditions it is more attractive than is bucktail.

But neither the tying nor the use of cohoe flies is even nearly fully understood as yet. Few flies have been tied with hackles, yet wet-fly fishermen have used hackles in nearly all flies, even silver-bodied flies, for generations, and it seems fairly certain that they must serve some useful purpose. The cohoe fisherman's disregard of them is probably based partly on the shape of the needlefish and partly on an unwillingness to veil the silver body. There is little doubt that the silver body generally plays an extremely important part in the success of any fly; it attracts the fish, draws his attention, and the polar-bear wing gives substance and poise to the fly when the fish is close enough to take. But a fairly small hackle tied at the head of a 2½- or 3-inch "Long Dee" hook, which is one of the best hooks for cohoe fishing, would leave plenty of silver exposed. And on very bright days a bright silver body may be a disadvantage; I have caught fish on flies with a body of black floss ribbed with silver, and have seen them caught on flies from which the tinsel had been stripped, leaving only the naked black shank of the hook under the bear hair.

Perhaps, too, there are better wing materials than the various colours of polar-bear hair. Whole saddle feathers, both dyed and natural, mixed with the hair, make an excellent wing. Peacock herl is valuable, and the light and dark saddle feathers of the red jungle cock are good. Turkey tail, golden pheasant tail —there are a host of good feathers that make fine long strips for winging, and the possible combinations are infinite in number; a score of flies must be tied and tried for every one that will prove to be of permanent value, and the thing must grow and develop from season to season.*

It is not exactly a question of imitation; the natural, for all practical purposes, is nearly always the same—the needlefish. That some flies are sufficiently good imitations under certain conditions is proved by the fact that they are taken freely and quickly; but the same flies may be followed and refused when the fish are apparently feeding just as freely. The principal factor probably is the light; perhaps not the intensity, but the quality of the light. The colours most commonly used are probably green, blue, orange and red, and it is quite evident on some days that the fish is coming to the green rather than the blue, or to the orange rather than the green. Occasionally all flies seem equally good, and occasionally a special shade of green or blue seems to kill when other shades will not. Altogether, it is an interesting problem, and one that fly fishermen, with their everlasting ingenuity, will certainly come near to solving in the end. One could wish that the fish did not come so well to the trolled fly, so that the stimulus to solve the problem would be stronger. To make a long cast, accurately and well, raise the rod point to set the hook almost as the fly touches the water and feel the strong plunge as the run starts in

---

* There has not been much development of cohoe flies since 1939. Polar-bear fur is almost universally used and shades of blue and green over white are the most popular. Some attempt has been made to find colour combinations to match varying light conditions, but I am not sure how successful this has been.

"the natural . . . is nearly always the same . . . the needlefish"

an immediate response, is a delight of action and sensation above most.

Not the least attraction of fly fishing for cohoes is the opportunity it offers for catching fairly large salmon on trout tackle. There is many a stirring account of such battles in angling literature, and in most of them the angler has started to his day's work quite without thought of salmon; the fastening of a big fish to the 2x cast and the small teal and red is both a shock and a pleasant surprise; the response of the nine-foot rod to its unequal task is also a surprise and usually a cause of the greatest anxiety. But in cohoe fishing men and women actually do go forth with nine-foot, five-ounce rods and the very definite intention of exposing these delicate weapons to the mercies of a ten- or twelve-pound fish. There is nothing to be said against this practice; indeed, it reflects great credit upon the angler's determination to get the most out of his fish, but it is perhaps carrying the thing a shade too far. With a five-ounce rod the angler is too little in control of the situation and must tire his fish rather by studious yielding to its whims than by meeting aggressively each type of resistance and turning it to his own uses.

Probably the lightest rod that will stand the strain of cohoe fishing for an indefinite length of time and give the angler reasonable control of his fish is a ten-foot split cane of about eight or nine ounces. Hardy's "Crown Houghton" is an excellent rod of the type, and the "Halford" is equally good; both these rods handle strong fish of ten or twelve pounds quite nicely, though they give the angler occasional moments of surprise at his own temerity. They will also make some sort of a show of handling a 2/0 fly when conditions are not too unfavourable, though they will not do it any too gracefully and easily for the best of men, and there is a degree of uncertainty about the recovery of a long cast that should recommend them chiefly to the solitary caster or to one who trolls a great deal and casts very little.

A 2/0 fly is a good morsel of weight and of air resistance, and to control it fully in a wind is work for an eleven- or twelve-foot rod of good backbone. For the past two or three seasons I have used with great pleasure and satisfaction an eleven-foot Wye rod, which will handle a 2/0 fly and anything up to thirty yards of line, without too much straining. If anything, the rod is a little short, and I believe a 12-foot "Wood" or even a thirteen- or fourteen-foot double-handed rod would be a little better for the man who is really determined to catch his fish by casting and not by trolling. The extra length is not important in casting, since casts of over twenty or twenty-five yards are seldom necessary and can seldom be made in time to cover a break, but it can play an important part in the business of working the fly once the cast has been made. The two main requirements of a cohoe rod are that it shall throw a 2/0 or heavier fly quickly and accurately to distances of twenty or twenty-five yards, and that it shall be long enough to give the fisherman plenty of help in bringing the fly through slack water with a lively movement. The shorter the rod—so long as it is long enough and powerful enough to handle a 2/0 fly—the better it will fill the first requirement; the longer it is, the better it will fill the second requirement. So it is necessary to make some sort of a compromise, and the best probably is a twelve-foot single-handed rod of the "Wood" type. All fittings, it is perhaps worth adding, should be of rustless or non-corrosive metal.

The No. 2 St. John, made in non-corrosive metal, is as good a reel as one could wish for the job. For use with rods of eleven feet or more it should carry thirty or forty yards of No. 5 fly line and seventy or eighty yards of backing. For smaller rods, 35 yards of B line with 100 yards of backing is quite enough; the normal limit of a cohoe's first run under the pressure that can be applied by an eight-ounce rod is under a hundred yards, though the exceptional fish with conditions in his favour may force a little more. Whether to use a double-tapered vacuum-dressed fly line or a cheaper level line is a debatable point. But the conditions of casting are quite exacting, and a good double-tapered fly line will last two or three seasons even in salt-water use if it is properly dried every night and well greased the next morning.

Three-yard casts tapered to 9/5 are commonly used, but these are unnecessarily light, actually too light for a 2/0 hook, though generally strong enough to land the fish. Probably 4/5 is as good a weight as any, and level gut of this weight really casts better than the lighter tapered casts.

Altogether apart from this salt-water fly fishing is the brief week or so of excellent sport that one can find in the rivers after the first fall rains. If these come in October and fairly suddenly, the cohoes run up from salt water almost immediately and I have often taken them in the Campbell, well above tidal water, with the sea lice still on them and the undigested vertebrae of needlefish in their stomachs. They take very freely, and it is quite unnecessary to use a large fly or even a silver-bodied fly. A light mallard and silver on a No. 4 hook is probably as deadly as anything, but flies dressed on six, eight and even twelve hooks are taken, and such standard trout flies as Jock Scott, Montreal and Parmachene Belle do very well. It is easy and very pleasant fishing in the rising water, and the fish take hard and fight splendidly. Such subtleties as greased line and the deep-sunk fly are quite unnecessary; a long cast, covering the water and fishing across slowly an inch or two below the surface in a simple, orthodox wet-fly manner, will catch more fish than one needs or wants. Actually, the fish can be caught in this way right up to the time when they have all spawned and died, but they deteriorate very quickly after they get into fresh water, and usually the percentage of ugly red spawners is too high to make fishing a real pleasure for more than a week or ten days after the first fish come in.

The usual fly-fishing methods are not always successful in salt water. Sometimes one sees hundreds of fish cruising everywhere, just breaking the water with their noses, like rising trout; when they are doing this they are feeding on a small, pink crustacean commonly known as the pink feed. A few individuals may come to an orange polar-bear fly or to Farlow's "Beedles" dressing of the pink shrimp, on a No. 6 hook. It is interesting fishing, but seldom really good; the imitations so far developed are probably not sufficiently convincing.

Spoons, plugs and minnows are generally worse than useless when the fish are on the pink feed, but when they are feeding on herring these are nearly always a good deal better than the fly. Conditions, also, can make fly fishing extremely unproductive; on some days and in some places the fish are found deeper than usual and perhaps more widely scattered. At such times and in such places it is often possible to catch them by using a light lead or setting a thumbnail spinner at the head of the fly, but there is probably not much point in sticking to the fly at all; one may as well be honest about it and put on a small spoon or a minnow.

When fish are plentiful and taking herring fairly freely, one can get very good sport by casting a No. 4 diamond spoon and a half-ounce lead. A three-inch devon minnow also kills fish extremely well at times, and many spinners are quite good. When the fish are more scattered and deeper, it is often necessary to troll, and for this again the No. 4 diamond spoon is an excellent lure. Trolling of this sort, with leads not heavier than two ounces, can be almost as interesting as trolling with the fly, and frequently makes a good day out of a dull one. There is also a great deal of deep trolling for cohoes, usually with large spoons or larger plugs and leads weighing from four or six ounces up to a pound, and often metal lines as well, but good fish though the cohoes are, a lead of even four ounces is really too much for them and such fishing is hardly worth considering.

Another method, extremely popular in Puget Sound and growing more popular in British Columbia, is "spinning" with a herring strip. This is an extremely deadly method which requires a good deal of skill, and is well worth trying. The disadvantages are that one has to handle natural bait, in the shape of strips cut from the sides of fresh herrings, and that other and less attractive denizens of the deep than the salmonoids have a habit of attaching themselves to the hook.

The tackle used is extremely simple; a bamboo pole, fitted with rings, a hundred yards of Japanese gut, any reel, a light gut leader, small hooks and one- or two-ounce leads. There are many ways of cutting the herring strips and, being a novice at the game, I am probably treading on delicate ground in describing one to the exclusion of others. But the way that seems to me to produce the most attractive result is the following: Make a deep cut along the backbone of the fish, from a little behind the gills almost to the tail, then another starting a little farther back from the gills and down near the belly, to join the first in a point near the tail. Join the start of each cut by a slightly slanting and very clean cut, right down to the ribs; without taking the knife out of this cut, draw it half an inch towards the tail through the flesh, then turn it up sharply until it is just under the skin, and draw it back in a single movement right down to the point of the triangle. If the job has been properly done there will be a long, tapering strip of skin and scales, entirely free of flesh except for the front half inch, in which one sets the hook.

The gut line is stripped off the reel into a coil in the hand or in the bottom of the boat, and the cast is made from the coil. The bait is allowed to sink well down in the water, then drawn up in a series of long jerks by stripping in line through the rings. Usually the cohoe takes on the "stop" at the end of a jerk, so that the strike is hard and sudden. It is a good method, the better because there is always an excellent chance of hooking something unexpectedly big—a thirty- or forty-pound feeding spring salmon, for instance.

The art of catching cohoes by attractive and sporting means

is very far from fully developed, and there are many waters that have been little explored by the angler. In Duncan Bay and most of the waters south of Seymour Narrows a seventeen- or eighteen-pound cohoe is a very big fish. North of Seymour Narrows, off Johnstone Strait and Queen Charlotte Sound, there are bigger fish. I have caught them up to twenty-four pounds off the mouth of a small creek just south of the Nimp-kish and I have seen a twenty-nine-pounder caught in Baronet Pass. Perhaps larger cohoes are not altogether needed; the eight- and ten-pounders do well enough. But the crash of a twenty-pounder jumping clear of the water in his first run has a memorable savagery, and to be casting close to the kelp when such fish are about is a strong experience. There seems a ruthlessness, a momentary surge of overwhelming power, in the strike of a twenty-pounder to a fly that is lacking in the strike of a fish much smaller. Good feeding bays will be found sooner or later in the more northern waters, and when they are found the taking of spring salmon on the fly, now a comparatively rare occurrence, will be more frequent. Perhaps there will then be found fishermen to point out that the strike of a thirty- or forty-pounder has in it that which the strike of a mere twenty-pounder can never have.

## REFERENCES

Davis, H. J. Care and Diseases of Trout, U.S. B.F., Investigational Report No. 35, 1937.

Hobbs, D. F. Natural Reproduction of Quinnat Salmon, Brown Trout and Rainbow Trout in Certain New Zealand Waters. New Zealand Fisheries, Bull. No. 6, 1937.

Hodgson, W. Earl. *Salmon Fishing*. Black, London, 1906.

# III

## *Migration*

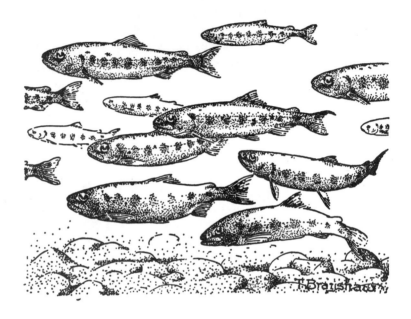

THE migrations of fish and birds have, until fairly recently, been reckoned among those lesser mysteries of the natural scheme that man has been ready— so respectfully and modestly ready—to consider insoluble. The salmon migrations have seemed especially miraculous because their causes have been so well hidden in the depths of the sea and their effects have been so clearly visible in the comparative smallness of rivers and inland waters. Salmon have received credit for everything from an infallible homing instinct to a superhumanly retentive memory and a very nice power of reasoning. Much of the strong fascination that the sport of angling has had for good minds has sprung from this mystery of the salmon and the slightly lesser mysteries that the movements of nearly all fish have always been. The growth of trees, the movements of birds, the lives of animals, all these happen in the air, where man also moves and lives. It is natural that they should have been the first to be clearly understood, but the very fact that they are now understandable argues that there are no mysteries or miracles in the natural order of things, that everything concrete—not to press the point too far—is completely accountable.

It is too much to say that every step of the salmon's migration from and return to its parent stream is fully understood. In broad outline the thing is sufficiently clear; many of the details are still open to legitimate scientific doubt, but the clearness of the outline directs the way to understanding of the details.

The parent-stream theory—that is to say, the belief that every salmon which survives to maturity returns to spawn in the stream where it hatched from its egg—is really the foundation upon which the mystery has been built. It is an amazingly sound theory; every marking operation that has been undertaken has shown clearly that the overwhelming majority of salmon actually do return to their parent streams to spawn. The exceptions are so few that they do nothing to shake the theory; but they have done a constructive service by suggesting that, since the thing is not perfect, it is useless to expect to find that the guiding force behind it is some flawless, probably hereditary, instinct wholly within the fish itself.

The next great step was the realisation that the ocean feeding grounds of the salmon are known. For many years it was accepted that the salmon left their rivers and went off to feed "somewhere" in the ocean, probably somewhere in the far north. I have contributed my own little share to the spread of this idea—it had a pleasing vagueness that stimulated the imagination—and I think that the majority of anglers, even today, still accept it. Actually, it is now well known that Pacific salmon spend their ocean lives somewhere along the continental shelf of western North America. This shelf is a perfectly clear and definite thing; a strip of comparatively shallow water running along the coast of the continent for several hundred miles and out from shore for a distance of about thirty-five miles, where it begins to slope, at first gradually then sharply, down into the depths of the Pacific Ocean.

For the present purpose it is only necessary to consider that part of the shelf which runs along the west coast of Vancouver Island and north from there to the Queen Charlotte Islands. Along this part of the shelf, and extending beyond it out into the Pacific, there is a current that sets, day and night, summer and winter, year in, year out, always northwestward, never southeastward. In normal weather it runs at 1 to 1½ knots; against a strong westerly wind it slows to half a knot; driven by a southeast gale it runs at 2 or even 2½ knots. The continental shelf in this area is not uniformly flat, but has on it a considerable number of elevations, which the fishermen call banks. Behind these elevations the constant current forms submerged eddies, exactly as eddies form in a stream behind the rocks, and in the eddies the smaller forms of marine life, having little or no motive power of their own, tend to collect. Small fish, such as herrings and pilchards and other forage of the salmon, also collect in the eddies to feed on the drift; and the salmon themselves turn in to feed on the herrings and pilchards.

This knowledge, which the fishermen had dimly before the scientists saw it clearly, set the position of the feeding grounds and in large measure accounted for it. Somewhere in this area was the end of the feeding migration. It remained only to learn how the young fish found their way to the grounds, what were their movements while feeding and how they found their way back to their parent streams in time to spawn.

Between 1925 and 1930 the Biological Board * of Canada conducted tagging operations from points on the continental shelf between the south coast of Vancouver Island and the north coast of the Queen Charlottes, and the conclusions of Mottley and Pritchard, based on the results of these operations, in large measure provide the answers to the three questions stated above. Though several species of salmon were tagged in the course of the operations, the bulk of the work was with spring salmon; and since the results of the work were clearest and most nearly conclusive for this species, it seems best, in attempting to describe them, to write only of spring salmon, though the main conclusions can probably be applied, in variously modified and perhaps more complicated forms, to the movements of the other salmon.

The seaward migration of young salmon, once it is well started, is a positive movement; the fish actually swim down with the current instead of merely drifting down in the stream. While the movement is in progress, feeding may or may not continue; probably it does whenever the small fish stop to rest in eddies or sheltered water, though knowledge of the feeding habits of the sockeye suggest that this species, at least, might not find in the streams much feed to its taste. If there is any suspension of feeding it probably ends as soon as salt or tidal water is reached, and the movement then becomes, instead of a positive migration, an intensive search for food which soon takes the young fish away from the immediate influence of the river. From this point it is necessary to deduce the direction of the movement by a simple piece of reasoning; the records show that virtually every fish tagged in the sea and subsequently recovered as a maturing or mature fish has travelled southward from the point at which he was tagged; in other words, the spawning migration is a southward movement. Since this is the case, and since the parent-stream theory is essentially sound, it

* Now The Fisheries Research Board of Canada.

follows that the feeding migration is always a northward movement.

A young spring salmon, feeding and working away from the mouth of the Columbia in a northward direction, will eventually reach the sphere of influence of the constant northwestward current along the west coast of Vancouver Island. Actually, tagging records and scale readings show that Columbia River springs of the ocean type are likely to reach the influence of the current late in their second summer, and stream-type fish late in their third summer. This means that they have spent rather more than a year in this portion of their journey, and it seems logical to suppose that through the whole of it they have been influenced chiefly by feeding conditions. Exactly why the feeding conditions draw them northward has not yet been explained; there may be a definite migration or drift of the feed, or progressively improving static conditions, or a belt of temperature, or any one or more of a dozen other possibilities; whatever it is, it will be explained sooner or later, and in the meanwhile its effect is abundantly clear; it draws or carries or leads the fish northward.

Once they have reached the influence of the northwestward current they must inevitably be carried still farther from the parent stream, unless they make some effort to hold or swim against the current. Since their only concern at this stage is to feed, they do not make any effort to resist the flow, and further tagging results show that through the remaining months or years of immaturity the current encloses them and carries them with it. They will stop frequently for shorter or longer periods where the feed has collected in the shelter of one or other of the banks; at times, following the movement of a school of herrings or pilchards, they may actually swim southward for a considerable distance; but all this will happen within the current and though it may slow the drift of the fish to an average speed far below that of the current, the sum total of their movement over any significant period of time will always be northward.

At some point in the third, fourth, fifth or sixth summer of most of these fish, a new factor begins to influence the movement. They begin to mature—that is to say, the sexual organs begin to develop. It has been shown that the sexual development of fishes stimulates them to activity, and that in the case of salmon this activity takes the form of swimming against the current. So at the onset of maturity the Columbia River spring salmon feeding off the west coast of Vancouver Island begin to head into the constant northwestward current. At first the reaction is not very strong, and the movement is frequently broken or delayed by feeding. It also fluctuates to some extent in proportion to the strength of the current, and as fish feeding in the shelter of the banks are not exposed to the full flow of the current, the migration may be still further slowed. But over a period of time the movement of a maturing fish along the west coast of Vancouver Island will be always southeastward, into the current and towards the parent stream.

As the sexual organs continue to develop, the stimulation to activity becomes more powerful, and the movement is more definite. Eventually, it brings the fish within range of the current of the parent stream, which then takes the place of the northwestward current and the tides as a stimulant, and directs the ascent to the actual spawning grounds.

Though the location of the areas in which tagging operations were most extensively carried on gave the results rather special application to the Columbia, the numbers of tagged fish recovered from other streams were sufficient to show that the theory is generally applicable. The percentage of fish from the Columbia falls off progressively as the tagging bases move farther north; off Vancouver Island the Columbia contributes fifty per cent of the total; off the west coast of the Queen Charlotte Islands the Fraser, a river comparable in size and influence to the Columbia and lying well to the north of it, begins to show strongly in the returns with a proportion of ten per cent, while that of the Columbia falls off to thirty per cent. Off the north coast of the Queen Charlottes the Columbia's proportion drops to twenty-four per cent and that of the Fraser increases to thirty per cent. Though no fish were tagged much north of here, it is obviously reasonable to assume that the Columbia's contribution will rather rapidly decrease while that of the Fraser will steadily increase until that river's sphere of maximum influence is also passed. The many smaller streams lying between the mouths of the two great rivers and to the north of the Fraser naturally do not show in comparison, but there is no doubt that their fish are carried northward in much the same way and turn southward at the onset of maturity.

It is not easy to prove exactly what draws each fish or group of fish out of the general stream of southward migration when the parent stream is reached. The drawing power of the two big rivers must be very great indeed, and there is not much doubt that individual fish of other rivers respond to it at times; but the overwhelming majority quite clearly do not. It seems probable that certain conditions, influencing the time of seaward migration, the extent of that migration and the slower or more rapid development of the sexual organs, tend to bring a fish within the influence of its own river at a time when it is at a sufficiently advanced stage of maturity to respond to the river's flow of fresh water; the temperature of that flow and possibly even its chemical content may act upon the fish to stop it and turn it at that particular point.

The response of fish at slightly varying stages of maturity to the flow of the parent stream may be assisted by the schooling of fish from the same parent stream before maturity. Williamson and Clemens state that: "Two salmon, Nos. 5054 and 5058, were tagged at Kuyuquot on June 5th, 1927, and were both recaptured at Iwaco, Columbia River, 270 miles distant, on August 8th, 1927. A similar case occurred in the

1926 experiment at Barkley Sound. Two fishes tagged on May 12th, 1926, were recaptured at West Beach, Whidby Island, 110 miles distant, on August 21st, 1926. It would appear that the fishes had kept company during their entire migration. They were not necessarily travelling alone, but may have formed part of a school that made the journey." Perhaps a layman may be allowed to deduce from this that the two fish may have belonged to a school formed either during the early stages of fresh-water life, or at the start of or during the migration to salt water, and broken up only on arrival at or near the spawning grounds.

Enough of mystery remains to stimulate good minds; there are still gaps bridged by conjecture, and the scientist has learned to treat those gaps with exaggerated respect. It is well that the layman should do the same, but at least the picture is clearer; there is reason in it—more of reason than of mystery but not, by any smallest fraction, less of wonder.

The new knowledge has many practical applications. It suggests very clearly, for instance, the solution of the problem caused by Japanese offshore fishing. The fish spread all over the continental shelf but not beyond it. An agreement by Canada, the United States and Mexico to enforce against other continents a limit to the extent of the continental shelf instead of the present three-mile limit, while continuing themselves to respect the old limits within the wider limit, would settle the question once and for all. It would conflict with what is at present considered an international law, but so does the present Mexican limit and so did the extension to twelve miles made by the United States during prohibition. Actually, this would be intercontinental rather than international law and so would not need a precedent; but international laws of this kind are set by the nations that have the big navies, and the limit of a continental shelf surely forms a more logical boundary than an imaginary line at a certain distance from shore.

It becomes obvious, too, that if the salmon of the Columbia

and other Oregon and Washington rivers migrate to British
Columbian waters and those of the Fraser reach Alaskan waters, any legislation designed to preserve the runs must be international if it is to be effective. Until recently the history of
legislation for conservation of the salmon runs has been largely
one of international jealousy rather than of international co-
operation. The wonderful success of the International Halibut
Commission in restoring the value of the halibut banks has done
a great deal for the cause of better co-operation between the
countries, and there is every reason to hope that the sockeye
commission at present working will solve its more complicated
problems as satisfactorily.

A further application of the new knowledge should come
when it has been expanded to explain fully the reasons why
fish turn off from the general migration at their parent streams.
At present the stocking of a stream with fry or eggs from
another stream is seldom successful. Experiments have shown
that fish transplanted in this way are likely to become "lost" in
the ocean and to return either to the original parent stream or
to one of the great rivers that throw fresh-water current far
out to sea. It seems possible that successful transplantings can
only be made by careful matching of streams and types of fish.
The date of spawning, the average winter temperature of the
streams—which controls the length of the incubation period of
the eggs—the time of the seaward migration, the tendency of
the fish to mature after a shorter or a longer period in salt
water, the temperature and flow of the stream at the time of
the spawning migration—any or all of these may prove to be
important factors. Now that the way has been shown, they will
be examined and compared; and sooner or later successful
transplanting will become a thoroughly efficient means of
cultivation.

It would be possible to suggest or point to a dozen other
applications of a fuller knowledge, but none could be more
essentially significant than this last. Anything that grows and

matures and breeds under purely natural conditions is subject to the pull of so many apparently insignificant forces, any of which may be of vital importance in shaping the finished product, that to attempt to tamper with the process, without full knowledge, must always be dangerous. There is much to be done for the salmon runs of British Columbia, but at the present stage the most vital need, once there is proper restrictive legislation to ensure the maintenance of adequate breeding stocks, is for research work.

## REFERENCES

Mottley, C. McC. Pacific Salmon Migration. Contr. Can. Biol. Fish., N. S. 4, No. 30, 1929.

Pritchard, A. L. Pacific Salmon Migration. Biol. Bd. Can. Bull. 41, 1934.

Tide Tables for the Pacific Coast of Canada, 1938.

Williamson, H. C., and Clemens, W. A. Pacific Salmon Migration. Biol. Bd. Can. Bull. 26, 1932.

# IV

## *Future Possibilities*

CUTTHROAT TROUT.

THOUGH the possibilities of developing stream fishing for trout on the coast are very considerable and there is at least some chance that ways may be found of increasing the productivity of coast lakes, there is not much doubt that the salmon runs will continue to provide, as they do at present, the most important game fishing in the province. The experiments of Hobbs in New Zealand and Foerster at Cultus Lake, B. C., have shown beyond reasonable doubt that artificial propagation has little if any advantage over natural spawning under normal conditions. Even if this were not the case it has long been realised that artificial propagation could not possibly be conducted on a sufficiently large scale to counteract the commercial drain, and the sport fishery is at present essentially a by-product of the commercial industry.

It is impossible to overstate the importance of this relationship between the two fisheries. Even if at some future time the game fisheries of the Province become more valuable in terms of annual cash turnover than the commercial fisheries—this is a possibility dependent on having about half a million anglers spend an average of thirty or forty dollars apiece on their sport within the Province—they will still be a by-product of the commercial fisheries when comparison is made in terms of fish consumed. This means that, with the possible exception of a few isolated cases, building up the runs that provide game fishing means building up all the runs in the Province; in other words, the interests of rod fisherman and commercial fisherman are identical.

The history of the salmon runs of British Columbia, like that of most of the other natural resources of North America, has been one of extraordinarily rapid depletion. In 1876 the Province's total pack of canned salmon was 7,247 cases from the Fraser. At that time salmon ran to every stream in thousands upon thousands, and to the great streams in millions upon millions. The runs must have seemed to the most far-seeing of men as terrific a phenomenon of nature as a volcano or the tides or wind or snow or rain, something that the most frantic efforts of man could do nothing to check or destroy. But by 1897 the pack had risen to over a million cases,* and the number of canneries operating and the number of boats fishing was still steadily increasing. By 1903 Sir Bryan Leighton was able to write: "I fancy that the canning business is being overdone, and that it is bringing about a deterioration of stock." Other men, in closer touch with the situation than Sir Bryan was, must have been able to see even more clearly than he did that the drain was too great. There cannot be much doubt that the

---

* Since the pack at that time was composed very largely of sockeye this would represent about twelve million fish.

men who had the power to check the drain saw what was happening, but they were hidebound by the tradition of the continent and did nothing. At no time in the history of the continent has a check been applied soon enough to the destruction of a natural resource, and now after little more than a century of westward movement the thing is complete, has passed beyond the limits of the continent to the limits of the useful waters of the Pacific. This is not a lament; it is a simple statement of what has happened and what was bound to happen. The continent was nothing more than a series of natural resources—land, timber, fur, fish and game. Each resource was capable of a certain maximum sustained yield, its natural increase. Of each resource was demanded, and taken, more than this maximum yield until the resource itself was no longer large enough to provide a useful natural increase. The task of the present and the future is the rehabilitation of these natural resources until they are capable of a maximum sustained yield as great as, or perhaps even greater than, their former maximum. It is necessary to understand this in order to understand the condition of the British Columbian salmon runs at the present time.

The yield of the British Columbian runs continued to increase even after the disastrous landslide caused by railroad construction in the Fraser Canyon in 1913, to a peak of over two million cases in 1926 and 1928. But the increase in the pack did not in any way keep pace with the increase in fishing effort. In 1890 a capital investment of about 1½ million dollars produced a pack of 411,000 cases. In 1913 a 12-million dollar investment yielded 1,350,000 cases. By 1918 the investment had risen to nearly 30 million dollars, but the pack was only 1,600,000 cases. In 1929 a 36-million-dollar investment yielded 1,400,000 cases—an investment twenty-four times as large as in 1890 and a pack only three and a half times as large.

At the beginning of the present century, had the spirit of the times permitted such measures, it would not have been at all difficult to limit the annual catch to the amount of the annual increase. But at the present time, though depletion has reached such a stage and is proceeding at such a pace that the need for drastic measures is obvious to everyone, it is no longer a simple matter to limit catches. A great industry has been built up, far greater than the natural yield of the runs can support, and it is necessary to consider the tremendous amount of capital involved and, more important still, the loss of employment that must follow any limitation. That is why it has been thought desirable to examine other possible means of counteracting the drain, such as artificial propagation, restrictions on the fishery in form of closed seasons, closed areas and limitations of gear, and efforts to control or destroy predators.

Any hope that the sponsors of such measures may have felt that they were adequate to meet the situation can have been based on little more than wishful thinking. It is axiomatic that closed times and closed areas simply produce more intensive efforts in times and areas that are not closed. Artificial propagation, even had it been a vastly more efficient process than it has proved itself, was applied to less than five per cent of the run of a single species of fish. Predator control can never be complete, and there is very little in its history to suggest that it is a cure for all evils; as a supplement to other measures it must always be useful, but its use on a considerable scale is not yet proved economically sound or biologically sound—and this last point may well be of vital importance in view of the delicate balances that are always operating under natural conditions. The mentality that can put faith in such measures is one not properly conditioned to the circumstances. British Columbians cannot completely rid themselves of the influence of the fairy tales about their vast resources that they have been listening to for so many years; they do not want to face the fact that an industry employing thousands of men and millions in capital must be heavily reduced if it is to continue to produce at all. And so they cannot bring themselves to admit wholeheartedly and without reservation that the only significant cause of depletion is overfishing and that the only possible remedy is less fishing. Valuable years have been lost in playing with palliative measures, and the valuable years are still passing with nothing done; each year so lost means that the cut, to be effective, must be more drastic; and if a sufficient number of years are lost it may well be that the runs will be reduced below the possibility of rehabilitation, as the buffalo were reduced and the passenger pigeons and the great stands of timber.

The quickest and best method of restoring the salmon runs to the point at which a large annual yield might again be safely taken would undoubtedly be a complete closure of all fishing for each variety and type of salmon through a period of one full cycle at least. This might also prove the cheapest method in the long run, but it would mean such a heavy and immediate loss of capital and employment that it is not likely to be considered. The alternative is to carry on a reduced fishery over a very much longer period, and to effect the reduction so that it will ensure an adequate escape of spawning fish to every stream.

It is quite impossible to do this by means such as the weekly closed season at present in effect. Weekly closed seasons might benefit a run of salmon that was attacked at only one point in its migration, but it can do very little for the runs as they actually occur. For instance, a school of fish passing through Johnstone Strait during a closed period may be subjected to fishing in Discovery Passage on Monday morning, and to attack after attack all through the rest of the week on its way down the Gulf of Georgia. A school passing along a heavily fished length of the west coast during a closed period will be fished in the Straits of Juan de Fuca and perhaps again in Puget Sound before it reaches its river.

A fishing season shortened at one end or the other cannot improve matters, since it is likely to produce overcrowding of some parts of the spawning areas and complete destruction of

"an adequate escape of spawning fish"

the runs to other parts. And all such measures are certain to increase the intensity of fishing during the periods at which they are not in force. What is needed is an adequate escape of spawning fish, spread properly through the season in direct proportion to the intensity of the run at any given time.

Exactly what proportion of the run constitutes an adequate escape is not at present known, though the work commenced at Karluk Lake, Alaska, in 1921 by Gilbert and Rich should eventually give a very clear indication. Dr. Gilbert, speaking before a committee of the House of Representatives in 1936, expressed the opinion that a spawning escape of fifty per cent of the total run to any given watershed should, normally, be sufficient to maintain the yield of the run and also provide some safety factor. At present the law on this point in Alaska reads as follows:

"In all creeks, streams, or rivers, or in any other bodies of water in Alaska, over which the United States has jurisdiction, in which salmon run, and in which now or hereafter there exist racks, gateways, or other means by which the number in a run may be counted or estimated, there shall be allowed an escapement of not less than 50 per centum of the total number thereof. In such waters the taking of more than 50 per centum of the run of such fish is hereby prohibited. *It is hereby declared to be the intent and policy of Congress that in all waters of Alaska in which salmon run there shall be an escapement of not less than 50 per centum thereof, and if in any year it shall appear to the Secretary of Commerce that the run of fish in any water has diminished or is diminishing, there shall be required a correspondingly increased escapement of fish therefrom.*"

This law is the essence of conservation and could be applied with advantage, subject to amendment as research proceeds, to all waters where salmon run. Within the last few years there is some indication that the principle is becoming recognised and will gradually be put into effect in British Columbia. The work of Pacific Salmon Fisheries Commission on the Fraser

River is leading this way and there seems good reason to suppose that the investigations of the Fisheries Research Board in the Skeena watershed will eventually provide a base for wise escapement laws farther north. It is difficult not to feel that things are still moving much too slowly, but at least some regard is now being paid to the relationship of escapement to catch. And I believe the time is not too far distant when both the canners and the commercial fishermen will look on the catch as a by-product of the spawning run instead of, as at present, considering the spawning run a by-product of the catch.

One criticism of escapement laws is frequently made by fishermen and too often by fisheries officers also. It is said that a large spawning run does positive harm in that the late-running fish destroy the eggs of the earlier spawners. No doubt some losses do occur in this way, but it is obvious that the loss of eggs of the early spawners cannot possibly be anything approaching one hundred per cent and that the losses from overcrowding in the case of late spawners will be nil. Therefore, the total seeding is bound to be larger in a year of overcrowding than in a year when the escapement is so distributed that no nests are disturbed by subsequent spawners. Gilbert and Rich have argued this point extremely well. After stating their belief that in some years the increase in numbers of progeny resulting from an excessive number of spawners may not compensate for surrendering the economic value of the parents they write: "But we have no evidence that 'overseeding' of the beds ever occurs, with a diminished run in consequence. That the reverse is the case, we have a certain amount of evidence, and need only refer to the quadrennial run on the Fraser River, which persisted throughout historic times despite almost incredible crowding of the spawning grounds during the 'big years.' The more moderate spawning of the intermediate years produced only the limited runs of those years; and when finally the spawning escapement of a big year, because of a catastrophe, was during one season reduced to a fraction of its usual size, the big run disappeared completely and has never been restored.

"As bearing on this point, we have in evidence also the large and small runs of pink salmon (*Oncorhynchus gorbuscha*), which occur in alternate years in virtually every portion of its range. All the members of any run have developed from eggs laid down during the second year previous. Every big year, then, produces a big year, although with this species especially, the streams are crowded to capacity and beyond during years of heavy run. The waste here again is enormous, and the economic phases of the question may well be taken into consideration; but it is well to keep in mind that the net results of such excessive crowding of the streams are in the way of increased runs. To those, therefore, whose duties lie in the examination of spawning grounds, we recommended a certain hesitancy in certifying that the beds are 'fully occupied' by spawners or are 'overseeded.' "

The enforcement of an escapement law will present certain practical difficulties, especially where the runs are made to yield at several different points before reaching the parent stream, but ways of overcoming such difficulties must be found and used, even if they mean the closing of extensive areas or a complete change in fishing methods. There is in any case a great deal to be said against the present practice of catching fish out in the ocean or at some distance from the mouths of their parent streams. Such fishery results in the capture of large numbers of immature fish, which have not attained their full weight. It also produces an inferior quality of fish, since the stomach and intestines are full of food and the digestive action, continuing after death, causes deterioration of the flesh before the fish reaches the cannery. Against these objections, it may be said that it tends to spread the work of making the catch among a greater number of individual fishermen and over a longer season than would be the case if all fish were caught off the mouths of their parent streams.

Though these are primarily economic problems, a tendency to confine the fishery to waters near or within the mouths of rivers would make the application of an escapement law very much simpler. It is essential that the total catch of fish running to any one stream at any time in the season be known and that it be kept properly related to the number of fish escaping. The counting and estimating of the spawners will need a considerable staff of trained observers, and thoroughly efficient methods will only be developed through experience. But basically the scheme is thoroughly practicable, and it is the only one that can be said to be logically bound to achieve its object.

In comparison with the cost of maintaining hatcheries, the cost to the industry of catches limited in this way would be small. If, for instance, the Fraser River canners were limited in any given year so that they packed only 100,000 cases of sockeye instead of 120,000, the fish represented by that reduction would deposit 480 million additional eggs on the spawning beds. Granting that artificial propagation is twice as efficient as natural spawning—which it certainly is not—the hatcheries would have to handle 240 million eggs to achieve a comparable result. This would necessitate the construction of five new hatcheries, each as large as the largest in the Province, and the immediate cost of handling such a quantity of eggs would be in the neighbourhood of $200,000—with nothing allowed for construction, depreciation and maintenance of buildings and equipment, or interest on the capital investment. The reduction in the pack would represent a cost to the industry—or, rather, an investment by the industry—of $240,000.*

Once an escapement law has been put into effect, the game fishery as a by-product of the commercial industry will be safe. Meanwhile, it is essential that the yields and breeding stocks of game fisheries already proved valuable be maintained even at

* 1938 figures.

the cost of reducing commercial fishing in areas where it is likely to affect the runs that make such fisheries. Every resort is dependent upon custom that has been built up slowly and painfully and which may be completely lost by a few bad seasons. The commercial industry is worth about $15,000,000 a year, but to be worth this amount it must use at least a hundred million pounds of salmon, at an average yield of 15 cents a pound. Salmon caught as game fish yield more than ten times as much, and it is evident that any move which diverts the necessary proportion of fish from the less to the greater yield must be economically sound.

It is unfortunate that in a few small details such as this the interests of game and commercial fishermen appear to clash, when the broad interests of both fisheries are identical. Actually, of course, there is no clash even in the small details; the ultimate good of the province, as represented by a sustained maximum cash yield from its resources, is the ultimate good of both fisheries; the commercial fisherman is bound to feel the benefits of any increased value in the sport fishing even if its only result will be to provide greater room for employment in both fisheries. But there are other grounds for misunderstanding. The commercial fisherman feels that the game fisherman's pet, the trout, is a destructive predator—which is perfectly true; he is, but the effect of his depredations has been shown by Hobbs to make itself felt very little where the commercial man believes it to be greatest—in the destruction of eggs—and his destruction of salmon fry may well be balanced, at least, by his destruction of other predators such as sculpins and squawfish. The commercial man feels also that it is unfair and illogical that artificial propagation of trout should be continued when the salmon hatcheries are closed; it is not the easiest thing in the world to understand that trout are subject only to losses in fresh water and so are much cheaper to produce, or that a game fish can be worth more to a workingman than a commercial fish. And while the commercial fisherman is turning over thoughts like these, the game fisherman sees him as an all-devouring monster, destructive and wasteful of fish, serving masters whose only desire is to clean up and get out.

It would be well for both if there could be greater sympathy and better understanding. The commercial fishermen—and I do not mean the cannery owners—seldom become rich; they are forced to employ the methods they use, simply to make what is too often an inadequate living. Most of them are aware of what is happening to the salmon runs, and probably are even more anxious than the game fishermen that effective measures shall be taken before it is too late. Better co-operation between the two interests might do much to bring this about.

Once a proper escapement law is drawn up and adequate means of enforcing it have been found, no fishery and no type of gear, except one that is grossly wasteful of immature fish, can possibly affect the permanence of the runs. But there are threats from two other forms of "development" that must be met. The present wholesale methods of logging and destruction of such limited forest regeneration as takes place is a direct cause of heavy flooding and silting of spawning areas. Hobbs, writing of New Zealand where precipitation and floods are lighter, on the whole, than in British Columbia, states that "all floods tend to be harmful in that they increase the deposition of fine material in redds," and again: "Floods rarely affect the substantial modification of the contours of redds. When they do so they may cause losses considerable enough to account for the partial failure of a year class." It is difficult to imagine anything better calculated to cause floods than clear logging of thousands of acres; and a forest fire sweeping through the débris of such an operation, burning the soil to a fine powder, provides tons of silt ideally suited to the blocking of redds. This is no place for a discussion of methods of controlling logging and forest fires; it is enough to say that there are adequate methods and that the resource provides enough money to put them into effect. Proper control will do a good deal to prevent flood dangers from becoming really acute, but it cannot do much to repair the damage already done. Hundreds of thousands of acres that once fed dozens of streams a controlled flow of water, in summer and winter, are now bare of growth and burned to rock and gravel, so that the water flows off them unchecked in the wet months, producing quick and violent floods in winter and extreme low water in summer. Even in 1938 two or three hundred square miles on Vancouver Island were burned over—thousands of acres for the second or third time within a few years—and there is nothing to guarantee that fire will not pass that way again within the next ten years. Reforestation is vitally necessary; it is the only permanent, complete and reasonably economical remedy. But it is also a slow remedy, especially when reliance is placed on natural regeneration, and it can only come at all if there is complete fire protection. During the past twenty-five years more than fifty million dollars of direct forest revenue, which should have been spent on protective measures, has passed out of the control of the Forestry Department, to be spent for purposes in no way connected with its origin.

While reforestation is taking place and until proper protective measures have been developed, some program of stream control is needed. Really adequate measures are likely to be prohibitively expensive, but certain reasonably economical possibilities suggest themselves; the planting of beaver in certain streams could do much towards conserving water, and many streams could be improved very cheaply by the placing of obstructions calculated to cause log jams at strategic points. Both commercial fishermen and anglers have been altogether too easily persuaded that log jams in streams are harmful rather than beneficial. It is true that an occasional jam throws a stream out of a valuable channel or even obstructs the passage of fish to good spawning areas; but it is safe to say that nine log jams out of ten, or perhaps ninety-nine out of a hundred, are wholly necessary and beneficial. They conserve water in a drought and check its force in flood time. They scour pools, harbour feed for young fish, give cover and protection to spawners and fry and fingerlings. Without them a stream flowing through logged land is no better than a poorly constructed drain.

The second form of "development" that threatens the salmon runs is the use of water power. The storage and use of water for a really large project, where power is a by-product of such major objectives as irrigation, flood control, and erosion control, and which is designed to be beneficial to mankind for as far into the future as man can see, is likely to be sound. But to encourage the damming of rivers by any and every private company for a temporary mining purpose or for a short-lived logging operation is certainly not sound.

This is, undoubtedly, the age of hydro-electric power. Yet in this present year, 1946, one need not be a far-sighted prophet to anticipate an age when water-power will be as far outmoded as ox-power now is. Development of water-power too often necessitates the flooding of potentially productive land, marring of scenery and destruction of valuable fisheries. When it does so, its own value must be closely weighed against the value of what it destroys; and now that hydro-electric power can be considered little more than a temporary asset, its value must be weighed even closely against those of perpetual resources such as the salmon run.

Fortunately, ways and means of counteracting the adverse effects of water-power developments can often be found. The main essential is thorough investigation well in advance of the development—a seemingly logical preliminary that is usually disregarded. The Nimpkish River power project, for instance, would have destroyed all runs of salmon to the finest spawning areas on Vancouver Island, and it is very doubtful whether the resulting employment and production would have matched what was destroyed. Yet the project was abandoned solely because of the difficulty of finding bed-rock at the proposed site. The present development at Elk Falls, in the Campbell

River, will not endanger any commercial runs comparable to those of the Nimpkish, but it does threaten the future of the famous tyee run. It would probably not be difficult in this case, by taking a few simple precautions, to overcome the danger. Yet the project is being forced ahead without any proper investigation at all.

These are major problems in the development and proper use of natural resources and as such, though they affect its subject, are somewhat beyond the scope of this book. The real reason for stating them at all is that they usually seem to be beyond, and left well outside, the scope of everyone who should properly be concerned with them. But I feel there is the strongest hope for the future in the setting up of such bodies as the Pacific Salmon Fisheries Commission, at present investigating the sockeye salmon runs of the Fraser and in the sort of information that will come from Dr. A. L. Pritchard's investigation of the Skeena watershed. There is clear precedent for the success of such work in the success of the International Halibut Commission, which led to legislation that has already placed a dangerously exhausted resource on a permanent yield basis. Salmon research faces difficulties at once greater and smaller than those solved by the Halibut Commission, but the problems unquestionably admit of complete solution. The only factors that can cause failure are international jealousy, political interference or the failure of canners and fishermen to co-operate.

## REFERENCES

Babcock, J. P. *et al.* Report of the International Fisheries Commission Appointed Under the Northern Pacific Halibut Treaty. U.S.B.F., Doc. 1073, 1930.

Babcock, J. P. Fish Traps in Alaskan Waters. Hearings, 74th Cong., 2nd Sess., on H.R. 4254 and H.R. 8213, Jan. 15th and 16th, 1936.

Gilbert, C. H., and Rich, W. H. Investigations Concerning the Red Salmon Runs to Karluk River, Alaska, U.S.B.F., Doc. 1021, 1927.

Laws and Regulations for Protection of Fisheries of Alaska. Dept. Commerce Circ. No. 251, 1938.

Rich, W. H. Growth and Degree of Maturity of Chinook Salmon in the Ocean. U.S.B.F., Doc. 974, 1925.

# PART FIVE

*General Again*

# Enemies & Diseases of
# Game Fish

**SCULPINS.**

PORTSMEN are always likely to be more interested in predator control than in other forms of culture or preservation of their sport, perhaps largely because such control offers many of the same pleasures and satisfactions that are offered by the sport itself. In British Columbia, predator control—which is quite a different thing from predator extinction—offers some opportunity for sport and very great opportunities for improving sport, and it is a pity that game fishing is so generally available as to make coarse fishing of slight interest. Hunters in the United States and in many parts of Canada have set an example to anglers by vigorous—perhaps at times too vigorous—attacks upon crows, ravens, hawks, owls and other predators. But hunters have limited opportunities for following their sport and usually very short seasons, so that predator control offers a welcome opportunity for the expenditure of ammunition when guns would otherwise be resting among oily rags in leather cases.

That predators have an important effect on game-fish populations in British Columbia is shown by the expected survival and growth to maturity of only 0.25% of the salmon fry hatched, and less than 5% of the trout fry hatched. A great part of these losses would continue in spite of perfect predator control; the 95% loss of trout fry planted in a lake containing no predatory coarse fish is very largely caused by the depredations of the yearling trout that will make the future fishing in the lake, and so must be accepted and allowed for. But, generally speaking, some predator control is likely to be feasible and beneficial in most native-stock waters.

It is probably safe to say that the most destructive predators are fish; in the fresh-water areas of British Columbia the char, sculpins (*Cottus asper* and others) and squawfish (*Ptychocheilus*) have a share in reducing the chances of survival of both salmon and trout, and the trout themselves prey more or less extensively on both salmon fry and trout fry.

In view of the fact that practically all losses to predators occur after the development of young fish to the free-swimming stage, it is evident that the really successful predators must have exceptional speed, or power of concealment, or other habit to account for their success. I have watched large trout lying for hours on end with salmon fry and fingerlings all around them and within inches of them, yet making no attempt to attack. And, at the end of a watching period I have caught the same trout by dropping a fly over them, and have found nearly always that their bellies contained nothing at all, or at most a small quantity of insects.

I have caught many trout in rivers swarming with humpback and other salmon fry in early stages of development, and have found in their stomachs occasionally a glut of fry, more frequently small numbers of fry, quite frequently one or two fry mixed with other food, and very often a few insects or no food at all. The trout is probably the fastest of the predators, yet it is fairly obvious that he cannot succeed in catching small fish under all conditions, and that a very considerable proportion of individuals are either disinclined or unable to take advantage of conditions sufficiently favourable to enable other individuals to catch fry. There can be no doubt that the trout is a predator, but it seems very questionable that he is a sufficiently capable one to account for a very high proportion of the losses that take place.

I have not sufficient experience of the habits of other predatory fish to make even such a guess as this as to their relative efficiency, and no very satisfactory information seems to be available. The bullhead or sculpin (*Cottus asper*) is able to hide completely by settling himself down into mud or sand or between rocks, and I have, very rarely, seen specimens only three or four inches long dart up from such concealment to seize trout or salmon fry. Squawfish have a very evil reputation and are big enough and ugly enough to justify it. But the whole question of the relative efficiency of fish alleged to be predators is worth very close examination before the wholesale destruction of any species can be recommended. There can be no doubt that predator species exercise a very considerable control over the relative abundance of one another, and it might well happen that the destruction of one species would lead to a tremendous increase in the numbers of another far more dangerous species. A further, perhaps more remote, possibility is that predators are valuable in preventing deterioration of the salmon runs through hybridisation. It may well be argued that cross-fertilisation is most likely to occur when eggs expressed by a female fail, for one reason or another, to lodge in the egg pocket provided for them. So long as there is a decent abundance of predators there is very little chance that eggs drifting free in this way will be left to hatch.

Predator fish must also be considered both as competitors of desirable species and as forage providers. Small suckers are very generally believed to be valuable forage fish, and there cannot be much doubt that trout consume large numbers of young squawfish and chub and sculpins as well. But it is also arguable that such fish consume, either directly or indirectly, large quantities of more desirable forage than they provide. It is always worth remembering that the native predators were present and numerous in the "old days" of spectacular abundance of trout and salmon, that the natural balance of conditions then existing had produced that abundance. This suggests that until full information is available, control should be confined to attempts to readjust the balance that man has thrown out by selective, and too often excessive, pursuit of the more desirable species.

An experiment in predator control is at present being carried on at Cultus Lake, where the physical circumstances of the watershed, and a previous knowledge of survival figures to be expected, are likely to make possible at least some definite conclusions. An attempt is being made to reduce by netting the number of predators in the lake to the lowest possible figure, and it was hoped that by this means the survival rate might be increased from three or four per cent to twenty-five per cent. Though the experiment is not by any means complete, results so far suggest that a survival rate of about thirteen per cent will be the maximum obtained by such control; it seems fairly evident that some other factor, probably lack of available feed for the fry, enters at this point to increase mortality.

Whatever the results of the Cultus Lake experiment, it is unlikely that any means of coarse-fish control at once fairly complete and reasonably economical can be found for the large, open waters of the province. Netting must always be an expensive operation and would have to be conducted on a considerable scale and continued over a long period of time to have a permanent effect. No chemical has yet been found that can be relied on to kill off coarse fish without danger to commercial and game fish and other valuable forms of life. So there is not much doubt that fish and game clubs can do a valuable service by encouraging members to kill as many coarse fish as possible in most waters. At best such effort could not do more than readjust the balance that has been destroyed by selective game and commercial fisheries. And in addition to benefiting anglers themselves by increasing the numbers of trout available to them, it would do much to earn the gratitude of the commercial fisherman and make reparations for whatever damage the privileged trout may cause.*

A group of under-water predators that do some damage are the larvae of the larger flies such as stoneflies and dragonflies. The dragonfly larva can hide himself very cleverly and has been seen by many observers to take trout fry. But there is not much doubt that the value of such predators as these in providing forage, and more particularly in providing fishing of a good quality, vastly outweighs any damage they may do.

The warm-blooded predators are very numerous and many have bad reputations, sometimes deservedly, but more often undeservedly, and some that are probably quite efficient predators are so attractive in their habits and make so important a part of the angler's scene that they deserve every consideration. They divide fairly naturally into two main classes, those that prey on fry or fingerlings and those that prey on larger fish, and each class includes both mammals and birds.

Of the birds, the American merganser has probably the worst reputation among both anglers and commercial fishermen. In a detailed bulletin recently published, Munro and Clemens do much to correct this impression. There is no doubt that the mergansers take considerable quantities of salmon fry and even fingerlings when these are readily available, but remains of young salmon or trout or char occurred in only 74 of 363 stomachs examined, from areas all over the province. Sculpins

* The Skeena River salmon investigations, started during the war and still going on, seem likely to yield valuable information on predators.

are the principal food of the merganser and were found in 120 of the stomachs examined; it seems altogether probable that this more than balances the damage done to salmon and trout. At the height of the spawning season, mergansers feed almost entirely on salmon eggs, but it seems logical to suppose that an extremely high proportion of the eggs taken are waste eggs. Unburied eggs can have practically no chance of survival, and eggs buried to a depth of eight inches or more under gravel can scarcely be considered available to mergansers or any other predators. It would seem that the merganser, to obtain fertile eggs that would normally have survived, must dive down upon the nest and scoop up as many as possible virtually at the moment of deposition, before the female has begun to cover them. It is conceivable that they do so, though I have not seen any observer's record of the process.

Munro and Clemens show very clearly the involved nature of predator relationship in British Columbia. It is extremely difficult to arrive at clear-cut conclusions, but there can be very little doubt that the conclusion of these authors—that the American merganser in its present abundance is not a menace to commercial and game fish—is essentially sound. They suggest control of any undue abundance if a competent survey shows it to be necessary, but also point out that any attempts to exterminate the merganser would probably have undesirable results. A little unprejudiced observation will show anyone interested that mergansers are most abundant on coast streams not in the spring, when the fry are most readily available, nor even in the fall, when a great many salmon are depositing eggs, but during the winter months, when waste eggs and rotting carcasses of dead salmon make a readily available supply of food.

A bird whose economic status is probably quite close to that of the merganser is the heron. I am afraid I must admit an affection and admiration for the heron that probably nullifies anything I say about him; I would as soon fish alongside him as alongside any fisherman I know. But it is true that herons in British Columbia are far more generally frequenters of tide flats and beaches than of fresh-water streams. They take salmon and trout—often fairly large trout—but it is difficult to say in what quantities. From what observations I have made I should judge that of the salmonidae the small trout and cohoe fry and finger-lings are the most frequent victims, but sculpins are far more available and far more frequently taken than salmonidae in estuarial waters, while various small marine fishes are probably most available along the beaches. Fortunately, the heron is little persecuted so far, and it is devoutly to be hoped that he will continue to be unmolested except in those few places where it can be clearly shown that he does serious damage, near hatcheries and perhaps along small streams in time of drought.

Cormorants and gulls are salt-water predators and almost certainly account for heavy losses of young migrants. Cormorants are not, normally, numerous in fresh water, but I have seen them on fresh-water pools in the Campbell. They are extremely fast under water and can catch and swallow fairly large fish. They probably do a good deal to control predator fish.

The list of ducks that will take eggs or small fish is a very long one, and some of the other diving species of birds may well be at least as efficient predators as the merganser. Mallard and goldeneyes are numerous and busy on the spawning beds during and after spawning time but probably feed chiefly on waste eggs and fragments of dead salmon. The early salt-water losses of salmon that migrate to the sea in their first year—all humpbacks, nearly all dog salmon and a high proportion of spring salmon—must be very large and are probably concentrated in the first few weeks of salt-water life. The salt-water diving ducks and even the tiny murrelets and grebes undoubtedly cause a considerable proportion of these losses, but their efficiency must be dependent, to some extent at least, upon the attacks of predator fish to drive the small salmon towards the surface or into shallow water. It seems altogether likely that no predator breathing air can be as efficient, at least in attacks on small fish, as one that takes its oxygen from water.

Loons are predators and efficient ones, but they are such attractive birds that no fisherman would care to see their numbers greatly reduced. Most small lakes have a pair of nesting loons in the summer time and the larger lakes may have two or three pairs; the present abundance is not too great in most localities, though it would probably become so but for the attacks of bald eagles. The kingfisher is another attractive and efficient predator. Hewitt estimates that a kingfisher will kill about 1,500 small trout in a year, and this estimate seems reasonable if other species of fish are not readily available; but I have not noticed any excessive abundance of kingfishers in British Columbian waters, so it is logical to suppose that some natural force controls their numbers.

Crows and snakes can do serious damage when fry and fingerlings are cut off in small pools by drought, and owls may also do some damage in conditions of this sort. But the fault is with the conditions rather than the predators, and it is quite obvious that fish cut off by drought stand in any case a relatively poor chance of survival. Better stream control and more intelligent forest control would do more to save fish than predator control is ever likely to do.

The most splendid of the bird predators are the ospreys and the eagles. Ospreys are not too common even in the unsettled parts of the coast, and no one who has watched them fish would wish them to be less common. No osprey should ever be shot unless there is abundant evidence of an abnormal increase in numbers, which is not likely to occur. The bald eagle makes the osprey fish harder by frequently robbing him of his prey, and he also fishes for herrings, eulachans and salmon at all stages of growth from yearlings to spawning fish. He is not altogether a good fisherman though, and takes a great number of spent and dead fish. Whatever losses he causes are amply compensated by his control of loons, mergansers and all diving ducks.

One of the most interesting of all predators is the little water ouzel or dipper. Watching him bob up and down along the banks of a stream, or fly from rock to rock, one would never suspect him of designs upon anything larger than insects. But I have watched him often, swimming about in an eddy with his head down, searching, then diving quickly to chase, and catch, trout or salmon fry. He is, of course, in no way a serious predator, and he takes at least as many small bullheads as he does trout or salmon fry. But he is one of the most attractive birds of all the streams, and it is somehow satisfying to know that he, too, is a fisherman.

The four-footed predators are many—bears, coons, mink, otter, marten, fisher, stray house cats and even muskrats take fish when they can get them. Many of these are valuable fur bearers; the sight of any one of them is a greater thing in a fisherman's day than a half dozen trout or a ten-pound steelhead, and few of them are sufficiently numerous to do serious damage. It is safe enough to leave all of them, except the house cats which have absolutely no business outside a cage or a house, to the control of other forces than any simple desire to reduce predators. I feel in honour bound to say a negative word for the otter. Many naturalists have accused the otter of slaughtering fish regularly "for fun," in some sort of blood frenzy, taking a single bite out of each and leaving the carcass to rot. Three times I have been able to watch otters fishing, and each time a single fish was killed, brought to shore and eaten. I have seen the evidence of such restraint and unwasteful consumption perhaps dozens of times, and though I have seen live fish marked by their escape from otters I have never found evidence of so wholesale a slaughter as the naturalists describe. That something of the sort does take place I do not doubt; but it is not a regular, nor even a common occurrence, and when it does occur an observant man will probably be able to see that some other factor than a simple blood lust has been working—perhaps the stimulation of a female's presence at mating time or the sudden surprise of finding a large number of fish scattering before a dive. I have never found reason to believe that it is the nature of any predator to be wasteful.

The Dominion Government has attempted to control the number of hair seals both by placing a bounty on them and by shooting some numbers on the breeding grounds. A considerable number of sea lions have also been shot. Both these animals are major predators, preying on adult fish, and there is not much in nature to exercise a very vigorous control over their numbers. Complete extermination has not been attempted and would certainly not be desirable, as without the seals and sea lions many predatory fish of no commercial value would increase disproportionately, and their control would be a very difficult and costly matter. The desirable extent of predator control of this sort may be ascertained very accurately and easily by an examination of the feeding habits of the predators and calculation of their total abundance. Any reduction should be related as exactly as possible to the reduction of salmon and cod and other desirable species by fishing.

A really spectacular predator—if he is a predator—is the blackfish. He is the fourth of Herman Melville's octavo whales, the killer whale, and properly not the blackfish at all, though he is almost invariably so called in British Columbia. Blackfish are believed by fishermen to take great quantities of mature salmon, and there is a superstition that when the blackfish have visited a bay there will be no more good fishing for at least a day or two. It is possible that non-feeding fish such as tyees do go down to hide in the weeds when the blackfish are near, and perhaps stay there for an appreciable length of time. But I have caught feeding cohoes in Duncan Bay until dark on a night when the blackfish were right in amongst them, and caught more on the very next morning after the visit of the predators. If feeding springs and cohoes go off the feed for a couple of days whenever they see or hear blackfish, it is a bit difficult to understand how they make such tremendously rapid growth. Probably the blackfish does take salmon; the only stomach examination of which I have heard a report revealed not salmon but a seal, which suggests that here again may be a valuable means of control. However that may be, I hope blackfish will never be driven altogether from the inside waters. The sight of a school—cows and bulls and youngsters—snorting their heavy way down Discovery Passage, each dorsal fin rolling up and over and down again in the slow arc above the gleaming back, is a pretty fine thing. And when one or two individuals of the school choose to jump right clear of the water, showing their pure white bellies and sixteen or eighteen feet of length, slapping their full ten or twelve tons back down on the water, it's just plain exciting.

The great number and variety of the predators are probably their best defense. As predators they are nearly all interrelated, and it is quite evident that many are extremely valuable in providing the cheapest form of control over more dangerous species than their own. Most of them were far more numerous when the salmon runs were at their height than they are today, and in thousands of generations they were not able, as man has been able within a quarter of a century, to deplete the runs. Until the case against any individual species has been proved to the hilt, it will be as well if control is not allowed to go beyond the point of matching its numbers to the decreased numbers of fish available. Control of this sort is essential and should have been exercised from the start of the fishery—a logical compensation by man for what he himself takes. But it would be a poorer and a duller world if even one species—even the squawfish, say, or the house cats—were exterminated.

Trout and salmon are subject to a considerable number of diseases and to the attacks of many parasites. Both diseases and parasites are far more likely to cause serious trouble under hatchery conditions than under natural conditions, but they can and do occur under natural conditions, and anglers are frequently puzzled and worried by their manifestations.

The most serious disease of salmonidae is furunculosis (*Bacillus salmonicida*), which has affected Atlantic salmon and brown trout under natural conditions in England and Scotland and has caused heavy losses in hatcheries all over the world. It has been found under natural conditions in the Elk River, near Fernie, British Columbia, where it has attacked Rocky Mountain whitefish, some cutthroat trout and probably also Dolly Varden char. Under hatchery conditions in the province it has attacked springs and cohoes, hybrid Pacific salmon, brown, cutthroat and rainbow trout. It has been shown that rainbow trout are highly resistant to the disease, but they are not immune and can act as carriers. There is some evidence that Pacific salmon are also less susceptible than are brown trout and Atlantic salmon—the Atlantic salmon is particularly susceptible—but it seems probable that all salmonidae are sufficiently susceptible to contract the disease even under natural conditions.

Furunculosis is a bacterial disease and is a general infection. It frequently appears as open sores or boils all over the body, but may also attack kidneys and intestines without showing much exterior effect. The disease may be carried by food or by water that has passed over infected fish, or may be passed by a fish to other fish inhabiting the same water, or spread by carriers showing no external signs of the disease. It is to some extent controlled by floods and by low water temperatures.

Hatchery raised fish, while not necessarily more susceptible to furunculosis than wild fish, are, from the conditions under which they are raised, more likely to be attacked. Because the fish from a single hatchery may be sent out to several watersheds, and because it is difficult to detect carriers and, at times, infected fish, the planting of hatchery raised fish probably entails the greatest danger of a spread of the disease in British

Columbia. Warm-blooded animals are not susceptible and there is not much risk of the transference of the disease from water-shed to watershed by birds or other migrants. Pre-eyed ova may carry the disease but can be disinfected by treatment with acriflavine, according to British investigators.

The high resistance to the disease shown by rainbow trout, and the distinct possibility that cutthroat trout and pure-bred Pacific salmon are less susceptible to it than are brown trout, Eastern char and Atlantic salmon, suggest that the native species are the only ones that should be handled in British Columbian hatcheries. Many hatcheries in the United States have suffered from the disease at one time or another, and if importations from across the line are at any time necessary it is quite obvious that they should be absolutely confined to shipments of properly disinfected ova. It is possible that in exactly the right conditions furunculosis might get a hold on valuable waters in British Columbia and do really significant damage.

Other bacterial diseases such as gill disease, fin rot and ulcer disease attack hatchery trout fairly frequently, usually with less serious results than in the case of furunculosis. They may also occur among wild fish, but have not so far proved as dangerous as furunculosis. But bacterial diseases are usually very responsive to any abnormally favourable conditions, and their reaction to new environment is more or less unpredict-able; there cannot be much doubt that all shipments from hatcheries should be subjected to rigid examination and sam-pling, and that hatchery work should be conducted only under the supervision of properly trained—not merely experienced—men.

Anglers are frequently worried when they find parasitic worms in either the flesh or the intestines of the trout they catch. Such infestation is fairly common in trout of the smaller Vancouver Island lakes during the summer months, and though it may detract somewhat from a fisherman's pleasure in his catch it is normally not at all serious; it does not even make the fish unfit for consumption, since the parasites are destroyed in cooking and in any case would not find the human animal a suitable host—not that this thought is likely to be of any particular comfort to the prospective consumer.

Most parasitic worms of this type are using the trout as an intermediate host; the trout takes them when they are infesting molluscs or amphipods or other feed, raises them through a further stage of life history, and passes them on to a final host when he in his turn becomes the food of certain birds. Though presumably they cause some drain on the fish's strength, this is not normally very evident; I have caught many Kamloops trout in native-stock waters such as Little River, which were in perfect condition, fought well, looked beautiful, and left nothing to be desired when they came to the table, though their intestines were heavily infested with both round and tape worms. Contrary to the general rule, infestation of this type is more common in wild fish than in hatchery fish, since artificial feeding and the protection of hatchery trout from predatory birds prevent completion of the life cycle.

There are several forms of external parasites which attack fish; of these *Gyrodactylus*, which usually attacks the fins, is the most serious and may do a great deal of damage in a hatchery. The external parasites with which the angler is likely to be most familiar are the "sea lice" of the migratory fish, which are usually copepod crustaceans (*Lepeophtheirus salmonis*). They occur on most salmon in salt water, and are generally clustered at the base of the anal fin, but they quickly drop off in fresh water. This last is the point of greatest interest, since anglers usually judge the degree of freshness of steelhead in streams by the presence or absence of sea lice. Angling writers are frequently inclined to state that a certain fish was only "twelve hours"—or, more rarely, thirty-six or forty-eight hours —"out of the sea, since the sea lice were still on him." Actually, the Fishery Board for Scotland showed as long ago as 1906 that sea lice would cling to grilse for four or five days in fresh water, and probably the safe conclusion is that a fish with the sea lice on him has not been in fresh water for more than a week. The finding of sea lice on a fish is a very real satisfaction, though steelhead frequently remain in first-rate condition long after the sea lice have dropped away.

The fungus disease, *Saprolegnia parasitica*, differs from these other parasites in that it is a plant rather than an animal. It is considered that *Saprolegnia* was originally a saprophyte, developing only on dead animal matter, and that it has only comparatively recently adopted the parasitic habit. This emphasises the fact that normally *Saprolegnia* is only able to attack fish or eggs that are likely to die in any case. There cannot be much doubt that it is practically always present in British Columbian waters, or that in spawning time the water of salmon streams is full of the infection. The chief danger is caused by its attacks upon eggs that are injured or dead, since it grows upon these and soon spreads its white threads over healthy eggs, to choke them and attack them as soon as they become weakened. The best control for the disease is undoubtedly stream control, which would prevent silting of redds and the death of eggs. Good and adequate spawning grounds are also a factor in control, and there cannot be much doubt that bird and fish predators which quickly clean up any eggs that are improperly buried and therefore moribund are very valuable in checking the spread of the growth.

Probably the most interesting and important feature of predators and the diseases and parasites of fish is their frequently close interrelationship. The control of any one of the three is a complex problem which may very well involve the other two also; it is even possible, for instance, that the presence of a sufficient number of warm-blooded scavengers such as ducks, eagles, crows and bears would materially assist in the control of furunculosis if by some misfortune the disease ever got a firm hold in British Columbia. One of the best possible forms of predator, disease and parasite control is rigid prohibition of the introduction of non-native species. The native species have proved themselves well able to resist predators, diseases and parasites already present in the Province. Non-natives may prove to be competitors and predators, and may introduce parasites or diseases to which the native stock is not highly resistant.

It is difficult to imagine any problem more involved or difficult—or more important—than the control of natural balances of any sort. Civilisation must always upset the balance and is seldom able of itself to produce the mechanism necessary to readjustment; but nearly always there is a natural mechanism ready to hand and by controlling it and directing it, readjustment can be made. If only because it is difficult to guess what problems the future may set, the extermination of any predator —even if there exists one that at present serves no useful purpose—should be studiously avoided.

## REFERENCES

Blake, Isobel. External Disinfection of Fish Ova, etc. Fisheries, Scotland, Salmon Fish, 1930, No. 2, 1931.

Blake, Isobel, and Clark, J. C. Observations in Experimental Infection of Trout by *B. Salmonicida*. Fisheries, Scotland, Salmon Fish, 1931, No. 7, 1932.

Davis, H. J. Care and Diseases of Trout. U.S.B.F. Investigational Report, No. 35, 1937.

Duff, D. C. B., and Stewart, Beatrice J. Studies on Furunculosis of Fish in British Columbia. Cont. Can. Biol. Fish. VIII, No. 8, Series A, Gen. No. 35, 1933.

Hewitt, E. R. *Better Trout Streams*. Scribner's, New York, 1931.

Jenkins, J. Travis. *Fishes of the British Isles*. Warne & Co., London, 1925.

Melville, Herman. *Moby Dick*, 1851.

Munro, J. A., and Clemens, W. A. The American Merganser in British Columbia and Its Relation to the Fish Population. Biol. Bd. Can., Bull. 55, 1937.

Williamson, Isobel J. F. Furunculosis of the Salmonidae. Fisheries, Scotland, Salmon Fish, 1928, No. 5, 1928.

Williamson, Isobel J. F. Further Observations on Furunculosis of the Salmonidae, 1928. Fisheries, Scotland, Salmon Fish, 1929, No. 1, 1929.

# 11

## Tackle & Equipment
## for British Columbia

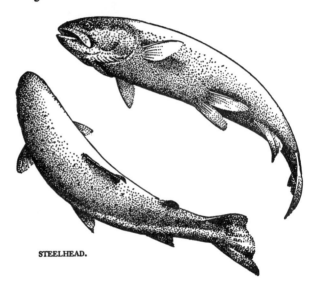

STEELHEAD.

CHOICE of fishing tackle and methods is, obviously, dependent upon the type of fish one hopes to catch and the type of water in which it is found. But it is also dependent upon the physical and mental characteristics of the man fishing and perhaps, above all, upon his early training and experience. It may be possible to show very clearly that a certain method of using a certain type of tackle should yield a greater pleasure per minute, per day or per season than other methods and tackle. But an angler who is used to the less satisfying method and tackle will not always find it easy to make the change; until he has attained at least a degree of proficiency in the use of the new method he is likely to find greater pleasure in his old ways. I have known a number of men who have made the change successfully, even quite late in life, but not without some effort. And the greater the proficiency with the old method the greater the effort needed to give it up.

Broadly speaking, what is true of changes between method and method is fairly true also within methods, between a stiff rod and a limber one—it used to be between split cane and greenheart—between dry fly and wet, between American tackle and English, and so on. In Canada, especially, there must always be discussion of the relative merits of American and English tackle, and there is not much doubt that such discussion serves many useful purposes; to attempt to avoid it in a book of this type would be a mistake.

I think that most anglers, whatever their own preferences or prejudices, are willing to agree that fly fishing—for trout and salmon, at all events—offers greater opportunities for the use and development of skill than does any other method. Since fly fishing also keeps the angler busy with an enjoyable and difficult task—that of casting and working or drifting his fly— whether or no he is catching fish, it is probably arguable that use of this method yields a greater amount of pleasure and satisfaction for each fish caught than does any other method yet discovered.

The basic methods of fly fishing are two: Dry fly, in which the fly is usually cast upstream and allowed to float down with the current, and wet fly, in which the fly is cast downstream and across, allowed to sink, and worked round in the current by the draw of the line. In fairly recent years two other methods have been developed: Nymph fishing, in which a sunk fly is cast upstream and allowed to drift down to feeding fish as though it were a dry fly; and greased-line fishing, in which the fly is normally cast across and slightly downstream on a slack line, supported just under the film of the surface by the floating line, and fished round to the angler's bank without any artificial movement from the draw of the line. All these methods have their earnest disciples, and I suppose that any fly fisherman must inevitably prefer one to the others; but I do not feel there is much room for controversy over the respective merits of each method as a sporting means of catching fish. Each is designed to fit certain conditions, and each in its ideal conditions is an effective and truly satisfying method; a good fly fisherman is one who can fish all four methods at least competently, though he may excel only in the use of one or two. The purist is merely one who elects frequently to deny himself a lot of pleasure.

There is a good deal in this matching of methods to conditions. When trout can be seen rising well to surface feed, practically begging for the dry fly, it is wasteful of sport and pleasure to take them on a wet fly. When they are bulging, taking nothing at all on the surface, response to a dry fly will be merely a lucky chance, and the nymph or the wet fly is what they should have. When there is a stretch of really fast broken water to be fished, searching with the dry fly becomes a chore; it is wet-fly water good enough to make for the rhythm of movement that can produce the wet-fly man's ecstasy. And if at some time the trout and conditions of water call for a fly fished near the surface, yet slowly and with only the movement that the current gives it, or if the summer steelhead are lying dourly in low water, then it is surely wasteful of opportunity and pleasure to know nothing of the greased-line method.

In some ways the different methods of fly fishing fit different temperaments in anglers. In dry-fly and nymph fishing, delicate and precise casting, steadiness and accuracy of striking and a fair knowledge of entomology are important; in greased-line fishing long and well-controlled casting is essential, but the greatest test of skill comes in the working of the fly and perhaps also in the holding of the hand from the strike, for the hook is set—perhaps moments after the fish has taken—by the pull of the current on a line that was kept slack all through the fishing of the cast. The demands of wet-fly fishing vary; sometimes, but not always, one must cast well. Generally it is necessary to have a good eye for water, for breaks and eddies and changes of current where the fish may lie. Quite often the fly must be subtly worked, deeper or nearer the surface, fast or slowly or not at all. And the river may also demand of a man that he be strong and steady on his feet, courageous and skilful to move to where he wishes to be.

I have written nothing of the playing of the fish. There can be no doubt that fish hooked on the fly, wet or dry, are freer to fight hard than those hooked by any other method. But the very reason for preferring fly fishing to all other methods is that the difficulties and demands of casting, knowing the ways of the fish, working or drifting the fly and striking are such that the playing of the fish becomes a relatively unimportant matter, though it remains a sufficiently vigorous performance to make a fitting climax.

Probably the supposed difficulty of casting a fly does more than anything else to keep men fishing worms, and salmon eggs and spinners and other unnecessarily clumsy baits and lures. I am not going to attempt to describe how to cast—that has already been as well done as it can be, in many fishing books— but I should like to say enough to show that casting is not really difficult. Anyone with a fair sense of timing can, within a week of first touching a rod, become proficient enough to go out and catch fish on the fly. The essentials are the right tackle, an intelligent teacher and a little daily practice. It is impossible to cast a fly satisfactorily without a proper fly line, since it is the weight of the line that does all the work; it is almost impossible to learn to cast in a year or so of haphazard flogging, even with good tackle; and it is impossible to learn the timing properly without a certain amount of practice, preferably on dry land. The fundamental secret of the over-head cast, which is the orthodox base of all casting, is that the back cast, which throws the line out behind the fisherman, is just as important as the forward cast which sets the fly on the water. The back cast must be made with sufficient force and lift to drive the line out straight behind; having done this, wait with the rod held perpendicular, as nearly as possible, then drive forward exactly as the line straightens out behind, but with slightly less force than was used in the back cast, since the line is already in motion and has only to be lifted from the air instead of from water or the ground. Practice is needed to learn the exact force necessary for both casts and the exact moment at which to start the rod forward, but the essential movements are essentially simple.

Fishing in most western waters demands knowledge of at least one cast besides the overhead—the roll or spey cast. This also is a simple affair, dependent chiefly on timing, but too many fishermen either have not heard of it or do not bother to learn it. It is simply a lift of the rod to bring fly and line free on the surface of the water, followed by a drive forward and down to roll the line out in a loop in front of the angler, without allowing the fly to pass behind him at all. Streams and lakes where bushes and trees come down close to the water's edge are almost impossible to fish properly without knowledge of this cast. The underhand cast, made exactly as the overhead but with the rod travelling parallel to the ground, is also useful, and the angler who is not ambidextrous would do well to learn to cast backhanded. Two other casts that serve as substitutes for or variations from the roll cast are the angle cast and the steeple cast. In the angle cast—which I have taken the liberty of naming myself since I have never heard of a name for it—the back cast is made along a line parallel to the bank of the river, but the forward cast is driven out at an angle to the line of the back cast, so that the fly falls well out in the stream. The steeple cast I have never seen made by any fishermen, and I have only been able to teach myself to do it in a clumsy, half successful way; the principle of it is that the line, instead of travelling out behind the fisherman, is driven straight up into the air above him and brought forward from there into a perfect cast. With all due modesty, I may say that I shall believe in the possibilities of the steeple cast only when I have seen them demonstrated.

Some men hesitate to start out upon a fly-fishing career because they believe that the tackle is necessarily very expensive. It is perfectly true that a certain minimum of equipment is needed, but it is possible to make up a thoroughly serviceable outfit for twenty dollars; one can find a workmanlike split-cane fly rod for ten dollars—still less for a greenheart or a second-hand split-cane—and for about two dollars a reel that will do all that is needed of it. The line is important, but five dollars will buy a double-tapered vacuum-dressed fly-line of good quality spliced to forty or fifty yards of backing, and the remaining three dollars are enough for a starting assortment of flies and casts. The fisherman who has to mind his dollars and cents will take good care of such an outfit and, with the addition of a few flies and casts from time to time, it will serve him well for many years. As hobbies and sports go these days, this does not seem a terrible outlay.*

On the other hand, one cannot usefully spend more than sixty or seventy dollars on a trout fly rod; that amount will buy one as good as any made; or much more than $15 for a good reel; or much more than $10 for a perfect line; which is a total of less than one hundred dollars for a first-rate outfit. The rich man can indulge in almost unlimited expenditure upon flies and casts, of course, and upon more and more outfits ranging slightly in weight and use from his original, but he will probably only make himself more comfortable, not more efficient, than his less fortunate brother.

I do not wish to suggest by this that it is a mistake to spend money on good tackle and on rods of varying power and

* Postwar prices would be about double those given above. But the last remark still applies.

weight with reels and lines to match, only that it is not essential to the enjoyment or efficient practice of fly fishing. I have invested my share of hard-earned money in tackle, and do not regret it. To have rod and tackle exactly suited to the water, the fish and the day is to add something to the pleasure, if not to the efficiency, of performance. And in a country with types of fly fishing as varied as there are in British Columbia an outfit of three fly rods is probably the minimum with which this can be achieved. I have found that the following rods are about right:

| Length | Weight | Fish | Waters | Methods | Max. useful cast |
|--------|--------|------|--------|---------|------------------|
| 8½ to 9 ft. | 5 oz. | Cutthroat trout Kamloops trout | Small streams, small lakes, all easy water | Dry fly, wet fly, or nymph | 60 ft. |
| 9½ to 10 ft. | 6 to 8 oz. | Cutthroat Kamloops Cohoes and summer steelhead (rarely) | Most lakes and rivers | General dry fly, wet fly, in heavy water or windy weather | 75 ft. |
| 11 to 12 ft. | 12 to 13 oz. | Kamloops (rarely) Summer steelhead Cohoe salmon | At Little River for Kamloops. Any water for cohoe and steelhead | Ideal greased-line rod. Comfortable with any wet fly up to 2/0 | 90 ft. |

Actually, the intermediate rod, particularly if it is a good powerful ten-footer weighing eight ounces or more, can be made to do the work of all three. And on the other side of the picture, one might add three more fly rods and still not have too many:

| Length | Weight | Fish | Waters | Methods | Max. useful cast |
|--------|--------|------|--------|---------|------------------|
| 7 to 7½ ft. | 3 oz. | Cutthroat Kamloops | Very small and brushy streams | Wet or dry fly | 45 ft. |
| 12 to 13 ft. | 12 to 13 oz. | Kamloops Cutthroat | Large and difficult lakes | Wet fly | 75 ft. |
| 13 to 14 ft. | 20 to 24 oz. | Cohoe salmon Summer and winter steelhead | Big rivers and salt water | Wet fly | 115 ft. |

But these, with the possible exception of the last, are rods that the average fisherman might seldom use. A little seven-foot rod is unquestionably a handy tool for poking around the small, heavily bushed streams that sometimes hold good fish, but the fishing in such streams is seasonal, requiring rather a precise local knowledge, and the angler who fishes them at all frequently needs no one to tell him which tackle to use. The long lake rod can scarcely be considered a necessity, though the angler with a good wrist and arm will find it gives him a considerable advantage in style and comfort in lakes where good working of the fly is important. The heavy, double-handed rod has an advantage over a single-handed twelve-foot rod in working a cohoe fly in salt water, and perhaps also in covering a fair sized steelhead stream in the spring or early summer months. It may also be a more comfortable tool for the man who feels that he is not powerful enough to handle the single-handed eleven- and twelve-foot rods that have become so popular in the past few years. But these are made in several weights, and usually with plenty of butt below the reel for a second hand, if necessary. And the advantage of having one hand free for the line is an important one.

All six of these rods, except possibly the long lake rod—which, I believe, is purely an English development—may be found somewhere in the catalogues of either English or American makers, and most of them may be found at all prices from twenty dollars or less up to seventy-five dollars or more.

I do not think there is a great deal to choose between a rod by a good English maker and one by a good American maker, though the fittings on American rods, particularly the ferrules, are likely to be light and weak, while those on English rods are often unnecessarily heavy. The cult of the very light rod—from $15/16$ of an ounce up to about 4 ounces—did much good to American rod making, but at the same time much harm. I believe it has now passed; certainly, it never served any useful purpose in British Columbia, and I doubt if it really did much good anywhere except in bars and smoking rooms. An 8½-foot rod weighing 4 ounces is about as light a rod as will do good work under conditions normally met, and a rod as light as this is really only necessary for searching water with a dry fly— which is seldom a satisfactory method in British Columbia.

It should be remembered that the greatest strain on a fly rod comes in lifting the line from the water and in casting, not in playing the fish. Up to a certain point a light rod will aid in reducing the fatigue of a day's casting, but if the rod is too light the extra effort of controlling and lifting the line without straining the rod will more than balance the advantage of re-duced weight. The old—and perhaps rather vague—rule of "let the rod do the work" applies excellently here, and to attempt to fish western streams, where long casting and heavy water are usually part of the fishing, with a three- or four-ounce toy is to accept unnecessary discomfort.

It is safe to say that the great makers such as Payne and Leonard of America, and Hardy and Farlow of England, turn out nothing but good rods; the only difficulty the angler will find is in choosing from among the many different types and weights and balances a combination that will suit his style and strength and purpose. Most of the rods from these makers are fairly expensive, and, as a general rule, cheap rods are not to be recommended. But by careful examination and selection it is often possible to find a good, cheap rod; such makers as Allcock's and Milwards in England make reliable rods at rea-sonable prices, and in America the Goodwin Granger Com-pany of Denver makes a standard rod, at $11.50, which for action and power and balance is unequalled by anything else I have seen at the price. The Granger Company makes other rods, up to sixty dollars in price; their whole range of fly rods is very sensibly planned, and the weights and balances of examples of the various price classes I have handled seem excellent.

The reel is not very important in fly fishing, but it should be of the narrow-drum type, not a multiplier, and of the simplest possible construction. Trout and salmon fly reels are made at prices up to $75, but I believe that there is no possible point in paying such a price. Twenty dollars will buy the largest size of salmon fly reel that one is likely to need, and it will be a reel that with normal care will last two lifetimes. From ten to fifteen dollars will buy an absolutely first-class trout reel, and there are plenty of good reels on the market at five or six dollars.

The line is the most important part of the fly fisherman's outfit, and there is no doubt that a double-tapered vacuum-dressed line is the best for all types of fly fishing. For the general run of western fishing, where fairly long casts are the rule, the old-fashioned type of taper is by far the best. The modern type, in which the line runs quickly from fine to very thick, holds its thickness and weight for less than twenty feet, then drops away into a long length of fine line, may be all right for tournament casting or for searching eastern streams with short, dry-fly casts; but it is extremely clumsy and uncomfortable to use where the average cast is fifty feet or more and the comfortable maximum may be as much as seventy-five feet. One does not care, at every cast, to draw the line in until the taper is close to the rod top and shoot such a length of line, and the result is that the short, heavy taper swings back and forth and jerks at the rod top like a lump of lead.

The best line I have ever used, in all weights, is Hardy's Corona. I do not think it is possible, or necessary, to make a better fly line than this, though perhaps the difference in price between the Corona and lines such as the Kingfisher or King Eider is greater than the difference in fishing quality. I believe the Kingfisher and the King Eider are actually the same lines, put out by the same maker; at least, I have been able to find no difference between them. The name Kingfisher is used in England and the name King Eider in Canada, and I have bought both indiscriminately for many years; they are a little stiffer than Corona lines and take longer to work into perfect condition, but they do their work splendidly and last almost indefinitely.

A good vacuum-dressed line always improves with use—and care; it grows softer, heavier, smoother and more supple, handles better, casts better, fishes better and looks better. Care of lines is quite simple, and really a matter of habit rather than anything else. Every fisherman should have a line drier of some sort, and make a point of winding the wet line off his reel on to the drier immediately after each day's fishing. Vacuum-dressed lines also need to be rubbed down regularly with some good greasing preparation such as Mucilin or Cerolene, which I believe are vegetable greases; I have not found animal fats or mineral greases at all good for lines. Most anglers nowadays prefer to fish a floating line with either wet or dry fly, and will grease their lines for this, if for no other purpose. But a line should never be greased when wet, and it is better to carry a spare reel and line than to grease a line to keep it floating after a half day's fishing. The amount of care used in greasing a previously dried line is more or less a matter of individual preference; working the greased line through the bare hands several times will help to spread the grease evenly, and polishing with a cloth or chamois leather also does good; but thorough drying and a single application of grease wiped over once with a cloth, after each day's fishing, will improve a line and keep it in excellent condition through many years of fishing.

Care of lines during the close season is important. The worst place for a line is on the reel. If possible, line should be wiped thoroughly clean of all grease and hung in loose coils in a dark cupboard; failing this, a line drier is a better storage place than the reel; or, if lines are wound off the reels on to a drier about once a month during non-use, they should keep in fair condition. A heavily greased line should never be left coiled on the reel for even a few days, as it is likely to become tacky if air is kept from it.

Selecting the right weight of line for a rod is a difficult

matter, since rods of the same weight and length vary so much in action, and some line makers do not always mean the same thing as others by the letters they use to indicate line sizes. As a general rule, I expect to find that I need a line one size heavier than that recommended for the rod by the maker, but even this rule does not always work out. Lines for the rods I have listed in this chapter, assuming that all the rods have decent backbone for their weight and length, would be about as follows:

| | | |
|---|---|---|
| 7 to 7½ ft. | 3 oz. | Hardy IDI. King Eider No. 1 Fine |
| 8½ to 9 ft. | 5 oz. | Hardy ICI. King Eider No. 2 Medium |
| 9½ to 10 ft. | 6 to 8 oz. | Hardy IBI. King Eider No. 4 Ex. Stout |
| 11 to 12 ft. | 12 to 13 oz. | Hardy No. 5. King Eider No. 5 |
| 13 to 14 ft. | 20 to 24 oz. | Hardy No. 4 King Eider No. 6 |

These lines are generally one size heavier than the makers recommend, but I have not found them too heavy for fishing in the ordinary way, and a heavy line is very necessary for good roll casting.

Gut casts are a big subject, but for general purposes the ordinary quality of round, clear gut casts put out by good makers is quite all right. Farlow's "Hewitt" stained casts have some slight advantage in very bright weather, but I do not think this is often very important in British Columbia. The size of the cast is dependent upon the size of the fly used more than upon anything else. 4x will not land fish on a No. 6 fly and Ox will probably not go through the eye of a No. 15 hook and is unnecessarily strong even for ten-pounders hooked on such flies. The best all-round sizes for fishing in the Province are 1x and 2x, with 3x for most dry-fly fishing and Ox or 9/5 for heavy, wet-fly work in fast water. There is a definite advantage in fishing at least as fine as 2x whenever possible. Gut substitutes will not handle a fly at all well, and in spite of their cheapness are not worth bothering with.

I have already written at some length about flies, but there is really no end to the subject. The contention of the informed, that fish are colour-blind, is one on which I cannot find sufficient evidence to argue either for it or against. But even the most fanatical of the "pro's" are usually willing to agree that fish see colours in different shades of grey—or pink or blue or green or whatever they are at the moment insisting is the precise tint of the fish's world—so the point is not very important; if a fish distinguishes between, let us say, ginger and orange, it does not matter much whether he is able to do so because he sees them as different shades of grey or simply as ginger and orange. But for all that, I am convinced that in most western fishing shape and size and (in wet-fly fishing) movement are probably more important than colour, and that a lively impressionism is probably more worth striving after than exact imitation.

There is no such thing, in my experience, as a knock-'em-dead, sure-success fly, nor any secret of the fly-tyer's art that is hidden from the common man. The most deadly flies I ever used were given me by a fisherman on a south of England chalk stream. They were three red variants and three dark variants, beautifully tied on No. 15 or 16 hooks, with the finest, brightest, hardest hackles I have ever seen. For nearly a year they lay unused in my box, and then one day I found myself in trouble with a big fish cruising in slack water and apparently smutting. Nothing I could show him, even my tiniest black ribbed with gold, would interest him. The big variants looked ridiculous, but I was determined to stay with the fish till I caught him or put him off his meal, so I laid one in his course. He took it calmly and deliberately, with that lazy confidence that passes for eagerness in a really good, difficult fish. He did all I could have expected of him, tearing up under the arch of a bridge, down and on again in the flow of the stream, forcing me to follow him and put down several good fish in the bend below, but I netted him at last, and went on with my variant. I did not expect it to catch more fish, but it did catch three more, all of them public characters, rising in difficult places.

For some reason I did not use the variants again until several weeks later, when another smutting fish refused everything I had. He took a variant, and I learned from then on to value a variant as a last temptation for a difficult fish; quite often it failed, but surprisingly often it succeeded. They are all gone now; four of them I gave away, the remaining dark one I lost in a fish, and the red was in my box until two or three years ago, but I cannot find it now.

These flies were tied by a lady tyer whose name I do not know, but who, I was told, could be persuaded to tie only a few flies at a time for certain favoured members of the Fly Fisher's Club. The reason the flies were good was sheer quality of material and workmanship. The patterns were simple and ordinary, little if at all different from the commonest types of variant. But the flies balanced and cocked and sat on the water beautifully, and the hackles were more brilliant and lustrous, cleaner and tapering to finer, sharper points than any others I have seen.

Such quality as this is not to be found in shop-tied flies. It would be impossible, without charging prohibitive prices, to use only perfect hackles and feathers, and the knowledge and experience required to select such materials, as well as the expertness to tie them perfectly, are wholly exceptional, amateur rather than professional, nearer to genius than to competence. Even so, many professional tyers do really good work and use excellent materials. The usual fault of shop-tied flies, particularly in the west, is that they are too heavily dressed; but angling writers have been raising their voices in this complaint for several generations, and it is now usually possible to find shop-tied flies that are not merely hooks lost in a clutter of feathers and wool and tinsel. Good flies are tied in British Columbia, both in Vancouver and at Kelowna, and visiting anglers can obtain good specimens of local patterns without difficulty.

There is still much to be said for amateur tying. The tying of the larger wet flies, on 6-10 hooks, is so easy and adds so much to the satisfaction of fishing that even a clumsy-handed man will lose nothing, not even his temper, in trying it. And amateur-tied flies, born of an idea, often a little more ragged, usually more lightly dressed even today than the shop-tied flies, take fish very well.

There are plenty of excellent books on fly dressing,* and I am not good enough to be able to add anything to them. But I may say that in tying wet flies for British Columbia—particularly for coast waters—low-water hooks, as used for greased-line fishing, are invaluable. Nearly all silver-bodied flies are better tied on them, and even seal's fur or wool bodies seem more graceful and natural. Besides having a better appearance, flies tied on these hooks are likely to be held longer in the fish's mouth, since the iron is lighter; the hook itself is very easy to set, and the long shank may sometimes mean the difference between hooking and missing a short riser.

Flies tied with bucktail and polar-bear hair are very popular in British Columbia, but though I have used them a good deal I have not found them more deadly than flies tied with more orthodox materials. Both bucktail and bear hair are valuable in fly dressing, but, as with any other material, they should be used only with the idea of producing some particular effect or impression. In British Columbian tyings they are too often used simply because they are what they are, as though they had in themselves some mysterious property that attracts fish. And since a very great proportion of bucktail and bear-hair flies are simply lures, their use tends to delay the development of more useful and interesting types.

I have not found much use, either, for the general run of shop-tied nymph and shrimp imitations. These are too often made of stiff, hard materials, lifelike on the store counter,

---

* *How to Dress Salmon Flies*. T. E. Pryce-Tannat. Black, London.
  *How to Tie Salmon Flies*. Maj. J. H. Hale. Fishing Gazette, London.
  *How to Tie Flies for Trout*. H. G. McLelland. Fishing Gazette, London, and others.

perhaps, but anything but lifelike in the water. For most true nymph fishing—that is, the drifting of the nymph without artificial movement—it is difficult, and seldom necessary, to improve on such standard dry flies as Tup's Indispensable and Greenwell's Glory, lightly dressed so that the hook will just sink them. These two patterns and a few simple wet flies such as the medium olive, tied on small hooks, have often done well for me in British Columbian waters.

At home, where going fishing meant taking a rod from under the billiard table and a bag or net from a hook in the hall, we used to remember to ask ourselves before leaving the house: "Rod, reel, line, casts, flies, net?" and to touch or glance at each item to make sure it was there. The net is missing at the moment, and it is not easy to think of a net that suits most British Columbian uses. Of the rod one can say, Let it not be too light. Of the reel, Let it be simple; of the line, Let it be heavy enough; of the cast, Let it be fine; of the flies, Have reasons for them; of the net, Let it be practical. In a boat any long-handled, simple net is practical, so long as it is big enough. But for stream fishing the net must be one that can be folded away into a case to be carried through brush, or it will soon be torn; it must be quite large, because the fish are large, and the handle must have a knuckle joint so that the net can be slung ready in strap or bag while fishing. I have not found the triangular shaped nets with folding arms wholly satisfactory, though they fill many of the requirements. But it is possible to buy a folding circular ring of light, hollow metal, and one of these, with a suitable net, a strong, light wooden handle and a knuckle joint, is probably as good as anything. For travel through the brush, net and ring can be folded away and put into creel or bag.

In addition to fly rods and tackle, the British Columbian fisherman needs spinning rods for spring salmon and winter steelhead, and, if he is going to try every type of fishing, one or two trolling rods. I have already written at some length of side-swing casting for the Nimpkish springs and for winter steelhead, but two other methods of casting, the English "thread-line" and the American "overhead" can be used with good effect for these fish. Though I have tried both methods, I have not been able to prefer either to the side-swing; chiefly, perhaps, because I first learned the side-swing method and am prejudiced in favour of it. The American method permits great accuracy and is very good along brushy streams, but there is a jerkiness of movement about it that I do not like. And from watching men well used to the method attempting to handle steelhead on the five-foot rods, I am convinced that much pleasure and ease in playing the fish are lost; there never seems to be enough rod to take up slack line caused by a change in direction on the part of the fish or a quick run towards the boat.

The thread-line method makes it extremely easy to cast long distances with light baits and is also very accurate, but I find the reel too "gadgety" and complicated, and dislike having to take a lot of precautions to prevent kinking of the line. Thread-line fishing is undoubtedly a deadly method of casting and working small spinning baits in low water, but this also seems to me an argument against its use in British Columbia. A few competent thread-line fishermen could cause serious depletion of migratory cutthroats in a very short while, and perhaps also spoil some good Kamloops waters. In spite of the attractiveness and fineness of the method, I believe its use should be barred, or at least restricted to winter steelhead fishing.

Of trolling I have had so little actual experience that nothing I say should be taken very seriously. But I believe an 8-foot, six-ounce rod should be about right for trout of under five pounds, while trolling rods for larger fish should weigh approximately one ounce to the foot—perhaps a little more for large spring salmon. Many trollers spoil the main object of their sport, which must necessarily be the playing of the fish, by the use of extremely thick and heavy rods, and this is, I think, because rods well suited to the work are not cheap or readily available. If trolling continues to be a fairly popular way of fishing, improved tackle and methods will probably be developed.

I find I have very little to say about gadgets; I am not mechanically minded, and cannot profess to have contributed anything at all to the general comfort of the fisherman. I prefer a fishing bag to a creel generally, though not when wading big rivers; when fishing I keep my gut casts in a little, round, aluminum box with two damper pads, as do most other fly fishermen; I kill most of my trout by knocking them on the head with my pipe, or did until a friend made me a beautiful priest of apple wood carved and painted in the likeness of a trout. I have never found a satisfactory fly box. This last is a real grievance that I feel someone should remedy. Dry-fly boxes are better than wet-fly boxes, and the best of them are the old-fashioned, black, japanned-tin ones; Hardy's "Halford" and "Montague" boxes are really excellent, though the black chips off them in time. But as to wet-fly boxes—the celluloid ones are too brittle, the aluminum ones bend and make the clips useless, the few that don't bend or break are too heavy. Hardy's "Neroda" boxes, which are made of some composition material, are the best I have found, but they are really quite heavy and bulky for the number of flies they carry. Perhaps the development of alloys in airplane construction will do something to solve the problem.

No fishing book is really complete without its description of some useful knots. There is one that the commercial salmon trollers use a great deal—but which I have not seen used by anglers—that is ideal for fastening a line to lead or swivel. The line is passed through the eye of the swivel, round and through again from the same side. Then the short end is passed round the length that leads back to the reel, and through the two loops. Any pull on this knot is bound to draw the first loop tighter and tighter on the short end of the line, so that it cannot possibly be drawn through. It is a neat, small knot, easy and quick to tie or untie, and it has little or no tendency to cut the

line. In emergency I have used it for tying heavy salmon flies
to gut too small for them, and it has not slipped or broken;
though I still prefer to use gut of the right size with a figure-of-
eight knot, I feel that this use is a supreme test of the qualities
of any knot.

I feel regretful about this chapter, as though I should have
been able to be more helpful, to make more splendid generalisations, yet remain more objective than I have. But the fact is,
I do not know all about all methods of fishing that are or might
be effective in British Columbia, nor have I tried out all types
of tackle from all the makers in the world. If I have slighted
any man's favourite method, I am sorry, because I know that
all legitimate methods of angling give some pleasure, though I
may feel that some give more than others. And if I have men-
tioned the names of some tackle dealers and omitted others
equally good, it is because I wish to write only of products I
know. It would have been possible to avoid, throughout the
book, mention by name of any tackle maker or any product,
but in doing so I should have lost concreteness. To write of an
8¾-foot rod weighing a shade over five ounces is to write of
an abstraction; there are thousands of rods in the world that
match the weight and the length, but most of them are probably very different from the rod I mean. To write of Hardy's
8¾-foot "Davy" rod is to tell the whole story; the rod exists
and can be handled or tried out or bought by anyone who is
interested.

# III

## *Limits & Ethics*

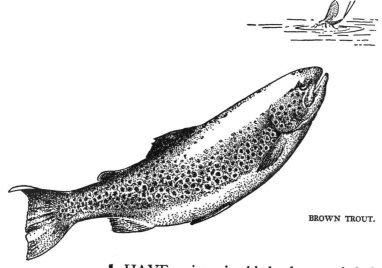

BROWN TROUT.

I HAVE written in this book a good deal about the angler's obligations to his sport, to other sportsmen, and to the state. It must not be forgotten that when angling rights are privately owned, the owners spend a good deal of money on the preservation of their value and restrict themselves and their friends to catches and practices that will help to ensure such preservation. Under public ownership there is always a very real danger that everybody's business and responsibility will become nobody's business and responsibility. The "if-I-don't-get-'em-somebody-else-will" philosophy is apt to take hold of men who are, normally, quite conscientious in their relations with their fellow men; and men who would not think of stealing private property will not hesitate to poach. This is true in commercial fishing as well as in angling. Actually, a crime of this sort against public property, when viewed dispassionately, is far more contemptible than most crimes against private property. It is an abuse of privileges, a thieving from the poor as well as the rich, from the future as well as the present—quite genuinely, if rather dramatically, a robbery of babes in arms and babes unborn. Unfortunately public opinion does not see it in this light, and though a gaol sentence is probably inevitable for a man who has picked a couple of dollars out of a millionaire's pocket, the man who has robbed a creek of its cohoe run, at a net return to himself of some hundreds of dollars and a net capital loss to the general public of several thousands, will generally get off with a fine that he can pay out of his past profits.

The creek robber, the dynamiter, even the poaching angler, are a good deal more likely to find themselves in trouble now than they were a few years ago. The effect of their work is pretty evident, and both commercial fishermen and anglers can see that "depletion" is something more than a scientist's bogey man that may scare their grandchildren. But seeing this is very negative virtue—really nothing more than an admission that the laws of the country should be enforced. If public ownership of angling rights is to prove itself by the preservation of the value of those rights, anglers will have to render far more positive co-operation.

The first essential—if anyone is to have any satisfaction at all out of public fishing waters—is proper consideration by every angler for the immediate rights of other anglers who may be fishing the same water at the same time. This is largely a question of good manners, and though I have not fished a great deal in the neighbourhood of large towns, I think it is fairly safe to say that most anglers in British Columbia show proper consideration for one another. Failure to do so is nearly always due to ignorance of and inexperience in fishing methods and conditions.

It is not altogether easy to lay down a set of rules on "how to behave while fishing a public water"; so much depends on the temperament of the individual. But it is safe enough to say to all but the very meek, "Over do the good manners." The main thing is to give the other fellow plenty of room; if he is fishing down a pool ahead of you, don't crowd him from behind. If you cut in below him, cut in well below—a hundred or two hundred yards, if possible, not just fifty or a hundred feet. As a general rule, don't cut in below him; let him work well down, then start in behind him and be content to stay there. It's easy enough to pick up fish behind a good fisherman, because he won't disturb the ones he doesn't get, and generally it is just as easy to pick them up behind a clumsy fisherman, because he leaves them all there for you. And if you are fishing down ahead and someone behind seems impatient—let him go on through. You'll take your time and cover the water better if you do.

Any angler who is at all experienced knows enough to be as friendly and as helpful as he reasonably can be to any other anglers he meets. Don't be mysterious and full of secrets; in any case you can't very well have any that amount to anything, and if you tell the other fellow everything you know he still probably won't be able to catch fish any better or any worse than his own skill will let him. Give him a fly if you've got a pattern that's taking and he hasn't, even give him a 3x cast if you've got one to spare and feel that his 2x is scaring all the fish away from him. But don't force either your gifts or your advice upon him unless he makes it pretty clear he wants them; and don't be afraid to be interested in his tackle and the way he's fishing it, even if he's murdering fish with a spinner and a worm when you know they'd come to a fly. Just take them with a fly, all along behind him; it's a more likely way of making a convert.

But to make manners on the stream worth-while, there must be some fish in the stream, and the first and greatest obligation of any angler fishing under state ownership is to do nothing that in any way threatens the future of whatever water he is fishing. This does not mean simply that he must abide by legal restrictions; he must be prepared at times to go beyond this and make regulations for himself. And to make such regulations he needs a certain knowledge of the condition of the water he is fishing and the essential principles of conservation governing its condition. In other words, he is under at least a moral obligation to understand what makes his sport and why.

Practical conservation may at times mean killing fish, and at other times exactly the opposite. The British Columbian Government at present sees fit to set a limit of twelve fish per day over the minimum-size limit of eight inches, for practically every water in the province. But while the future of a lake like Paul might be seriously endangered if anglers made a practice of returning a large proportion of sizeable fish to the water, any man who takes it upon himself to kill twelve sea-run cutthroat trout in one day's fishing on a water accessible by road is unquestionably endangering the future of that sport. It is the angler's business to know and understand things of this sort; if the Government does not know enough to protect his interests for him, he must protect them for himself.

In the same way, while it is usually unsound practice to return a spawned-out fish or a mending kelt to an artificially stocked interior lake, there is no excuse for killing ripe steelhead or cutthroats, or mending fish of either of these species, in coastal waters. The chance of survival or second spawning may be comparatively low, but there is such a chance and as far as is known at present, second spawning is not detrimental to the stock. Obviously, the resources of understocked waters and the sea are adequate to provide feed for an economical recovery.

Under public ownership there cannot be, except in artificially controlled and highly productive waters producing at their maximum capacity, enough fish for everyone to have all he wants. Therefore it becomes a further obligation of the fisherman to get the utmost satisfaction out of every fish he chooses to kill. The angler, whatever his method may be, fishes primarily for sport, not food; that is why he uses rod and line instead of going down to the fishmonger's or using net or dynamite or some more quickly effective method. Angling methods have been developed through the desire of anglers to set certain limits upon their own efficiency, so that the taking of fish may be a matter of skill and difficulty. The object of angling is not primarily to catch fish, but to get satisfaction out of attempting to do so, and out of succeeding through skill and knowledge. Ideally, competition between angler and angler has nothing whatever to do with the sport of fishing. The competition is between angler and fish, with the conditions made reasonably equal by the restrictions which the angler imposes upon himself.

It follows, then, that the degree of satisfaction the angler gets from his sport is quite largely proportionate to the rigour of the conditions which he has imposed upon himself; the more rigorous they are, as long as they do not make the catching of a reasonable number of fish quite impossible, the greater will be the satisfaction. There is a passage in J. W. Hills' *A Summer on the Test* which makes this point perfectly. Mr. Hills, writing of mayfly fishing on English chalk streams, says there are days when trout will take anything, when neither bad casting, thick gut nor wretched imitations will put them down. "But," he writes—with a sigh of relief that almost sounds from the printed page—"such days are rare. Looking back over many years, I can only remember a few. And, to put against such days, I remember many more when trout were wonderfully difficult, when fish were feeding steadily and yet accurate and delicate fishing met with scanty reward."

"When trout were wonderfully difficult"—not "damnably difficult," or "abominably difficult," but "wonderfully difficult." And difficult but not impossible; they were feeding steadily, taking the naturals, and therefore open to persuasion by the artificial; the rest was up to the fisherman; if he could find an artificial sufficiently like the natural to be convincing and if he could present it convincingly, it would be taken.

These are ideal conditions, by no means always to be found; they are conditions under which the killing of even one or two fish would yield a great deal of satisfaction, while failure to kill a fish at all would not necessarily detract from a day of intense pleasure. It is not possible to reproduce such conditions at will; but the individual angler can, by confining himself to the use of those methods which demand the most of him, do a great deal towards improving his chances of meeting with them; and he can at the same time assure himself of a maximum amount and intensity of satisfaction from all his fishing.

This book has been largely devoted to fly fishing, and I feel that I owe an apology for this to the many good sportsmen and good anglers who use other methods. But I have been forced to the conclusion that fly fishing is by far the most important and satisfactory method of angling in fresh water throughout British Columbia. It is true that in some interior lakes the fish are too deep for fly fishing during July and August, and that in these months other methods afford both necessary and desirable means for controlling the stock; it is true, also, that big trout in some of the very large lakes of the Province are seldom or never available to fly fishing, and it is desirable that these should be fished for and caught by other methods. But these are exceptional conditions, and their occurrence is usually considered unfortunate rather than fortunate; the average fisherman does not go out of his way to seek them, though he may use them, when they occur conveniently, for want of something better. And through the six or eight months of the trout season, fly fishing is available somewhere within easy reach of any part of the Province I have yet visited.

I have found also that I very much prefer fly fishing to all other methods; that this is due in some measure to habit and early training I am perfectly willing to admit, but I honestly believe that it is also a logical preference—that almost any man will get more and better satisfaction from fly fishing than from any other method. If this belief is sound, the angler who fishes state-owned water is under some moral obligation to use the fly whenever there is a reasonable chance that it will be effective. Fly fishing is not by any means invariably less deadly than other methods, but it is almost invariably more subtle, more delicate and more exacting. It is separated from all forms of natural-bait fishing by the fact that it is based on a complete deception of the fish; the artificial fly is not merely something attached to hook and line which must be fished in such a way as to seem a free and natural occurrence in the water, but it is something—of wool and silk and feathers—that would be of no conceivable use to the fish if it actually were floating free in the water; yet the fish must be persuaded that he desires it enough to take it, and the deception must last long enough to permit the angler to set the hook.

The casting of a fly is a prettier and more satisfying operation than any method of casting other natural or artificial baits that I have yet seen or used. The working of any type of fly is more difficult and more interesting than the working of natural or artificial baits for feeding fish. And the striking of fish that have taken the fly is a good deal more difficult than the striking of fish that have taken baits of any other kind. The only possible exception to these sweeping statements is in the case of upstream worm fishing, which is one of the most difficult and attractive methods one is likely to come across. But it is a method seldom used in British Columbia.

These advantages of fly fishing, combined with the general effectiveness of the method, seem enough to make its use—at least in angling for trout—sounder than the use of any other method. Logically, the fly fisherman should be able to derive more satisfaction from the hooking of fewer fish in the course of a day's fishing than the troller or bait fisherman, and I am inclined to believe that this is the case; so much so that it is perfectly possible for the fly fisherman to have a thoroughly interesting and enjoyable blank day.

The real fly fisherman does not simply go out fishing. He goes out to catch fish by one particular method, the use of the artificial fly, unweighted, unencumbered, unadorned by spinner or any other improvement. If he cannot catch trout by this means he is usually content to go without them—and in British Columbia he will not often find himself fishless. There will always be times when he could do better with worm or creeper, natural minnow or caddis or caterpillar or any of the hundred other possible natural baits, or with spoon or spinner or phantom or any of the hundred possible artificial baits. But to use any of these would be to fail in his object every bit as completely as though he had worked all day with the artificial fly and caught nothing; and he would, in addition, have deprived himself of the pleasure of a day of casting and working his fly.

When he wants to catch fish and is honestly convinced that he cannot catch them on the fly, he may be perfectly content to try other methods. The winter runs of steelhead, for instance, are not, normally, likely to respond to flies fished in the ordinary way, and some men may feel that there are forms of bait-fishing more attractive than using the deep-sunk fly; I suspect that such an opinion would be based on an inadequate knowledge of the deep-fly method, but good arguments can be put forward for the devon minnow or the prawn. Fly fishing for tyee salmon—at least in its present stage of development—is not a particularly productive or attractive method, so one can turn willingly enough to the big spoons.

I do not think that all methods of fly fishing are equally attractive, or that all other methods of fishing are equally unattractive or necessarily unattractive at all; only that when there is a reasonable chance of catching fish on the fly, to fish for them by any other method is wasteful of pleasure and also, if fish are caught, of fish. In the course of the rather intense self-examination that this chapter has made necessary I have listed the various fishing methods for the main types of British Columbian game fish in the order of the satisfaction their use affords me. The implication of the list is that I find none of the methods unattractive and am prepared to use any one of them, provided I am convinced it will do no harm and that those listed above it stand absolutely no chance of success. Perhaps I should admit though, to keep the record quite straight, that if it looks as though I shall have to go below No. 3 or 4 on any list I am likely enough to seize an opportunity to be virtuous and stay at home to get some work done.

*Steelhead*
1. Greased line
2. Deep-sunk fly
3. Wet fly
4. Dry fly
5. Devon minnow
6. Prawn
7. Spoon or spinner
8. Fly with spinner
9. Spinner with bait
10. Bait alone

*Kamloops or Cutthroat*
1. Dry fly or upstream nymph
2. Wet fly
3. Silver-bodied wet fly
4. Upstream worm or natural bait
5. Devon or natural minnow
6. Rolling fly imitating alevin, salmon egg, etc.
7. Natural bait downstream
8. Bait and float (lake fishing)
9. Spoon or spinner with bait
10. Trolling

*Pacific Salmon*
1. Wet fly (cast)
2. Devon and spinner (cast)
3. Spoon (cast)
4. Wet fly (trolled)
5. Natural bait or herring strip (cast)
6. Trolling with spoon
7. Trolling with natural bait

Such hairsplitting lists as these cannot very well have any general application, and the whole matter is really one for the individual fisherman to decide for himself. But he should give the matter some thought, and make some attempt to get the most out of his fishing. Where a water is especially suited to a certain method, and will not be harmed by the restriction of other methods, it may well be good policy to impose such restrictions. When a method shows itself to be a definite threat to the future of the fishing, in spite of restrictive legislation already in force, it obviously must be barred; no fishery can stand, for instance, anything approaching intensive use of salmon roe, and I very much doubt if the natural stock of any trout stream can stand the drain of spinner-and-worm fishing. But these methods have, in any case, little to recommend them beyond their effectiveness, and most keen fishermen are not much concerned with them. For the rest, even in the broad question between fly fishing and other methods, any change must come through the desire of the mass of fishermen. If they become convinced, sooner or later, that firmer restriction of methods will mean more and better fishing for everyone, they will undoubtedly go after such restriction and get it. Meanwhile, it is the business of the authorities and the fish and game associations to see to it that bag limits and seasons are set in such a way as to protect future breeding stocks from depletion by any legal method of angling.

I have tried to avoid the use of the word "sportsmanship" in this chapter, because I feel that this also is a personal matter. One man may choose to be a sportsman, and another may choose to say "to hell with it," and go out and chuck a stick of dynamite or a clump of salmon eggs into a good pool. Both are probably attractive fellows if one knows them well—simply with slightly differing points of view. But such things as the enjoyment of a day's fishing and future breeding stocks and the value of good fishing to the country, are concrete and comprehensible to anyone. To mix sportsmanship in with these things is to make it expedient; and I doubt, somehow, that expediency should enter into sportsmanship.

# IV

## *The Future*

KILLER WHALES.

THE game fisheries of British Columbia serve two important needs: They are at once a source of recreation to a considerable proportion of the population and a means of attracting much needed tourist traffic, as well as some residents of independent means. In a commercial era which has not yet fully realised the importance and the material value of proper recreational facilities for its people, the second need is usually considered the more pressing of these two. In my opinion this is a gross confusion of values, but the fact remains that it is practically impossible to talk constructive development on anything approaching an extensive scale unless one justifies it first in terms of tourist trade.

This is not at all hard to do. British Columbia is potentially the greatest trout and salmon country in the world and is geographically placed to draw from an almost unlimited number of non-resident anglers. Even in its present state, her game fishery is drawing a steadily increasing number of non-residents —in 1937 there were issued 2,970 season licenses at $5.00 and 1,841 day licenses at $1.00; in 1946 over 10,000 season licenses were issued at $7.00. I have no doubt at all that the fishery could be made good enough and attractive enough to satisfy about half a million visiting anglers every year. Probably development to this point is not necessary, or even desirable. But the population of the North American continent is quite clearly in for shorter working hours and longer holidays. Facilities for travel will continue to improve and the pressure on all existing recreational facilities will steadily increase. There is a real service to be done in development of such a perfect recreational area as British Columbia, and it is an immense economic opportunity.

Within the past ten years, full control of the British Columbian game fishery in non-tidal waters has passed into the hands of the Provincial Government. The chief arguments in favour of the move were that the division of control between the Dominion and the Provincial Governments had proved unsatisfactory, and that local interest and local knowledge should be applied to local problems. The force of the second of these arguments is somewhat doubtful, since the Dominion Government maintains the only biological research stations in the Province, but the idea appealed to local anglers, and there is not much doubt that the Province will continue to control the fishery.

At present the control is negative rather than positive. The fishery is under the administration of the Game Commission, which has no trained and experienced game-fish men in its service and which is, rather unaccountably, managed by the Attorney General's department. The only funds available, as far as I know, are those from the sale of angler's licenses, and these funds are at present being spent chiefly in plantings of game-fish fry, in limited patrol work, and in some salvage of fish trapped by low water in summer.

I have tried in this book to outline the principles of conservation and development, and to suggest that they are not by any means so simple or so well understood as is generally supposed. I do not think that any sound programme of conservation and development can be worked out and properly applied by the present system of administration, or by anyone except a trained biologist or a committee of biologists with complete information at their disposal. Even the committee would need a single head, and this man should have at least the same standing as the deputy ministers of the various departments of the Provincial Government now have. If possible, his post should be even farther removed from the influence of politics, and certainly it should be protected for at least a period of years from political interference.

Such a position would require a man of exceptional qualities as well as exceptional knowledge. He would have to command the unlimited confidence and respect of anglers and sportsmen's organisations, and be capable of working towards large ends through a long period of time. He would have to be able to meet the public and explain his work and its object in comprehensible terms, but at the same time he would have to be very firm in resisting sectional pressure. It is undoubtedly possible to find a biologist with these qualifications, but his work would command a considerable salary, if only because the competition from the United States for the services of such men is extremely high.

The first few years of a proper administration of the game fishery would have to be devoted mainly to surveys and research, with the enforcement of proper restrictive legislation to maintain existing stocks, and limited development wherever present knowledge shows that it can be safely and economically undertaken. The results of the surveys and research work, together with all possible records of catches and angling conditions, would form the basis for a long-term plan of development.

The provision of funds for research and development should scarcely be a matter of difficulty. There can be no doubt that most resort owners and guides who are dependent for their livelihood upon the fishery would be glad to pay a direct tax, based upon the volume of their business, provided they were certain it would be put to such use. The resident anglers of the Province, who now pay only a dollar a year for the right to fish anywhere in the Province, would accept an increase under the same condition. No license at all is required at present for fishing in tidal waters, which are under control of the Dominion government. Control in this regard should be given to the Province and a single fee, applicable to fresh or tidal waters or both should be charged. I believe that might well be as high as five dollars, though children under eighteen should not be required to pay.

The fishery divides naturally into three main parts: Interior trout fishing, coast trout fishing and coast salmon fishing. A short survey of the more accessible waters of the interior would be enough to indicate the lines of a program of immediate, if cautious, development. Different waters could readily be made to yield different types of fishing and different sizes of fish; some lakes could be restricted to fly fishing and others could be developed principally for the troller. Research work should be taken up where it was dropped in 1936, and should be carried through until a comprehensive program develops.

Coast trout fishing needs immediate restrictive measures and very intensive research work. There is no reasonable doubt that the runs of migratory trout can be improved very considerably as soon as life histories are properly understood; and the number and accessibility of coast lakes justifies considerable research work into the possibilities of increasing their productivity. With the amount of good holding water and good fishing water available on the coast, there is no reason why this trout fishing should not become a much more important part of the fishery than it is at present.

The coast salmon fishery presents a problem of immediate difficulty because commercial competition is so important, but the future of the commercial fishery is at least as dependent upon a rigid policy of conservation as is the future of game fishery, and it is difficult to believe that proper restrictions will not be imposed in time to save it. Most work for the salvation of this part of the game fishery must be dependent upon the promptness and efficacy of whatever measures are taken for the preservation of the commercial fishery. But whenever these measures seem insufficient and there is direct threat to the runs that provide most of the game fishing, a policy calculated to counteract the threat should be developed. This also would call for some research work, chiefly tagging and life-history work, but measures restricting commercial fishing whenever it directly threatens game-fish runs are not at all beyond the bounds of possibility, since the greater value of salmon caught as game fish might easily justify such restrictions economically.

Hand in hand with the job of preserving and improving the fishery must go the work of presenting it properly to the public. This, again, comes within the province of the ideal single administrator, and calls for a good deal of delicacy and foresight as well as straightforward promotional ability. Anglers are men out for rest and peaceful recreation, and anything too frankly commercial will turn them away. The rather crude tactics of regular tourist bureaus and their tendency to make extravagant claims and to offer vague information is not likely to build sound business.

Improved communications would do a great deal to present the fishing properly. I do not think that this need is so pressing or so extensive as is generally supposed in the Province; anglers will go over very bad roads almost cheerfully if they expect

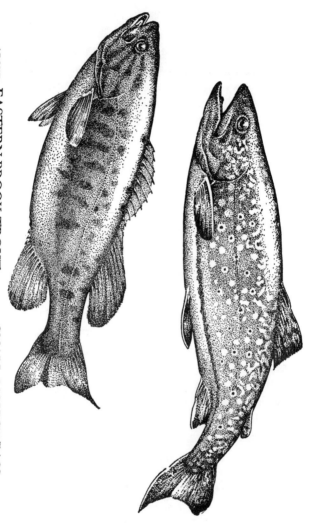

ABOVE: EASTERN BROOK TROUT. BELOW: SMALL-MOUTH BASS.

good fishing at the end of them, and they have learned from
bitter experience that the best fishing is likely to lie at the end
of the roughest roads. But there is a need in the Province for
good main roads, and the general opinion is that the proper
expenditure of funds available in the past would have produced
such roads before this. Public opinion is sufficiently aroused
on the point to give reason to suppose that future road-building
programs will be wiser and sounder.

What the development of the game fishery needs, apart from
the main roads which should give reasonably quick and easy
access to distant points, are passable roads, pack trails and foot
trails to many waters now inaccessible, and foot trails along
the banks of good streams. A few of these should be constructed almost immediately, but the great majority would only
be needed as development proceeded. In the same way, government cabins constructed at strategic points and available to the
fisherman would be of the greatest value, and nominal rents
would pay for their maintenance.

The present non-resident angler's license fee of seven dollars
per season seems wholly satisfactory though possibly the policy
of selling day licenses at one dollar should have been continued.
A reasonably low license fee is a valuable advertising point,
and if at any time an increase seems necessary it should be made
indirectly, through increased taxation of guides and resort
owners. The right to fish four million acres of water for seven
dollars a season is a good buy, and a good buy is something that
appeals to everyone; any apparent increase would reduce this
effect and might cause more irritation than the gain would
justify. Whatever the fee charged, the purchase of the necessary license should be made as simple and convenient as possible for visiting anglers. The present system, which makes it
illegal for non-resident anglers to carry rods or fishing tackle
anywhere within the boundaries of the Province but provides
no opportunity for the purchase of licenses at border points, is
absurd and has caused unnecessary annoyance.

The whole question of efficient and courteous service is a vitally important one. What the visiting angler needs is full, accurate and up-to-the-minute information, and every effort should be made to provide him with it. Any attempt to mislead by, for instance, stories of past catches that are no longer possible in the waters in question, should be quickly checked. In the course of development it should be possible to establish central information bureaus in cities like Vancouver and Victoria, which should be in constant touch with the main resorts by radio or telephone. In these offices the latest information as to the condition of any water in the Province should be kept on file and made available to any inquirer. In time, the service could be extended by the establishment of suboffices at important border points and smaller towns. The central bureau would also have a mailing list of all anglers who had at any time taken out non-resident licenses; it could then keep them informed of developments and improvements made throughout the Province, as well as of any change of conditions at their favourite waters.

In the actual use of the fishery, guides are perhaps the most important factor of all. There is at present no system of licensing guides or checking their qualifications, though big-game guides are licensed and must prove themselves competent in order to obtain licenses. It is obviously impossible to produce by legislation men such as Herbert Pidcock and Bill Nation, who build up a fishery and its traditions at least as much by their own personalities as by their excellent qualifications as fishermen. But it is necessary to encourage good men to go into the profession, and at the same time to give visiting fishermen assurance that they are employing men who have at least some qualifications. At present there is no such assurance, and I have actually seen a guide, receiving $8 a day for his services, in such difficulty with tide and wind that the man he was rowing had to take over the oars. A licensing system would prevent this sort of thing, and so protect both visiting anglers and competent guides. It would also encourage the guides to organise an association, which might well prove a major factor for conservation.

It would be necessary to issue at least three classes of license: Class C licenses should be issued to guides who can prove themselves safe and capable boatmen, with some fishing knowledge; Class B licenses to guides who can show that they thoroughly understand the fishing and conditions of one locality; Class A licenses restricted to men with a thorough knowledge of all types of fishing, and sufficient general ability to adapt such knowledge to conditions anywhere in the Province.

On the coast especially, there is a real need for at least a limited number of Class A guides. Each year a few large yachts come up, to wander among the straits and inlets of the inside passage in search of good fishing. Too often they do not find it, or find it with difficulty, and as a matter of fact, without competent local knowledge of the habits and movements of the native game fish, such a search is nearly always certain to fail. The expense of a cruise with a large yacht is heavy, and the addition of the wages of a competent guide would be a relatively small item; I am quite certain that it would always pay the owners handsomely to take aboard a properly qualified guide immediately upon entering British Columbian waters and to retain his services throughout the trip. But some guarantee of the man's qualifications is absolutely necessary, and qualified men must be readily available; that is to say, they should be registered at some central office in Vancouver or Victoria, so that they can be found and sent out with the yachts when needed.

A guide for this type of work would need a sound knowledge of trout, salmon and steelhead fishing, and of the times and quality of the runs to different localities. He should also have some knowledge of channels, safe anchorages and other problems of navigation where local knowledge is useful, even though he would not, of course, be expected to take any sort of responsibility for the safety of the yacht. To get the best out of some streams he would have to be a capable riverman, able to take a canoe or skiff through normal rapids safely and easily. And if there were any question of trips to lakes or streams at some distance from salt water, he would need to be a fair woodsman. In addition to these positive qualifications, he would need a good fund of enthusiasm and fishing experience, to be able to tackle the problems presented by waters he had not previously fished.

At present there are probably not available, in the whole of British Columbia, a half dozen men with all these qualifications, and I doubt that there are a dozen with even the necessary fishing knowledge and experience to make really first-rate all-round guides for coast waters. Probably the nearest approach to a service of this type at the present time is that offered by the Malibu Club, of Princess Louisa Inlet. I have no personal knowledge of the organisation, which, I understand, started during the war years and has developed since. Mr. L. R. Nelson, the managing director, writes me that the Club has "a charter fleet of 65 yachts available at Newport, California; Seattle, Washington; Vancouver, B. C.; and here at the Malibu Club." He adds: "We have available at the Club a large assortment of fishing tackle for rent, as well as boats and guides for our guests and visiting yachtsmen." Princess Louisa is one of the finest of the many beautiful inlets along the British Columbian coast and I understand the Club has thoroughly modern and comfortable accommodations there. An organisation as ambitious as this one appears to be should do much to solve the problems visiting anglers have had to face in the past. In fairness, I should add that Painter's Resort at Campbell River has always made every possible effort to assist visiting yachtsmen and other anglers who wish to try out the less accessible waters of the coast.

There are undoubtedly big possibilities in flying by both private and charter planes unless the government decides to restrict their use. There has been some suggestion that this should be done, on the grounds that the wealthy sportsman has an unfair advantage and that lakes and streams will be fished out long before they become accessible to the general public. I find it rather hard to believe that such a natural development could be arbitrarily blocked or that there is really serious danger of depletion by airplane anglers; but I am fully satisfied that the closest possible check should be made when planes come out of fishing areas and that when flying becomes widely popular it will be essential to maintain airplane game patrols.

The use of airplanes as a means for stocking inaccessible waters has also been proved. Fish have been dropped in various forms of containers, both with and without parachutes, and from various heights, and sufficient proportions have survived to suggest that most of the methods used are practical. This is a spectacular means for doing a simple thing, and nearly always gets a good deal of publicity; it might, for that reason, suggest itself to irresponsible authorities. But it is vitally important to remember that the stocking of any lake without a preliminary survey of available spawning areas and of general conditions is absolutely undesirable; if the lake is sufficiently accessible to permit such a survey or to make stocking of immediate importance, it is probably also sufficiently accessible to make stocking by ordinary methods quite easy. There may be a few exceptions to this statement, but they are not enough to suggest that stocking by airplanes is of real importance, especially as the survival from such plantings would probably be one more variable factor to complicate the exact calculations necessary in proper fish culture.

Few things are more important in the presentation of the fishing than the country itself—its people, scenery and general characteristics. British Columbia is a country still dependent chiefly on the production of raw materials, and she is likely to have to remain so for many years. Her people—those that the angler is likely to meet—are loggers, fishermen, miners, trappers and guides; they are quiet, intelligent people of many nationalities, but essentially Canadian; they are North Americans, but not Americans, and are different in many ways from men of similar occupations in the United States. These differences are important to people who come up to Canada from the United States; they like to notice them and remark on them and to feel, through them, that they are actually away from home, in a strange country. There is a simplicity, calmness and slower pace in the Canadian life that is understood and appreciated.

The scenery of British Columbia is big and, where it is unspoiled, magnificent. Where it is spoiled, it is badly and dangerously spoiled. The hideous effects of high-lead logging and the fires that inevitably follow the system are depressing and shocking and, altogether apart from the economic waste they represent and the damage they cause, are a definite liability to any country that is trying to develop a tourist industry. So much splendid country has already been destroyed, and there is so little sign of any real change of policy in this respect, that it seems useless to add to innumerable protests. But it is a fact that there is no need at all for logging in the immediate vicinity of streams and lakes; by paying proper attention to the contours of the ground it would be perfectly possible to leave strips of timber adequately protected from wind. And some more rapid means than natural regeneration, checked and destroyed again and again by fire, must be found for the restoration of important areas already logged. Few trees grow more quickly than the British Columbian maple, and avenues of these along the roads and stands near lakes and along the banks of streams would do much, within a few years, to restore some of the lost beauty.

The backgrounds in British Columbia are always beautiful and are likely to remain so; they are the hard mountains, indestructible by any abuse that man has yet been able to develop. As yet, too, there are hundreds of lakes and streams back in standing timber that the logger has not reached and is not likely to reach for a while. These are wholly beautiful, wholly peaceful and natural; one can go to them, often quite easily, and find the real British Columbia, huge and still among great trees, with the country always climbing away towards mountains and the bright streams full of fish, their edges travelled by mink and coon. Back in such country there are deer and elk tracks still on the gravel bars of the streams, and perhaps a bear will be fishing around the bend or feeding in the next patch of salmonberries. With a fresh cougar scrape in the hemlock needles of the trail and a pair of bald eagles circling above the timber, it is easy—perhaps too easy—to forget the things that are happening to the country outside.

As I said I would, I have written of the future in terms of the tourist trade. I believe that everything I have written of the possible development of the resource holds good if it is regarded as a recreational facility, not to be kept sacred to residents of the Province but to be shared by all who wish to come. Recreational facilities of this size and scope can no longer be regarded as luxuries, but as necessities, to round out the lives and give health and relaxation to the producing population of the continent. The steadily increasing wealth and leisure of the ordinary man is already creating a demand for entertainment facilities of all kinds that will have to be met promptly and adequately. Spectator sports, movies, beer halls, dance palaces mean little to a man who comes to his leisure with a desire to do something himself. Fishing and hunting meet the need exactly and it is not difficult to realise that within fifty years the fish and wildlife resources of the continent will be strained to the very limit, unless every possible effort is made now to maintain and develop them.

In a sense, this game fishing of British Columbia is the last unspoiled natural resource in the whole of Canada and the United States; it is still capable of an important sustained yield, conservation measures can still be easily and cheaply applied, and ways of improving and increasing the yield at reasonable cost readily suggest themselves. It does not seem possible that the anglers of this generation will allow any force, however powerful, to prevent their handing on to the next generation a resource more valuable than the one they have found.

# V

## The People's Right to Good Fishing

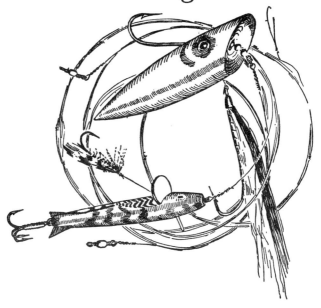

I F the angler has certain obligations to the State, the State has equally definite obligations to the angler. The government of a young State is primarily a trustee appointed by the people to look after all natural resources, whether they are to be developed by private or by public ownership. The trusteeship implies, above everything else, that the resources shall be managed in such a way as to provide maximum benefit not to individuals, but to the people as a whole.

The term "maximum benefit" has also certain definite implications, especially in the case of a self-reproducing natural resource. The duty of the trustee is to encourage and facilitate the use of the natural increase, but at the same time to check firmly any tendency which threatens the resource's power of sustained yield. Only when there is plain and ample proof, in advance of action, that depletion of a resource is a necessary preliminary to more valuable development, can there be any release from the second part of this duty.

In the case of such simple natural resources as the game and commercial fisheries of British Columbia, the terms and implications of the trust are even more definite. Governments, from their earliest history, have had full control of these resources. The people have agreed to submit to whatever taxation may be necessary for maintenance and development, and to obey whatever restrictions may be imposed for preservation. Thus there has been ample opportunity for the development of a sound and consistent policy of use within the limits of the yield, and at the same time freedom, power and the necessary financial means for the improvement of the resources to a greater capacity of yield.

But there is, unfortunately, a single weakness in the nature of the trust. The people are at once founders and beneficiaries. As founders they exert too great control over the trustees; as beneficiaries they are too much inclined to demand instant benefits at the expense of future security. The trustees have failed to restrain the beneficiaries from abuse of their property, because they are afraid that the founders may put them out if they do.

That is why public ownership of natural resources has, on the whole, proved less sound than private ownership. Systems of private ownership of game fisheries have shown themselves extremely effective in conservation. There were trout in the Test and the Itchen, for instance, when the Romans were in Britain. No human effort was responsible for the creation of the streams, for their original production or their potentially continuous yield. The right to use the yield was taken and held by force, or made over to private individuals by gift of the crown, and passed to its present owners through a series of purchases. This system has not merely maintained the original productivity of the streams, but has increased it tremendously. But enlightened government, which presumably did not exist in the middle ages or even in the nineteenth century but which certainly should exist now, is in a position to do the same thing —if only it will accept its responsibilities and assert its powers. In a country such as British Columbia, where the ratio of resident population to fishing waters is very low and likely to remain so for perhaps hundreds of years, it is obviously possible to maintain and increase the productivity of the fishery to the great benefit of the whole people. For this reason, if for no other, the people of the Province, having handed over to their trustees a going concern, may legitimately insist that those trustees are under an actual and moral obligation to maintain it as a going concern for present and future generations.

But there is a broader question than this. Some people consider that all blood sports, in which category the gentle practice of fishing with an angle undoubtedly belongs, are objectionable; they deny the right of anyone to kill any bird, fish or animal for sport. Of those who take this stand a fair number are, by ordinary standards, cranks; others are professed intellectuals; and a few, at least, are people of strong and generous sympathies and a noble quality of mercy, who may or may not be misguided. The three groups together form no more than an inconsiderable minority in any State I know. The cranks, who base their arguments upon direct lies and wilful distortion of facts, are not important. The truly merciful people—at least, all of those I have met and talked with—have but small knowledge of natural conditions or of how the blood sports are conducted; they are usually struggling against their own fearful imaginings rather than against anything that actually exists. The professed intellectuals who oppose or despise blood sports are likely to be similarly hazy upon rather important points, but with much less right. They are often people of some power in leading thought, and would like to be even more powerful; and they are genuinely anxious that mankind should have a better and fuller life. Such people should be open to argument and, having power, should be concerned to understand fully that of which they would speak or write. For them as well as for the curious—or bewildered—angler himself, it seems worth arguing the people's claim, good or bad, to fishing at all.

The first argument—and rather a complete one—is that the people enjoy fishing. The answer is that they shouldn't enjoy it, and that if they do they are barbarians, which obviously they should not be. This is likely to be supported by contemptuous and bitter talk of the blood lust, and the hunting lust, of sadism and unnatural—or too natural—enjoyment of prolonged suffering. Much of the fierceness of such attacks derives from the fact that field sports—shooting and fishing and hunting generally—have been the pleasures of the rich rather than of the poor, at least in the Old World. This is now far less true than it was, even in the Old World, and in the New World it has never been true and seems quite unlikely to become true. But the strength or weakness of the arguments put forward is not necessarily affected by the fact that the reason for advancing them is essentially unsound. There cannot be much doubt that any thinking man who takes his enjoyment in ways that cause death, preceded by at least some degree of suffering to living creatures, must take time to examine the nature of his enjoyment pretty thoroughly.

It is not possible for man, at least in the present state of his knowledge, to understand exactly the mental and physical sensations of birds, fish or animals, nor has he any satisfactory means of estimating the intensity of these sensations. But from watching and trying to understand, one inevitably reaches certain conclusions. I have watched animals and fish a good deal, quite often without lethal intent and with, I hope, a thoroughly objective mind. One point has impressed itself upon me more thoroughly than any other. All the wild animals I have watched live only in the immediate present; past and future pleasures are not with them, past or future terrors cannot be a part of the present. I have watched deer feeding calmly within a hundred yards of one of their number freshly killed by a cougar; I have seen a grouse, clean missed by both barrels, swing round the shoulder of a ridge, settle within fifty feet of me and begin at once to feed, unhurriedly and without a sign of nervousness. Many times I have returned trout to the water and watched them swim off upstream, a little hesitantly at first as though expecting the restraint of the line or still off-balance from their brief excursion into the air, but not panic-stricken or in haste; and quite often I have seen one swim directly to the place where it was caught and begin at once to feed again.

From such observations as these, I am well satisfied that fish and animals are not affected by man's most abject sensation, which is the anticipatory fear of pain or death; nor are they affected as he is by the memory of pain or the sight of death.

On the other hand, there can be no doubt that animals, birds and fish feel pain; it is altogether necessary that they should do so, or the normal reactions that ensure the preservation of the race would not occur. Almost certainly they do not feel pain so intensely as do even the most primitive members of the human race, and unquestionably their power of recuperation is much greater. But still, they feel pain; and they know fear—not fear of death or future suffering—but immediate fear of an immediate, visible threat to themselves, fear of present pain or present restraint, and even fear of something directly associated with pain or restraint, such as the nearness of man or other predators, though this last is normally neither prolonged nor intense.

These are points that the man who fishes or shoots should never allow himself to forget; minimise the intensity as you will—and there is logical justification for doing so—the fear and pain remain inevitable if field sports are to be followed at all. They remain also if man is to be anything but a vegetarian—commercially caught fish do not suffer less, but more, than rod-caught fish; or if man is to protect his vegetable crops—a deer or rabbit wounded by a farmer suffers as much as one wounded by a hunter. But the unwritten rules of field sports guard to a certain extent against such suffering; the rod fisherman knows his obligation to kill his fish quickly as soon as they are out of the water, and the hunter his obligation not to attempt fluke shots or to allow the escape of a wounded animal. If these unwritten rules are less well observed under public than under private ownership of sporting rights, governments and sportsmen's organisations must take a hand in educating or compelling hunters and anglers to observe them.

Having admitted that fear and pain are caused by hunting and fishing, it is necessary to find whether any benefit results from them, and if the benefit is measurably greater than the suffering of the animals and fish. I think no one would deny that it is thoroughly desirable that man should go out along the streams and into the woods and fields, or that he should get to know something of the ways of animals. In doing so he improves his health, relaxes his mind, gains immeasurably in depth of experience and breadth of knowledge. It may be said that he can do all these things without killing or causing suffering; but the fact remains that he does not. Why should he? With rod or gun in his hand he is part of the scene, empty-handed he is a spectator. In the first case his powers of observation and sensitivity will be intensified, in the second they will be dissipated by lack of purpose—I am writing now of the average man, not of the trained observer.

It is necessary to emphasize the fact that the sportsmen's pleasure or satisfaction is in no way directly dependent upon the causing of pain and fear. The normal man who fishes or shoots—I do not deny that there may be a few exceptions—is not driven by any blood lust or hunting lust or by his innate sadism (for sadism probably is born into the normal man); his pleasure is compounded of many factors—some mental, some physical—whose power would be lost if he were able to visualise the struggles of his hooked fish as in any way similar to the death struggles of a human being, or the sensations of his hunted deer as akin to those of a hunted man. The exact type and degree of pleasure derived from field sports by their devotees necessarily varies with the individual, as does the exact type and degree of pleasure derived by its devotees from, let us say, dancing. The comparison will bear extension. Dancing is considered to have been, from earliest times, an expression, a stimulation, a glorification or what you will of love—or, in the terms of the intellectuals, the sex lust. From crude expression, frenzied stimulation and vulgar glorification, dancing has developed to its present position as one of the highest, if not the highest, of the ephemeral arts. Even in its best and purest forms, dancing cannot be altogether divorced from the sex lust—if it is it becomes an insignificant, emasculate and decadent performance —but appreciation of the higher forms is such that the devotee experiences a variation of intense emotions, none of which is necessarily directly or consciously associated with sex lust. The same is exactly true of angling and, perhaps to an extent varying more widely with the individual, of other field sports; the highest forms of angling, practiced by competent performers, have almost exactly the same degree of relation to the blood lust as the purest of ballet has to the sex lust. And angling is actually better entertainment than dancing for the masses of people in at least one important respect—they can be participants, not merely spectators, of even the highest forms, though here too capacity must vary. And even the lower forms of angling are not as closely connected with blood lust as are the lower forms of dancing with the sex lust; anglers would have at least to use spears, and so cease angling, to get down to this point.

Men turn to field sports in search of intensity of experience

not so easily or so safely attainable in other pursuits. Perhaps
the strongest point in human experience occurs when a young
and vigorous man, possessing a sufficiently live sensitivity, is
suddenly and closely faced with violent death. Most men and
most women experience such moments as this before they are
thirty—perhaps in crossing a street, perhaps in war, perhaps in
the mountains or on the water or, as happens to men often
enough in British Columbia, in the eternal split-second of the
fall of a five-ton fir log. The moment is not one of blank fear,
but of an ecstatic physical and mental sensation of swift movement—reaction, probably, but yet in brilliant consciousness.
The quickening of the blood stream, tightening of the throat,
tenseness of muscles, sharp clearing of thought and intense
focus upon the moment are all good, not evil, experience. After
the moment is past the knowledge that body and mind have
responded is satisfying; fear may come later, from brooding
upon the over-closeness of death, and with it perhaps a resolve
to avoid any possible recurrence of the situation. But in spite
of the fear and in spite of resolutions for the future, the vivid-
ness and the strength of the moment are nearly always pro-
claimed in a clear memory of it and a constant willingness to
recount the details.

Comparatively few men past extreme youth place themselves
willingly in such situations; but they seek the sensations, and
find them, in sport. Nearly a hundred years ago Mr. John
Jorrocks, that able if somewhat biased philosopher of sport,
pointed out that: " 'unting is the sport of kings, the image of
war without its guilt, and only five-and-twenty per cent of
its danger." Fortunately, neither angling nor hunting can quite
claim five-and-twenty per cent of the danger of modern war-
fare. Both forms of sport do at times expose their disciples to
physical danger, but angling is far less dependent upon such
moments and the fascination of fly fishing and the other gentler
forms of angling is entirely independent of them. But the high
points of all forms of angling, through what is perhaps a tem-

porary distortion of values, have the tenseness, strength, and power of stimulation of moments of physical danger.

That it can provide so easily and at so little cost such intensity of experience is perhaps a sufficient justification for angling. But the sport has produced and is producing far more than this. Mechanically, fly fishing is a delicate yet stronge exercise, delicately yet strongly performed; this is of value. And it has its moments, often stretched into hours, of beauty seen and realised. The beauty of water, moving or still, and in different lights, the beauty of mountains and timber, of rocks and weeds and insect life, all more intensely observed because there is purpose in the observation. The beauty of a fine fish jumping against white water, the sheen of a fish freshly landed, and the graceful shape—not gasping and flopping as the intellectuals picture it, but still and smooth and touched to unbelievable beauty by the strange element—all these create emotion that is good, not evil.

The direct or indirect contributions of angling and anglers to knowledge, through research, are already important and increase with every year that passes. Much of the knowledge so gained is directly applicable to useful purposes, but even when it is not it still has value simply as knowledge of ways of life and types of life that would otherwise remain hidden. And if man owes any debt of gratitude for the existence of the world in which he finds himself, surely it is best paid by attempting to know and understand all the workings of that world, whether or no such comprehension serves an immediate purpose.

But perhaps the best evidence of the aesthetic value of angling is in the contributions of the sport to art and literature. The contribution to literature is the more important and significant, but there has been enough of angling in British art alone to justify the production of a thick quarto volume devoted to the discussion of it. A surprising number of artists have felt the appeal of the subject, and some of them—Sargent, Turner, Hogarth, Alken, Leach, Morland, to mention only a few—have borne good enough names. Norman Wilkinson, one of the great dry-point artists of the present day, may be said to be angling's own.

The literature of angling is vast. As long ago as 1883 there were well over two thousand known works on the subject, and presumably the fifty-six years since that date have multiplied this total. Most of it is not great, although Walton, Scrope and perhaps a few others have produced books that stand out simply as literature and have been read by a wide public for many years. Much of it is technical, often good writing in well-planned forms. Too much, perhaps, is prosy reminiscence. But a very high proportion is good by any standards. Grey's *Fly Fishing*, Kingsley's *Chalkstream Studies*, Hills' *A Summer on the Test* and *River Keeper*, the best of Patrick Chalmers, Romilly Fedden's books, Henry Williamson's *Salar*—all these are well worth the attention of readers who may care nothing at all for fishing as a sport.

Such listings are dangerous. They cannot be comprehensive, and the choice is wide enough for the omissions to be significant. But to forget for the moment the quality of the literature; merely its quantity is ample evidence of how much of pleasure and satisfaction, intellectual far more than physical, there is to be derived from angling. That so many men have seen fit to sit down and write of their sport is a strong tribute to its fascination; for the making of a book, though it may be pleasant, is never altogether a light task. The number and general excellence of the technical books show more clearly than does anything else the grip of the sport upon good minds and the almost unlimited possibilities of development and refinement that are in it. The books of reminiscence are evidence of emotion remembered in tranquillity, and even the poorest of them show a surprising depth of interest in the subject and a willingness to search other forms of knowledge for anything that may have a bearing upon it. The considerable number of really good non-technical books on angling suggests that the sport has qualities

that are less tangible than mere technical difficulties, and that
the expression of these can be a valuable thing. The mere fact
that angling has inspired even a few really great books gives it
a place above criticism.

The essential point is the breadth and diversity of the subject
and the deep devotion to it. It produces intelligent thought and
good, clean work. It is responsible for refinement of craftsman-
ship in the making of tackle and flies—the making of flies for
Atlantic salmon has become a high art in its own right; its
traditions of workmanship and beauty demand something of
the skill and devotion that were given to the making of illu-
minated manuscripts, and actually have almost as little practical
application to the catching of salmon as beautiful illumination
had to the legibility of the manuscript. Above all perhaps, there
is the direction of man towards knowledge and intimate observation that would otherwise escape him; knowledge of water
and its behaviour, of fish, insects and birds, as well as of animals
in their relation to one another.

## REFERENCES

Chaytor, A. H. *Letters to a Salmon Fisher's Sons*. Murray, London,
    1910.
Ellis, Havelock. *Dance of Life*, 1923.
Scrope, William. *Days and Nights of Salmon-Fishing in the Tweed*,
    1843.
Shaw Sparrow, W. *Angling in British Art*. Lane, London, 1923.
Surtees, R. S. *Handley Cross*, Bradbury & Evans, London, 1854.

# APPENDIX

## *British Columbian Fly Dressings*

QUITE a number of flies, most of them wet flies, have been developed for British Columbian waters by local anglers. The most important of these are Bill Nation's flies for the interior lakes. The following are the standard dressings of this series:

### 1. *NATION'S SPECIAL*
Tail   6 strands tippet.
Body   Rear third flat silver. Rest black floss.
Ribs   Oval silver tinsel.
Wings   Mottled grey turkey strips, few strands tippet enclosed.
Sides   Jungle cock and dyed red swan (red in September only).
Hackle   Fine speckled gallina.

### 2. *NATION'S FANCY*
Tail   15 strands tippet.
Body
Ribs } as above.
Wings   Light mallard, few strands tippet enclosed.
Hackle   (Tied on No. 6 hook) Fine speckled gallina behind wings. (Tied on No. 4 hook) Light badger ahead of wings.

3. *NATION'S BLUE* (*coupled bluets*)

    Tail   Solid spear blade light mallard.
    Body   Rear third flat silver tinsel. Rest pale blue floss.
    Ribs   Oval silver.
    Wings   Light mallard with blue overstripe (pale chatterer shade).
    Hackle   Badger, set ahead of wings.

4. *NATION'S RED* (*coupled red dragons*)

    Tail   Light mallard.
    Body   Rear third flat silver tinsel. Rest scarlet wool.
    Ribs   Fine flat silver.
    Wings   Long strips dark mallard.
    Sides   Red swan.
    Hackle   Badger, set ahead of wings.

5. *NATION'S SILVER-TIP*

    Tail   6 strands tippet.
    Body   Rear fourth flat silver tinsel. Rest black floss.
    Ribs   Oval silver.
    Wings   Light mottled turkey, few strands tippet enclosed.
    Sides   Red swan (coast water only; omitted for interior).
    Hackle   Speckled gallina.

6. *NATION'S GREEN SEDGE* (*No. 6 hook only*)

    Tail   Red swan.
    Body   Green seal's fur (vary shade to suit seasons, bright green fur treated with peroxide).
    Ribs   Oval gold tinsel.
    Wings   Light mallard or teal strips.
    Hackle   Light badger, set ahead of wings.

7. *NATION'S SILVER-TIPPED SEDGE*

Tail  Red swan.

Body  Two turns flat silver, rest green seal's fur (sun-bleached to shade needed).

Ribs  Oval gold tinsel.

Wings  Light grey mottled turkey.

Hackle  Badger, set ahead.

8. *NATION'S GREEN NYMPH* (*hook sizes 3, 5, 7 most useful*)

Tail  Clump of tippet.

Body  Green wool built up to $\frac{3}{16}$ inch (shade and colour of body varied as needed).

Ribs  Oval gold tinsel.

Hackle  Ground-hog tail hairs laid over body, shorter hairs (same) under.

9. *NATION'S GREY NYMPH* (*hook sizes 4 and 7 most useful*)

Tail  Clump of tippet.

Body  Built to $\frac{3}{16}$ inch, light mallard wound over size 4, emerald green wool over size 7 (former imitates mature nymph, latter the yearling).

Ribs  Oval gold tinsel.

Hackle  Ground-hog tail over, ground-hog rump or desert-fox rump under.

10. *NATION'S BLACK* (*hook size 7*)

Body  Slender, black machine silk.

Hackle  6 hairs brown coast bucktail over, four under.

Mr. T. Brayshaw's patterns are by far the best yet tied for fishing at Little River and other places where large Kamloops trout are feeding on sockeye smolts. The two dressings given below are usually tied on two hooks in tandem, the tail hook a size larger than the upper hook. Mr. Brayshaw writes: "Hooks should be joined by double, treble-twisted gut—one right twist and one left twist—otherwise, when wet, the tail hook has a tendency to turn round. There should also be a few turns of silk over the tinsel to prevent it breaking when a fish bends the fly up."

## DRESSING I

Body   All flat silver tinsel.
Wings   Moose hair, largely white or white tipped with dark brown.
Hackle   Badger.

## DRESSING II

Body   Flat silver to shoulder. Shoulder scarlet floss silk, ribbed oval silver.
Wings   A few strands peacock herl, covered with two furnace hackles, jungle cock cheeks, topping over all (a few strands of blue macaw sometimes added).
Hackle   Under hackle scarlet. Over hackle blue macaw.

If the migrating smolts are small, a dressing somewhat similar to No. II may be tied on a No. 2 low-water hook. Furnace hackles in wing may be varied with badger, teal, golden pheasant centre tail or other suitable feathers. The extra long shank of the low-water hooks is useful in most silver-bodied flies.

For coast fishing I nearly always tie my own flies, and vary the dressings a good deal. The following is a list of those whose dressings I do not vary and which have become sufficiently important to me to need names. So far as I know, no tackle dealer carries a regular stock of them.

1. *SILVER BROWN* (*No. 6 or 8 Low-water hook*)
Tail   Indian crow breast feather (small, whole feather).
Body   Flat silver tinsel.
Hackle   Dark red game cock.
Wings   Slender strips golden pheasant centre tail.

NOTE: A very useful cutthroat fly, particularly for maturing fish in August and September. Also takes summer steelhead and cohoes in fresh water.

2. *SILVER LADY* (*No. 6 Low-water hook or larger*)
Tail   Tippet (small whole feather).
Body   Flat silver.
Hackle   Badger.
Wings   4 strands bronze peacock herl, teal strips, badger hackles laid along these, topping over all.
Alternative Wing   2 blue hackles, good sides out, paired strips, golden pheasant centre tail, barred summer duck. Topping over.
Cheeks   Pale blue chatterer.

NOTE: Excellent for summer steelhead either as an ordinary wet fly or a greased line fly. Also takes cutthroat trout very well.

3. *BULLHEAD*
Tail   Light mallard.
Body   Flat silver tinsel.
Wings   Light mallard, thick, enclosing 4 strands bronze herl. Sometimes also a few polar bear hairs.
Hackle   Badger, heavy, set ahead of wings and standing stiffly out from shank of hook. May be varied with dark red, claret or blue hackle.

### 4. *GAMMARUS* (*No. 6-10 hooks*)

Tail   Small topping.
Body   Olive seal's fur, veiled by brown hackle wound over.
Ribs   Oval gold.
Hackle   Jay (blue).
Wings   Hen pheasant centre tail strips.

NOTE: Really a simplification of the Golden Olive salmon fly; there is also an English trout fly, known variously as the Victor or Invicta, which is much like it. It is a good shrimp imitation and useful for any trout in any water.

### 5. *DARK CADDIS* (*No. 6 hook*)

Tail   Dark mallard.
Body   Very dark green seal's fur.
Ribs   Oval gold.
Hackle   Furnace or dark olive.
Wings   Blae or dark mallard.

NOTE: Closely related to Greenwell's Glory. A good summer fly in many cutthroat streams.

### 6. *CEDAR BORER* (*No. 6-8 hooks*)

Body   Mixed emerald green and blue seal's fur.
Ribs   Bronze peacock herl, gold thread.
Wings   Green peacock herl.
Hackle   Light blue tied ahead of wing.

NOTE: This is a freak-looking fly, but trout in coast streams seem to take the brilliant blue-green borer beetles whenever they find their way into the water and it is rather comforting to have even the roughest imitation. The above dressing takes fish well under these conditions.

### 7. *BROWN CATERPILLAR* (*No. 4 or 6 hook*)

Body   Olive seal's fur.
Ribs   Oval silver tinsel.
Hackle   Long soft dark red wound palmerwise.

NOTE: A good stock wet fly, very easily tied.

### 8. *BLACK CATERPILLAR* (*No. 6 or 8 hook*)

Body   Black seal's fur.
Ribs   Bronze peacock herl, oval gold tinsel.
Hackle   Black wound palmerwise, or one side of any bronze feather wound palmerwise. Effect should not be too tidy.

NOTE: This is the best flying-ant imitation I have ever used. Other caterpillars, tied in the same way with seal's fur of different colours and matching hackles, are also good. Orange and fiery brown particularly valuable.

In addition to these I have found the low-water Lady Caroline invaluable both as a shrimp imitation for cutthroat trout, and as either an ordinary wet fly or a greased-line fly for summer steelhead. The dressing is as follows:

### *LADY CAROLINE* (*No. 6-8 Low-water hooks*)

Tail   Golden pheasant breast feather.
Body   Fiery brown and olive seal's fur (mixed).
Ribs   Flat silver tinsel, gold and silver thread (last two may be omitted).
Hackle   Blue heron (may be omitted).
Throat   Golden pheasant breast feather.
Wings   Dark mallard flat along body.

NOTE: This is a complicated dressing for a trout fly; hence the suggested omissions. It is very doubtful that the refinements really make much difference to the fish.

Two other very good flies for migratory cutthroat are Play-fair's Shrimp and the Tinsel. There are many dressings of the Tinsel, but I believe the brown and black barred feather from the male hooded merganser given in the one below is the best of all for the purpose. The fly is chiefly useful in the spring, and I have satisfied myself that it is best tied without hackle or tail. Mr. Geoffrey Playfair's Shrimp I have not used, but it is an excellent and simple pattern, and Mr. Playfair tells me that it kills very well in estuarial waters.

## PLAYFAIR'S SHRIMP
Body    Hare's ear.
Wing    Polar-bear hair, dyed brown, tied in again at the tail.

## TINSEL
Body    Flat silver tinsel.
Wings   Light strips of brown and black barred breast feather from male hooded merganser.

Most of the dry flies I have used in British Columbian waters have been standard English and American patterns, such as the bi-visibles and palmers, and the Halford and Dunne imitations of ephemeridae. But the sedges are important and at least one, the *GREY-BODIED SEDGE*, is extremely valuable in both coast and interior waters. I have not been able to learn what is the standard dressing of this fly, but the following dressing has done as well for me as any:

Body    Medium grey wool (or chenille or mole's fur) (No. 8-10 hooks).
Ribs    Black floss, heavy.
Wings   Hen pheasant centre tail.
Hackle  Large pale ginger.

Two other large sedge imitations are as follows:

## 1. *OLIVE SEDGE*
Tag   Gold tinsel.
Body   Dark olive green seal's fur, ribbed black floss, veiled by olive hackle wound up.
Wings   Dark mallard.
Hackle   Olive.

## 2. *TRAVELLING SEDGE*
Tag   Gold tinsel.
Body   Dark olive seal's fur ribbed black floss.
Wings   Hen pheasant centre tail.
Hackle   Badger behind wings, furnace ahead.

General Noel Money, of Qualicum Beach, who is by all odds the finest and most experienced steelhead fly fisherman in British Columbia, has been kind enough to give me the following dressings of his most successful flies. They may be tied on any size of hook from 2/o to No. 4, though I understand that the best sizes for summer fishing are usually Nos. 1/o-3.

## *GENERAL MONEY'S FLY*
Body   Black silk.
Ribs and Tag   Gold tinsel.
Wings   Red swan, with or without topping over.
Hackle   Yellow.

## *DICK'S FLY*
Tail   Topping.
Ribs and Tag   Gold tinsel.
Wings   Dark mallard.
Hackle   Yellow or coch-y-bondhu.
Cheeks   Jungle cock.

*PRAWN FLY* (*Hook sizes 4/0-No. 3*)

Ribs and Tag   Silver tinsel.
Body   Orange wool.
A long red hackle, tied palmerwise along the body.

General Money is of the opinion that shape and size are more important than colour, though he believes it is just possible that the fish respond slightly better to a red fly. His usual custom is to start fishing a red fly and change later to a dark fly if a change seems desirable.

Dressings of cohoe flies are of almost infinite variety and are usually very simple—two or three colours of bucktail or polar bear hair, with silver body, short tail and no hackle. Both flies are tied on 2½ inch Long Dee hooks and the dressings are as follows:

*COHOE GOLDEN*

Tail   Orange polar bear.
Body   Flat silver.
Wings   White bear fur, olive bear fur.
Sides   Red jungle cock hackles, flat along the wings, full length, bronze peacock herl laid along these.
Topping over all.

*COHOE BLUE*

Tail   Tip of large blue hackle.
Body   Flat silver.
Wings   White bear fur, blue bear fur.
Sides   Blue hackles and badger hackles, flat along wings, full length.
Heron hackles over all.

I had hoped also to be able to give the standard dressings of a number of local flies which, through their great popularity, should have mention in any book on British Columbian fishing. Unfortunately I have not been able to learn exactly what dressings of these flies are considered standard. There is a good deal of variation, apparently dependent on the whim of the tier, and even the names of the flies are likely to vary in different parts of the province. Since I seldom or never use any of these patterns myself, it seems inadvisable to risk reading off the dressings from casually purchased specimens. The following is a list of the names of some of the better-known local favourites. Amateur tiers will be able to order sample flies from it and deduce from them sufficiently accurate dressings:

*SIWASH*
*SILVER MINNOW*
*YELLOW BELLE*
*YELLOW PERIL*
*CAREY'S SPECIAL or*
  *THE DREDGE*
*CAREY'S PARMACHENE*
  *BUCKTAIL*
*PATSY*
*BRYAN WILLIAMS'*
  *GREY-BODIED SEDGE*
*BRYAN WILLIAMS'*
  *GREEN-BODIED*
  *SEDGE*

*BRYAN WILLIAMS' YEL-*
  *LOW-BODIED SEDGE*
*BRYAN WILLIAMS'*
  *DARK-BODIED SEDGE*
*CUMMING'S FANCY*
*BLACK O'LINDSAY*
*KAMLOOPS SPECIAL*
*BROUGHAM'S*
  *NICOMEKL*
*BROUGHAM'S CLOW-*
  *HOLM LAKE*
*RHODES' FAVOURITE*
*PARMACHENE BEAU*
*PROFESSOR (wool body,*
  *black head)*

There are a number of good tackle dealers in British Columbia from whom local flies may be purchased. Amongst them are Harkley and Haywood of Vancouver, whose store is, in my opinion, the equal of any on the Pacific Coast, Lisle Fraser of Vancouver, J. B. Spurrier of Kelowna, Roger Monteith of Victoria and Lenfesty and Wilson, also of Victoria. The visiting angler can depend upon intelligent service and advice in any of these stores.

# TABLE SHOWING PHYSICAL CHARACTERISTICS BY WHICH BRITISH

| Species | Anal Fin Rays | Gill-Rakers | Branchio-stegals | Pyloric Caeca | Vetrebrae | Scales in Lateral Line | Scales from Adipose Fin to Lateral Line |
|---|---|---|---|---|---|---|---|
| Humpback (Pink) (*O. gorbuscha*) | *15* 13-17 | *28* 27-33 | *11-12* 10-15 | 165-195 | usually 65+ | *170* 150-198 | |
| Spring (Tyee) (*O. tschawytscha*) | *16* 15-19 | *23* 20-28 | *16-18* 13-19 | 140-185 | usually 68+ | *146* 131-151 | |
| Cohoe (Blueback) (*O. kisutch*) | *13-14* 13-16 | *23* 19-25 | *13-14* 12-15 | 45-80 | usually 63+ | *127* 121-136 | |
| Sockeye (*O. nerka*) | *14-16* 13-16 | *36* 30-39 | *13-15* 11-15 | 66-92 | usually 62+ 56-67 | *133* 125-139 | |
| Dog (Chum) (*O. keta*) | *13-14* 13-17 | *24* 20-26 | *13-14* 12-16 | 140-185 | usually 64+ | *150* 126-151 | |
| Kokanee (*O. nerka kennerlyi*) | c. 14 | 30-40 | — | — | — | 125-140 | |
| Steelhead (*S. gairdneri gairdneri*) | *10-12* 9-13 | 19-21 | 11-12 | — | 63-64 62-65 | 131-134 124-146 | |
| Kamloops (*S. gairdneri kamloops*) | *10-11* 9-13 | 18-21 | 11-12 | — | 63-64 62-66 | *145* 130-150 | |
| Mountain Kamloops (*S. gairdneri whitehousei*) | 10-11 | 18 | *11* 10-11 | — | 62-65 62-67 | *153* 139-164 | |
| Coast Cutthroat (*S. clarkii clarkii*) | *9-11* 8-12 | *18-19* 14-21 | 10-1 | — | 62-63 60-64 | 150-158 143-180 | |
| Yellowstone Cutthroat (*S. clarkii lewisi*) | *10-11* 8-12 | c. 18 | 10-12 | 43 | 60-61 | *165* 150-175 | |
| Mountain Cutthroat (*S. clarkii alpestris*) | 10-11 | c. 19 | *11* 10-11 | — | — | *218* 200-230 | |
| Atlantic Salmon (*S. salar salar*) | *8 or 9* 7-11 | — | — | — | 58-59 57-61 | c. 120 | *12 or less* 10-13 |
| Brown Trout (*S. trutta trutta*) | *8-10* 7-11 | — | — | *49* 35-73 | 56-60 | c. 125 | *14 or more* 13-16 |

Figures in italic indicate averages or variations normally met with.

igh scale count in lateral line distinguishes humpback
om other Pacific salmon. In case of abnormally low
unt (150-151) confirm by counting 1st row above lat-
al line. In humpback 170+ others 153 −.

istinguished from humpback by lower scale count.
om cohoe by high pyloric caeca count. From sockeye
low gill-raker count. From dog by high anal and
anchiostegal count. Tail heavily spotted.

istinguished from all Pacific salmon except sockeye
low pyloric caeca count. From sockeye by lower gill-
ker count. Upper half of tail sometimes spotted.

istinguished from all Pacific salmon except humpback
high gill-raker count. From humpback (if gill-rakers
ss than 33) by lower scale count. Tail lightly speckled,
t spotted.

istinguished from other Pacific salmon as spring
lmon. From spring salmon by low anal and branchi-
tegal counts. There is an overlap in both these but
nfusion between these fish not likely to arise.

nfusion between this fish and Pacific salmon not
obable. Distinguished from all except sockeye by
gh gill-raker count. From trout by anal fin ray or
l-raker count.

THIS GROUP IS DISTIN-
GUISHED FROM ALL TROUT
(including *S. salar*) AND
CHAR BY 13 OR MORE RAYS
IN ANAL FIN.

eelheads, Kamloops and mountain Kamloops are dis-
nguished from each other by progressively higher
ale count as species become farther removed from
astal waters. Geographical distribution normally
parates these varieties. Where through transplanting
does not, differences will probably disappear and dif-
entiation may be impossible after a few generations.

Rainbow group distin-
guished from cutthroat
by lack of hyoid teeth
and generally lower scale
count. From *S. salar* and
*trutta* by high anal fin ray
count (10+) and high
vertebrae count.

e same remarks apply to the varieties of this species
to the varieties of the rainbow group.

Cutthroat group distin-
guished from rainbow by
hyoid teeth and high
scale count. From *S. salar*
and *trutta* by high anal fin
ray and vertebrae counts.

THIS GROUP IS DISTIN-
GUISHED FROM ALL PA-
CIFIC SALMON BY 12 OR
LESS RAYS IN ANAL FIN.

rger scales than brown trout. Distinguished by count
12 or less scale rows between adipose fin and lateral
e.

aller scales than Atlantic salmon. Distinguished by
unt of 14 or more scale rows between adipose fin and
eral line. Since these fish are not native this feature
y change.

Distinguished from na-
tive trout (cutthroat and
rainbow groups) by low
anal fin ray and vertebrae
counts. Probably also un-
spotted caudal fin.

# Index